MW00587575

GROUP LIVING *and* OTHER RECIPES

GROUP LIVING

and

OTHER RECIPES

Lola Milholland

*Spiegel
and Grau*

S&G

Spiegel & Grau, New York
www.spiegelandgrau.com
Copyright © 2024 by Lola Milholland

All rights reserved. No portion of this book may be reproduced, stored in a retrieval system, or transmitted in any form or by any means—electronic, mechanical, photocopy, recording, scanning, or other—except for brief quotations in critical reviews or articles, without the prior written permission of the publisher.

Interior design by Meighan Cavanaugh

Library of Congress Cataloging-in-Publication Data Available Upon Request

ISBN 978-1-954118-57-7 (hardcover)
ISBN 978-1-954118-58-4 (eBook)

Printed in the United States on 30% postconsumer recycled paper

First Edition
10 9 8 7 6 5 4 3 2 1

To my mom, my dad,
and the Holman House

CONTENTS

Recipe List   ix

Prologue: That's Group Living   xiii

Butter Sculpture   *1*

Bitter and Sweet   *20*

Tender   *43*

Driftless   *69*

Offer Me S'more   *91*

Rigid Liquid   *120*

In the Thicket   *146*

Kanom Ko Rona   *166*

Nuclear Family   *193*

Tripping   *218*

Compost   *235*

Always Coming Home   *262*

Acknowledgments   281

Notes   285

About the Author   291

RECIPE LIST

CONDIMENTS AND VEGETABLES

Zak's Chili Oil with Fermented Black Beans   *xxi*

Chris's Chili Flakes   *xxiii*

Junko's Daikon *Namasu* (Quick-Pickled Daikon, Carrot, and Ginger)   *40*

Lola's Radicchio Salad for Nancy with Spicy Cilantro Dressing   *143*

NOODLES AND RICE

Theresa's Garlicky Panfried Pasta   *17*

Chris's *Khao Tod* (Crispy Broken-Rice Salad)   *190*

Sakiko's *Hiyashi Chūka* (Cold Sesame Noodles) with Jammy Eggs, Peas, and Pickled Radish   *214*

Amy's Matsutake Rice and *Onigiri* (Rice Balls)   *231*

FISH, MEAT, AND EGGS

Yuri's Miso Cod *Nabe* (Hot Pot)   *38*

Chris and Zak's *Tom Kha Gai* (Chicken Coconut Curry Soup)   *66*

Franny's Chicken Adobo   *88*

Corey's Usual Bullshit (Spicy Ground Pork, Tofu, Mushrooms, and Greens)   *118*

Lola's Jammy Eggs   *216*

DRINKS, DESSERT, AND BREAKFAST

Amalia's Cantaloupe-Seed Horchata   *163*

Amanda's Rhubarb-Strawberry Crisp   *259*

David's Seedy Granola   *277*

My father liked his fruit very ripe, so whenever one of us came across an overripe pear we gave it to him. "Ah, so you give me your rotten pears! What real jackasses you are!" he'd say with a hearty laugh that reverberated throughout the apartment, then he'd eat the pear in two bites.

—Natalia Ginzburg, *Family Lexicon*

Prologue

THAT'S GROUP LIVING

When my mom was about to turn seventy, she announced to my brother and me that she was going to do a stand-up comedy set at her birthday party. To my knowledge, she'd never done stand-up before in her life. I was nervous. I told her that she'd need to practice a lot, that I was pretty sure comedians didn't just get on a stage and start riffing— that they ran through their material over and over, until they knew it inside and out. She gave me a knowing smile and said nothing. I wasn't sure if this meant she'd rehearse or not, but I could tell she was tickled by my concern. It dawned on me that she might not actually care how her act was received; she was turning seventy and would do what she wanted.

For her party, she erected a circus tent on the land trust where she lives in a communal lodge in southwest Wisconsin and invited everyone she knew. My housemates—past and present— flew from Portland, Oregon, to join, and we all cooked together for days. I run a small food business and had packed twenty pounds of our fresh noodles in my luggage so my longtime-roommate Chris and I could make platters of *pancit palabok*, a saucy Filipino noodle dish, which we served alongside jars of my brother Zak's homemade chili oil. Chris's partner, Erin, made an enormous salad arranged to look like a grinning face. Our friend Cynthia and my sweetheart, Corey, pitched in to form nettle empanadas at my mom's request. Her friend Eric and his son Nico butterflied several lambs and roasted them on spits.

The tent sat in a clearing on a ridgetop, with deciduous woods around the perimeter. When dinnertime came, more than a hundred of us sat down to eat at long folding tables like we were at a church spaghetti fundraiser—or a commune potluck. We clinked glasses excitedly and talked with full mouths; old folks slapped their knees and young kids crawled among the bony, bouncing legs. The night was warm for mid-May, and I was in short sleeves. As darkness began to fall, the thin twilight was replaced by a rising full moon so bright I had to turn my back to it. *Of course she scheduled her party for the full moon*, I thought. It beamed like a spotlight.

When all the dishes were cleared, my mom took the stage for her set. The tent walls were rolled up, so air flowed past the tables of friends and family. Dozens of people sat on folding chairs, cheeks glowing from wine and beer, looking toward her with grins already plastered to their faces. Zak and I stood just outside the tent, side by side, looking in. I felt such intense vicarious embarrassment I wanted to run into the nearby woods, but Zak compelled me to stay with a firm, unconditional look.

Our mom stood at the microphone, looking breezy in a tight, stretchy turquoise dress, her long salt-and-pepper hair down. In different ways, Zak and I both look like our mom. All three of us have full lips and long oval faces. She's half-Filipino, and we're one-quarter, so her hair is black, streaked with white, and ours is brown; her skin is darker, ours paler. Zak has her slim, athletic build. I have her toothy smile, but I'm four inches taller and measurably less frenetic, magnetic, and direct. She has a potency you can sense from across a room.

Swishing in her dress, she appeared comfortable in her skin, undoubtedly nervous but clearly excited. She opened by describing her childhood in the fifties. "It was the era of *Father Knows Best*," she sneered. She described teasing her hair, wearing girdles, saluting the flag, offering penance for all her dirty thoughts as she ogled Jesus's lithe body dripping from the cross. She was leaning forward at the hips, jutting her chin out, and slicing her open hand through the air in her best George Carlin impersonation. All seven of her siblings had come to rural Wisconsin from as far away as Los Angeles, Boston, and Manila. The three who remain devout Catholics squirmed in their seats, more uncomfortable than I was.

"In the sixties, I became a disinheritor," she announced proudly, a finger pointed at the crowd. A few people cheered like sports fans—"Yeah! Yeah!"—but most remained quiet and alert. She'd tried to throw away the dominant belief systems she'd grown up with, she explained. At the top of her list: Catholicism, patriarchy, and patriotism.

"But did I throw away too much from my parents' generation?" she asked. "Did I throw the baby out with the bathwater? Was there something from that time that I didn't appreciate? Something valuable I left behind?"

She held a pregnant pause, looking around at the audience of friends and family, searching their rapt eyes for an answer.

"No!" she screamed. "I didn't disinherit enough!"

What have I inherited from *my* parents' generation? My childhood looked very different from my mom's. I was raised by someone who'd disavowed Catholicism, patriarchy, and patriotism, in a household with a quality of transience and openness that felt transgressive. Guests were constantly coming and going, sometimes staying for weeks or months at a time. I loved it. Unlike my mom, I don't want to throw my upbringing away. I want to sort through the remains and build on what feels solid in the face of a world I find troubled and precarious.

Very early in life, I recognized that I take after my parents in many ways. The most obvious is my intense relationship with food. Both my parents love to cook, eat, and drink. When their plates and cups are empty, they daydream about cooking, eating, and drinking. But it took me a long time to realize that both my brother and I are following their lead in another way just as central to our lives: we live communally. In fact, we live together.

Since my early twenties, I've lived with Zak, several close friends, and, more recently, Corey, in a large home in Portland. Over more than fifteen years, we've become like a commune in collective spirit but without the structure, the utopian dream, or ninety-three Rolls Royces.

In my twenties, this seemed ordinary, not so different from the circumstances of many of my peers. In my thirties, it became more uncommon. But somehow, I still didn't perceive our living situation as notable until Zak took up a new refrain. (He loves refrains and collects them the way someone else might hoard memorabilia.) From the beginning, Zak has been the occasional grumbler of our group, grouching when someone's stuff is littering the table or when the tomatoes they've abandoned on the counter attract fruit flies. But now—in his own nod to stand-up—I'd hear him announce in the voice of one of his favorite comedians, Neil Hamburger (a dejected lounge-act type), "*That's* group living."

Let's say I found a beloved ceramic bowl chipped. "*That's* group living," I'd hear Zak's voice saying, even when I was alone.

Group living—*yes*, that was what we were doing; I just hadn't named it before. Yet in naming it, it took on a new shape, and not the one I wanted or expected. A handful of stereotypes sprang all too easily to my mind: a horde of eighteen-to-twenty-four-year-olds with no consideration for one another lazing about a filthy, smelly house; a cult of personality rife with sexual abuse; hippies fooling themselves into thinking slop is transcendent; and any freaky mixture of the above. Isn't group living *always* a hassle?

These stereotypes feel out of touch with reality to me. I mean that in the broadest sense: Most people in the world live in communal settings. To stigmatize group living is to dismiss the pressures of the housing crisis; the need to reimagine women's unpaid domestic labor; the fact that loneliness and isolation menace all ages; and the racist, classist roots of the nuclear family and single-family home. But I mean it in a very personal way as well. Every day, I look forward to dinner at our house. By cooking for and eating food made by other people, I give and receive each day, which feels as central to my life as inhaling and exhaling. I salvage my sanity by laughing with my housemates, and I depend on their perspectives to help me outgrow my own. *That's group living too*, I protested.

Sisterly defiance surged in me. Suddenly, I had something to prove.

M y defiance gradually took an unexpected form: I wanted to
make a commune cookbook, a now-defunct genre that flour-
ished in the United States in the sixties and seventies. Perhaps
the most famous example is *The Tassajara Bread Book*, which rein-
troduced whole-wheat baking to home cooks. Many of these cookbooks were self-published by back-to-the-land hippie communes
and Zen monasteries. Whenever I visit thrift stores or garage sales,
I look for them, but after a month or two, I'll let them go, because
who wants to make "yeast cheese" or adzuki bean pizza?

Why a commune cookbook? In some ways, our house
descends from the hippie communes of the past. Could a cookbook provide a way for me to sort through that nearness and then
create some distance? To describe my reality with the same
attentiveness as the hippies once recorded theirs, and, in the process, to show something different and new? To challenge stereotypes without pretending they don't come from a real place? To
write better recipes—ones without errant adzuki beans—that
people will want to cook and share? To reclaim Zak's refrain?

To my delight, there's a recipe for group living in Lucy
Horton's wonderful *Country Commune Cooking*, published in 1972.
It comes from one of New England's longest-lasting New Age
communes, a group initially known as The Brotherhood, which
was led by a guru who received spiritual transmissions from a
retired bus driver named Elwood Babbitt. The recipe is called
"Brotherhood Spirit in Flesh Soup":

> Get everyone together and get a good feeling between
> you. Work out anything and everything that lies unex-
> pressed. Realize that you are Spirit—and that the

health and balance of those you feed depend only on your *Thoughts*—that balance and order of the body depend upon balance and order of the Mind Positive. The ingredients are of secondary importance, and always in a divine relativity. This soup was made by Alan, Martin, Tam, Lynne and others, and Duh Bear.

1. Two big pots half full of boiling water.
2. Add 2 cups of pinto beans and a little later several handfuls of barley.
3. To each then add a lot of sautéed onions. At this writing the soup isn't done, but we'll add 12 canning quarts of squash, carrots and tomatoes from last summer's garden. Also some green beans someone gave us. Later some salt and seasoning, kelp powder, and a few tablespoons of miso to each. Follow your own *Awareness* most of all.

This soup will feed 130 along with two pots of brown rice and two pots of millet. Pots are about 3 or 4 gallons.

Finally, one last ingredient to be used throughout—*Love.*

I assume that, like me, you're now groaning (good grief, canned squash—yuck!). And maybe laughing ("Work out anything and everything that lies unexpressed"—thank you, that sounds easy!). And maybe also feeling perplexed (you're going to feed 130 people with two cups of pinto beans?!). I'm forever delighted by this disclosure: "At this writing the soup isn't done."

I love this recipe for its brazen commitment to itself. I love how every inappropriate use of capitalization makes me cringe: *Spirit. Thoughts. Mind Positive*! *Awareness*! *Love*! This recipe embodies some of the exact stereotypes about group living that I instinctively want to distance myself from: apparent openness masking rigidity, self-righteousness, carelessness in appropriating Asian cultures and ingredients, mind-over-matter rhetoric that manages to sweep all structural inequity under a rag rug, and unappealing food.

And yet—if I'm being honest—I also just love it. It catapults me into the past, into a steamy kitchen with someone named "Duh Bear," who's possibly a dog. I'm reminded of the sense of humor that so often accompanies these books, which somehow take themselves very seriously and not seriously at all. I'm reminded of my mom at her birthday party, pointing her finger at her friends and family. She'd posed herself a question: Had she disinherited enough? But she was also asking it of us all, as sincere as she was mocking: Had I? Had we?

Unlike *Country Commune Cooking*, this book provides no specific recipe for group living. In the end, I didn't write a commune cookbook, in parody or homage. The title *Group Living and Other Recipes* is a wink to my brother, as well as a joke on the hippies who wrote recipes for how to live and on myself for being in proximity to them and for feasting under their circus tents.

How we structure our homes isn't a one-size-fits-all situation. There's no single authoritative recipe. *Now* is always the right time to reimagine home and family, and group living represents a galaxy of approaches. My intention is to explore it, not write it off or valorize it. I want to complicate the stereotypes even as I write in their shadows. After all, what is human history if not one giant attempt at group living?

Throughout this book, I've included sincere (and delicious) recipes from the people I love, adding a whiff of the commune cookbooks after all. Sharing food has always been at the center of my life, a way of communicating beyond language: What do we carry with us from our previous relationships to people and places? What tastes good to us? What makes us feel good? These recipes were given to me, and now I offer them to you. Please make them and share them. Bring my home into yours!

Zak's Chili Oil with Fermented Black Beans

Recipe by Zak Margolis, adapted from
Barbara Tropp's China Moon Cookbook

MAKES 3 PINTS

The glue that holds my household together is this complex, addictive chili oil. Zak first encountered it in college when his then girlfriend, Emi Takahara, made it. The first key ingredient is *douchi*—black soybeans fermented with a mold culture similar to the one used to make miso. You can often find *douchi* in East Asian markets in tightly vacuum-sealed bags or in cardboard tubes. Without the beans, this chili oil would still be tasty, but it would be less complex.

The second key ingredient is homemade chili flakes, which are smoky, aromatic, and *spicy*. Our roommate Chris taught us how to make fresh chili flakes—*prik pon* in Thai—and we've never gone back (recipe follows). As Chris says, "Chili flakes are crucial to the Thai pantry. My mom made them from scratch because when you buy chili flakes, they're not toasted the way she likes. Toasting the chilis before you flake them brings out a whole other level of aroma and flavor."

Homemade chili flakes are incredibly simple to make, but if you aren't on your game, you can turn your kitchen into a mace chamber, so it's important to be attentive. We use dried Thai chilies for their spiciness, but the same process will work with any dried chilies, and each will have a distinct flavor and heat level.

Zak's notable changes to Barbara Tropp's original recipe were to increase the garlic fivefold and decrease the volume of peanut oil. My favorite thing about eating this oil is scooping up the plentiful goop on the bottom, including those whole garlic cloves that mysteriously become both shriveled and plump. I like to make a lot with friends and divide it. I've included proportions for a small amount, but this recipe is easily scaled up—I often quadruple all the ingredients to make six quarts—and the steps remain the same.

2 cups peanut oil

⅓ cup plus 2 tablespoons toasted sesame oil

⅔ cup dried red chili flakes (recipe follows)

20 cloves garlic, peeled and smashed

⅓ cup Chinese fermented black beans (*douchi*), roughly chopped

4 tablespoons fresh ginger, peeled and cut into matchsticks

In a large heavy saucepan over low heat, bring all the ingredients to a gentle simmer. Cook for 20 minutes, checking occasionally to make sure the oil doesn't bubble aggressively. Remove from heat and let come to room temperature.

Wash 3 glass pint jars and let them air-dry. Scoop the precious goop from the oil and carefully distribute among the jars. Then pour the remaining oil over the top. Put the lids on and store in a cool dark place for up to 3 months.

Chris's Chili Flakes

Recipe by Christopher Rabilwongse

**MAKES ABOUT 1 CUP—SCALE UP
OR DOWN AS NEEDED**

3 ounces dried Thai chilies, whole, stems removed

Sprinkles of salt

Heat a wide cast-iron skillet or wok over medium-low heat. Add a single layer of dried chilies so they don't overlap and a sprinkle of salt (which helps prevent the chilies from smoking). Begin stirring the minute the chilis hit the pan. Never stop stirring. You'll smell a rich, fragrant toasted-chili aroma as they darken from bright scarlet to russet. Keep stirring and watching closely for about 1 minute. Once you see the first sign of a chili turning black and many of the chilies have darkened a shade, take them off the heat and scoop them onto a baking sheet to cool, leaving the salt behind. Black means you've gone too far. Burned chilies will create tear gas in your kitchen, so be watchful. Let the toasted chilies cool. Repeat as needed with remaining chilies and pinches of salt.

Once cool to the touch, put toasted chilies in a food processor and blitz until they become flakes approximately the same size as the seeds. This takes about 1 to 2 minutes in my Cuisinart. (A Vitamix is too powerful and creates chili powder instead of flakes.) Use these to make chili oil. Keep the extra flakes in a jar on your counter to sprinkle on things.

GROUP LIVING *and* OTHER RECIPES

BUTTER SCULPTURE

One spring day in 1992, I came home from second grade and learned my parents had given my bedroom to three Tibetan monks from Dharamsala, India. My parents' friend Rhonda had called just a few hours earlier, asking if the monks could stay at our house starting that night. Every bedroom in our house was already filled, but that didn't discourage my parents, who love singular experiences. Since my uncle Paul was staying in our spare room and my brother, Zak, had been displaced by guests in the past, my parents offered my small room for Tenzins Dudhul, Norgay, and Norbu to share. During their three-month visit, I slept on the couch in the living room.

Every day, the monks would go to the Portland Art Museum and work on a sand mandala in public view, piping colorful sand into intricate geometries on a felted table. It looked to me like a map of a temple, filled with secret corridors and flower gardens. Each monk started from the center and worked in silence toward the edge. Building the mandala was part of a festival that Rhonda was organizing to raise awareness of China's occupation of Tibet.

Tenzin Dudhul was the youngest of the three monks. He was unbelievably handsome, in his early twenties, strong and agile, always grinning with luminescent teeth and mischievous eyes, his black hair shaved close to the scalp, his forehead a perfect postcard. I had the crush of a happy-go-lucky seven-year-old who wants nothing more than to be in the presence of her objective. I called him "doo doo," which made his grin stretch even wider.

Aside from Dudhul's smiling face, I have few vivid memories of their visit, only a sensory collage: I recall the softness of the gauzy white cloth they tied to doorknobs as blessings. I can smell butter everywhere—melting into their astringent Lipton tea, sizzling in a pan to fry the gritty wheat noodles they made by hand, and being mixed with mineral pigments to fashion tiny ceremonial butter sculptures. I can see the red and gold of their robes, which mirrored the red and yellow tulips that bloomed along our sidewalk in April, and how those robes flew akimbo as they learned to ride bikes on our street.

I came along the day the monks swept up the mandala they'd constructed so carefully, storing it in an urn they wrapped in silk and carried in their arms. We took a motorboat onto the Willamette River under a gray, overcast sky. As I watched them dump the colorful sand into the slate water beneath the Hawthorne Bridge, I felt moody and annoyed. No one explained anything to me, but I understood very simply that this, like the creation of the mandala, was supposed to be important and beautiful. I found it sorrowful. They'd spent three months making something I thought was amazing and then willingly dumped it in a river. Flush, gone. Next, they'd leave, Dudhul would stop grinning at me, and I'd have my bedroom back, because all things are fleeting.

M ost of the people who stayed with us didn't make such a memorable exit, but impermanence was a strong theme of our household. Over and over again, my parents welcomed visitors and we made a life together—over days, weeks, months, years. Then the visitors would leave, and we'd start again, somehow never from scratch but always anew, with nothing to show for our time except what was patterned inside us. I became accustomed to the entrances and exits, which gave the house a lively syncopation.

As mainstream US culture shifted into the "my-own-private-bathroom" era, my parents flung the doors of our house open and invited people in. In addition to Zak, nearly eleven years older than me; my Filipino grandpa, Goyo; and my on-again, off-again Scientologist uncle Paul, my parents always said yes to exchange students. We hosted more than twenty while I was growing up. I can see Joachim, a French high schooler who dressed in oversized, ratty clothing and sported dark, floppy hair like a labradoodle's, splashing chaotically in the Deschutes River at the Warm Springs Reservation, where we'd camp every summer under larch trees barely shading us from the blazing sun. I remember trying to walk side by side on a narrow trail with Ellen, from Holland, who'd slathered herself in sunscreen and wore sunglasses, a hat, and long sleeves so no sun touched her skin as we climbed to the top of Angel's Rest, a promontory overlooking the Columbia River Gorge.

When a delegation of indigenous Tairona from Colombia came to tell their story and seek markets for their fair-trade coffee, my mom coordinated buyer meetings and my dad translated from Spanish. And when a larger group of Tibetan monks came through town with the Lollapalooza music festival, my dad unearthed a dozen cheap foam mattresses and set up our living room for a sleepover party.

It was also common for my parents' friends to appear just before dinner, uninvited but always welcome, with a partial bottle of wine in hand. Both my parents loved to cook, and though their lives were hectic, we ate dinner with whomever was with us. It might sound like chaos, but it felt like security. There was always room at our table.

M y mom, Theresa, has a purposeful way of moving through space, with punchy pitter-patter steps like a hummingbird in human disguise. She's small and strong, half-Filipina, half-Polish, with black hair, wispy eyebrows over smiling eyes, a stoner's faintly stained teeth, weathered hands, and knobby finger joints from working at a laundromat as a teen and a lifetime of digging in garden dirt.

Born in 1946 and raised in Schenectady, New York, my mom dropped out of college in 1965, moving first to Miami and then, on a whim and with five dollars in her pocket, across the country to Los Angeles. There, under the unrelenting sun, she survived her twenties: she waited tables at a strip club, finished her college degree, took a lot of drugs, married a poet-cum-acrobat, became a preschool teacher, and had a son, Zak. When her marriage ruptured in 1975, she moved to Portland, Oregon, where she loved the cover of the wet, towering temperate rainforest. She joined the natural-foods industry early by managing a Portland co-op called Food Front.

My mom has the uncommon pairing of extreme competitive-
ness and a tender, empathic heart—a pairing that works because
she found herself competing with corporate America. Her tem-
per is a sudden hurricane followed by sunny skies, a transition
that leaves her peaceful and others damaged and distraught. At
home, she's almost always barefoot and, in the mornings, in a
T-shirt without underwear. "Don't forget to let your vagina
breathe," she told me so often as a little girl that, in kindergarten,
it took several visits to the principal's office for me to remember
to wear underwear.

Most of my friends' moms were secretive and restrained. My
mom, on the other hand, took me and my friends to a Blazers
game, leaned in close with wheaty beer on her breath, and told
us that a certain basketball player had just made her "cream her
jeans." Then she winked, and all four of us held those words in
our heads, like a mysterious wrapped object, until, years later, we
finally creamed our own. She believes kids know more than
adults give them credit for and that they can handle complex
ideas. She calls Jesus Christ "the bloody cadaver," and when I
was growing up she used the word "hypocrite" to describe people so often that I came to believe it was the common state of
being human. *She's a hypocrite. He's a hypocrite. I'm a hypocrite.*

Before she retired, my mom worked ardently, first in natural-
foods grocery stores and later for the largest organic-dairy-farming
cooperative in the United States. When she wasn't on the clock,
she was either physically active—gardening, hiking, canoeing,
biking—or she was smoking weed and daydreaming, girlish and
goofy. Sometimes, she did both, intertwined: jogging to nearby
Peninsula Park, me on a pint-size bike at her side, until we reached
the rose garden, where she'd lie under the lollipop trees, smoke

weed, and giggle. At home, she rarely took a shower to wash off her BO. Instead, if she was going out, she'd dab a little Le Baiser du Dragon on her wrists and under her chin and smell like earth and onions, breathing vaginas and dark flowering vines.

M y parents met in Portland in the mid-seventies at an arts-and-crafts street fair called, unfortunately, Literuption. My dad, David, has clear, deep blue eyes like Crater Lake and pale skin that burns easily, so that for most of the summer, he's a bubble gum shade of pink. His hair is long and flowing, falling to his mid-back—seemingly never growing any longer, only curlier, as the years pass. His eyebrows shoot in every direction, like tentacles feeling for a steady surface. His easy laugh comes out like a shout: "HA!" When he dances, he strides in place, occasionally kicking out a leg and punching the air to the beat: "HA! HA! HA!" His body temperature runs hot, so he wears shorts, even in snow, and despite winter rain is always in sandals with socks. He travels by bike or bus and takes circuitous routes he insists are the fastest way.

Born in Colorado in 1946, my dad was raised in rural southern Oregon and then eastern Washington, a child of the arid high desert. He joined the Peace Corps at the age of twenty-one and spent two and a half years in Guatemala helping to build schools and supporting leaders of the local agricultural cooperative. During that time, while my dad was away on a trip, a shady businessman swindled seventy families of their garlic harvest, leaving many destitute. My dad subsumed this tragedy into his body as private but unforgotten pain. Outwardly, he is ebullient and playful. One of his closest friends once described him as a diamond-shaped man, which I took to describe not his physical body but his metaphysical being—his Big Rock Candy Mountain philosophy that the next big thing is always coming his way, despite all evidence to the contrary.

My dad is a man of collections. His first was of Guatemalan textiles. Next came books by Pacific Northwest authors, poetry pamphlets, skinny Post-its for highlighting his favorite passages in books—anything, really, that could be tied to the written word—and then one thousand T-shirts, for every Podunk mosquito festival, public transportation opening, lesbian separatist commune, vegetable-distribution company, and Philippines-awareness campaign he'd encountered. He imbues his ephemera with the heavy weight of meaning—these objects revive lives that were vivid, wild, and too easily discarded or forgotten in the torrential mainstream. He cares deeply for individuality, which means he pays close attention to details and readily forgives misbehavior. He surrounds himself with writers, visual artists, filmmakers, historians, and political radicals, many on the edge of solvency. In his worldview, everyone matters, and every year he'd invite everyone in my class to my birthday party—"no one should feel excluded," he insisted.

My parents didn't have an easy relationship, but it was compassionate. In the late seventies, they moved in together because my dad needed a place to live. He didn't believe in monogamy. My mom could go either way and was happy to have a partner who loved and wanted to care for Zak. They agreed to an open relationship, to never getting married, to not having any children. He helped her make peace with her ex. Other decisions came later—to have a child (me!) after all, just before they both turned forty; to start a marketing business together (what were they thinking?); to terminate the business (what a relief!). My mom had many lovers. My dad kept his romantic life secret.

In 1990, when I was five, my mom borrowed money from her boss and put a down payment on a white two-story craftsman house on Holman Street. She planned to move there without my dad, but ultimately, they worked things out and he joined. The Piedmont neighborhood was filled with old houses, most built around the turn of the nineteenth century. A canopy of hundred-year-old black walnut, oak, red maple, hornbeam, and beech trees shaded the urban cement.

At the time, the collection of neighborhoods around Piedmont housed the most diverse community in very white Portland, including 80 percent of Oregon's Black residents. During the period of redlining, this was one of the few places in the city without housing restrictions. My parents were the early shiver of a wave of gentrification that would swell as Portland moved into the twenty-first century, displacing longtime residents.

The Holman House was built of wood. Old-growth timber beams ran the length of the basement, serving as the bones of the building. Under the large front porch, my dad found ancient chicken cages from an era of subsistence living; in the farthest corner of the basement, my mom found broken rifles; and halfway down the basement steps, behind a mysterious two-foot-high door that led to a patch of dirt, my brother found, of all things, a speculum. The Holman House held secrets of its own.

My parents ripped up the parking strip to plant onions. Inside the yard, my mom planted tomatoes, delphiniums, snapdragons, and lilies; my dad planted lilac suckers he dug up from a friend's mother's house and buried a bathtub filled with bamboo shoots for an incongruous patch of canes among the line of evergreen trees that buffer sound from Martin Luther King Jr. Boulevard, half a block away. They made all repairs, or enlisted relatives and unlicensed-contractor friends to help, which meant the rock wall leading to the basement was half-done and, for years, the kitchen skylight dripped whenever it rained.

Previous residents had wanted this 1905 house to feel more like the popular ranch homes of the midcentury, so they lowered the ceilings by four feet in the butter-yellow kitchen and in a nondescript "sitting" room next door. My parents took sledge-hammers to the ceilings and to the wall separating the kitchen from the side room, opening up one oversized room in place of those claustrophobic spaces. The house seemed to breathe, like a corseted person set free. Rhonda, the Free Tibet activist, became their interior designer. She added an island, lined the chimney in copper, and painted the kitchen walls the color of wild-salmon flesh, a shade that initially made my mom scream in horror. Rhonda's solution was to apply a faint coating of gold sponge. Now the walls also shimmered like fish scales. This loud kitchen became the heart of the house.

My dad's younger brother, Doug, came down from Port Townsend, Washington, where he and his wife, Nancy, had founded a cohousing community. He offered his skills as a designer and builder—his day job was working as a member of a construction co-op—to remodel our upstairs bathroom and to build a side porch off our new kitchen. From then on, we spent every warm summer evening eating dinner on the porch.

My parents had an unspoken philosophy about the house: *We only deserve it if we share it.* This resonated with another important code of conduct my mom insisted on: "Never loan anyone money. If you have money, just give them money. If they give it back to you, be thankful. But don't delude yourself: They don't owe you anything. You gave them the money, and that was your choice." This code made sense to me even though we lived paycheck to paycheck for years.

Neither of my parents was free of conventional cultural expectations, but both fought them. They could go overboard and contradict themselves—my mom vehemently disavowed marriage as a form of patriarchy but was also wildly excited for wedding invitations and romantic gestures. My dad scoffed at status symbols only to become obsessed with where people had gone to college and their family lineages. "We're hypocrites," my mom would concede. But they repeatedly enacted their firmest beliefs: Life surrounded by characters, even painful, heartbreaking ones, is preferable to isolation. One needs strange, unpredictable experiences to gain perspective and learn how to gauge risk. And—most important of all—examine your fears. Don't accept them as blackout curtains on the world. Never let them clench your heart. Be discerning.

Not to say that there weren't things in the nineties that my parents feared: the Gulf War and the US bloodthirst for oil; the tragedy of the AIDS epidemic; rampant deforestation; that Vice President Dan Quayle didn't know how to spell the word *potato*. My parents' list was long, and they made it clear that many people's lists were legitimately longer. It's just that guests, dinners, strangers—these were nothing to be fearful about, nor overly prepared for. My parents felt an obligation to be generous. The house had extra rooms, and it was no sweat to cook extra food at night. "Going out to eat is when it gets expensive," my mom would remind me.

I could see clearly that my friends in cleaner, quieter, more affluent houses were not more at ease. Some of my friends' homes felt like small kingdoms. Their parents were benevolent monarchs who governed with elaborate rules, which inspired elaborate forms of deception. Although these friends were more sheltered than me, they were also considered more vulnerable. Even as a kid I recognized this as a self-fulfilling riddle.

I understood the logic of my home. My mom never lost her commitment from her job at the laundromat to ironing, so there were always clean, crisp sheets and tablecloths—as good a foundation as you could want. Dinner was rarely ready when people arrived. There was no set mealtime. My mom put guests to work chopping garlic (always garlic) and washing lettuce for salad in a large hardwood bowl my dad kept nicely oiled. People were asked to help clean up after. None of this, "Oh, just relax!" Food was plentiful. If someone else showed up, you could always boil more pasta.

My dad didn't work the way my mom worked. He headed myriad projects, including editing an alternative arts-and-culture quarterly and running a nonprofit devoted to Oregon's cultural history, but these didn't generate consistent income. In fact, they sometimes did the opposite, sapping his money and digging him into a hole of debt he'd rationalize with the promise of tomorrow's windfall, which rarely came.

He was a stay-at-home dad, although no one ever used those words. I spent many afternoons tagging along as he ran errands. Our usual stops were his PO box downtown and Arvey Paper and Supplies in Southeast, where he'd gather colorful reams to print informational flyers on. While we raced around town, sometimes he'd take me to Martinotti's, an Italian grocery run by his friends Armand and Dixie, where I could choose from chocolates shaped like mushrooms and amaretti cookies wrapped in thin paper. More often, we'd stop at Nicholas for a Lebanese pizza—fluffy dough with mozzarella and black sesame seeds.

Portland sits at the confluence of two big rivers, the Columbia and the Willamette. To the west are the foothills of the ancient Tualatin Mountains; to the east, a long gentle slope rises to a perfect triangle volcano, Mount Hood. Beyond it stretches the high desert. The summers are filled with bright blue skies, technicolor flowers, dry air, and sunshine; the winters are unending, colorless, and wet.

One winter Saturday, when I was in middle school and feeling especially despondent, my dad put me in our golden Jeep and drove east. "We're driving until we reach sun," he told me. He'd packed a small cooler with tuna fish sandwiches and cans of grapefruit soda. He wore his usual khaki shorts, sandals with socks, and a cotton sweater with the sleeves rolled up. In the driver's seat, he sat upright and alert, his long brown hair staticky against the seat. He took us down the Columbia River Gorge; along the wide, strong river we could barely see through the blitzing rain; and past Mount Hood and Mount Adams, invisible in the sky, until we shot past the rain clouds and arrived in the bright winter sun that he'd grown up under. "HA!" he shouted, pleased with himself and ready for his picnic. This was his magic trick for me.

A few years after we moved into the Holman House, my mom started a serious relationship with a man named George who lived in Wisconsin. My parents soon had separate bedrooms. George began visiting more often and staying at our house. I treated him no differently than the other adults who came and

went. My parents continued to live under the same roof as roommates. They made parenting decisions together, I'm sure often
with difficulty. They were transparent with me about their drug
use, judging that I could understand the idea that marijuana was
illegal, and thus not something I should talk about in public, but
that it shouldn't be illegal, because the state got a lot of laws
wrong and the world was messy.

My dad's availability and willingness for parenting duties
made it possible for my mom to work tirelessly, which was a
blessing and a curse. The traditional roles were reversed: she was
the primary breadwinner and poured herself into her work. But
she was prevented—because someone needed to pay off the
mortgage and the credit cards—from ever stepping away and
taking a break. She felt both resentful and appreciative.

Behind closed doors my mom screamed at my dad, mostly
about deception and money. In the open, she screamed at him
about forgetting mustard for a picnic. A current of acrimony grew
between them. I couldn't understand my mom's anger and began
to feel touchy and bitter, but I also craved her attention and luxuriated in moments of shared laughter and meals, when the table
was filled with people and a whir of centripetal energy held us
together.

Impermanence is especially ruthless in puberty. My flat chest
gave way to breast nubs. My childhood fairy tales transitioned
to teenage melodramas. I was a butter sculpture, melting. I can't
separate the frustration and disappointment of this time of my
life from what was happening in my home. My mom had started
working for a dairy cooperative, Organic Valley, which was taking
her to Wisconsin, where George lived, for one week a month,

then more. When she was home, she worked ferociously. She started making a better salary, and we didn't live paycheck to paycheck anymore. My mom and dad untangled their finances, and the separation between them grew wider. I felt she was never home. She felt I never wanted to see her when she was. Zak had long since moved to college, Grandpa Goyo to the Philippines, and Uncle Paul to Boston. Guests were fewer and further between.

By the time I reached high school, our phone regularly rang with debt collectors chasing my dad. The moment I lifted the receiver, they'd berate me. I learned never to pick up. My dad grew more reserved, more concerned about my academics. I felt sadness oozing from us both like sticky, foul sap.

I became an unintentional Goody Two-shoes. When I was fourteen, my mom and I had a heart-to-heart. She cornered me in the living room one early Friday evening. I was already in my Joe Boxer pajamas, lying on the floor in front of the television, head tilted against the base of the couch. She summoned me up, and I mentally prepared myself for a familiar lecture about indolence and a reminder that when Zak was a kid, he hadn't been allowed to watch TV or eat refined sugar, except on Halloween. She'd become less strict in the ten-plus years between us, as her work obligations waxed and the fervor of the seventies waned, but she hadn't forgotten her old rules or her reasons for them. That wasn't the lecture for today, however. Instead, she got right to her point. She told me that I could take any drug in the world as long as she was the dealer. "Nothing is off-limits," she announced. "The only rules are that I have to supply it, and I have to know where you are and who you're with when you take it."

I'm not sure how other people would feel hearing that offer from a parent, but I told her, "I don't think so, Mama. I'm not really interested. That's your thing."

When I try to understand this answer now, what I remember was the sensation in my body. I didn't want to escape reality, to unhinge the rigid bits of my brain and expand outward. I wanted to clamp down harder. I wanted to control every impulse and contract inward. Mine was a teenage girl's brain, seeking perfection through a whittling knife. I've seen this in other girls. It's a road to eating disorders. It's a demonic riddle that no amount of intelligence or rationalizing seems to overcome. In my failure to misbehave, I felt pathetic. I contained both the wounded animal and the circling raptors.

In our shared restlessness, I saw the Holman House as another family member with its own unfulfilled expectations. Where were the parties? The pitter-patter of feet on hardwood floors? Why weren't the tablecloths ironed? Who was there to leave strange objects in strange cubbies? Why so much silence, so many unused rooms, so much pent-up disappointment?

By high school, my hummingbird mom had largely flown away, and the kinetic energy of adults who share a common focus had come unspooled. What seemed so easy and malleable before—the endless companionship, the lively dinners—was much harder. The chemistry was wrong; things rarely fell into place. After a long period of quiet, a delegation of organic agricultural researchers from Russia came for several days and slept on our foam mattresses. One night, the delegation leader, a former Soviet bureaucrat, drank himself into oblivion and then accidentally sliced his hand open with a serrated bread knife. There was no laughing about that.

At the start of my junior year, my mom and George brought their friend Diamond Dave for a visit. Diamond Dave was a street poet and radio personality from San Francisco who spoke exclusively in rhyming verse. You might, for example, say, "Hey, Dave, want to go see this art opening?" and he'd answer, "I'm up for it; I'm down for it; I'm all around for it," while wiggling his pointer finger in the air like a wand.

One morning, he shook me awake, saying, "The two towers. The great powers. Once so tall, watch them fall."

After a bleary moment, I shrieked, "Get out of my room!" shocked to find a seventy-plus-year-old Rumpelstiltskin hovering over me.

My mom was already in her home office, working. My dad gave me my usual tablespoon of cod-liver oil, a hot breakfast, and a kiss out the door. I biked to school, wondering at my weird wake-up, walked toward my locker, and landed in the embrace of a girl I knew but not well, who was weeping and holding me like I needed holding.

"What's going on?" I asked. "Is everything okay?"

"The Twin Towers have been attacked," she told me through sobs.

A long pause.

"What are the Twin Towers?" I asked her.

She could have told me about a UFO invasion, and I'd have been more comprehending. But over the rest of the school day, I became intimate with her meaning. Every one of my teachers, completely unprepared for the task at hand, turned the lights off and the TV on, so that for eight hours I sat in dark classrooms watching the Twin Towers repeatedly buckle, crumble, and crash. We watched the planes' moments of collision over and over. (And over and over and over.) We watched real people jump from the upper stories. I felt the specter of fear loom up, bleak and totalizing. *Don't let fear clench your heart!* But my heart did ache and throb. The world had shifted onto a new axis. One era of my life was over, ended by a foreign attack on domestic soil and a little old man jiggling his beaded hair and speaking riddles over my bed.

Diamond Dave stayed with us for an extra ten days after the September 11 attacks, waiting until he could catch a Greyhound south. Twice, he zoned out on the back porch while smoking and dropped a lit cigarette. My dad found him sitting there in a daze, oblivious, the wood at his feet smoldering. When he was gone, Diamond Dave had left his mark on the Holman House: a burn etched in the shape of a waning moon.

Theresa's Garlicky Panfried Pasta

Recipe by Theresa Marquez

MAKES 2 SERVINGS

My mom loves to serve a quick hot lunch to whomever is hungry and around. Whenever we had pasta leftover from the night before, she'd panfry it for us in garlicky butter until the noodles crisped on their edges, creating contrasting crunchy and chewy textures. Sometimes, she'd incorporate simple additions like ripe tomato or sautéed mushrooms at the end to make a more wholesome meal without too much extra fuss.

Did she take inspiration from the monks? The aroma of melting butter reminds me of their panfried noodles. From her mom's Filipino cooking? You can substitute rice for pasta in this recipe and you'll make the Filipino garlic fried rice called *sinangag*. Or is she just a beacon of common sense, because why would you reheat day-old pasta any other way?

1 tablespoon butter

1 tablespoon olive oil

¼ teaspoon salt, plus more to taste

4 to 6 cloves garlic, smashed

2 cups leftover cooked pasta, any shape, cooled

Freshly ground black pepper

OPTIONAL

Juice of ½ lemon

Chili flakes (page xxiii)

Grated Parmigiano Reggiano

In a broad skillet over medium-low heat, melt the butter and olive oil together until shimmering but before the butter takes on any color. Add the salt and stir to incorporate. Add the smashed garlic cloves and cook, turning them periodically until they turn golden. Watch carefully, as garlic can turn from tan to dark brown quickly. Remove the fried garlic from the pan and set it on a cutting board.

Add the pasta to the pan. Stir to coat in the garlic oil. Spread the pasta into a single layer across the surface of the pan. Don't disturb the pasta—leave it alone for 2 minutes so parts of it turn golden. Jostle and flip the pasta and leave it alone for a few more minutes. (If the pasta seems especially dry, add a spoonful or two of water.) Repeat this at least once more, until the pasta is fully reheated and crisped on its edges.

Mince the fried garlic cloves. Return most of the garlic to the pan and fold to incorporate. Continue to fry so the garlic gets crispy. Garnish with the last fried garlic bits, along with freshly ground black pepper, salt to taste, optional lemon juice, chili flakes, and a snow shower of freshly grated Parmigiano Reggiano. Eat while it's hot.

BITTER AND SWEET

'd assumed that turning twenty-one would feel important, but when the day came, in February 2006, I awoke to cold, sloppy rain and a feeling so powerfully blank it mirrored the wet, colorless sky. I'd been living in Japan for six months, where the legal drinking age is twenty, and I'd been buying alcohol from the moment I landed, making this milestone birthday feel especially anticlimactic. My friend Emily helped me rally. She'd asked her friend, who was coming to visit her in Kyoto for a week, to sneak marijuana through customs in a baggie in her vagina. The night of my birthday, the three of us—Emily, this new friend I was much indebted to, and I—bathed at a *sento* on a side street off Nishiki Market. One of the bathhouse's tubs had electric pulses in the water that supposedly eased pain. Every few seconds I briefly tasted electrocution.

Afterward, in the dark under an awning sheltering us from the rain, we smoked this most prized contraband, a single joint, in a country where marijuana possession can get you five years in prison. I felt the residue of the electric pulses amplify. I'd started smoking weed in college, away from the approving eyes of my

parents, always tentatively. As we wandered in the darkness and
drizzle down Shijo (Fourth Avenue), I lost myself in the visual
intensity of a place I'd been living in as a student for months.
The water of the Kamogawa River reflected neon from both
sides, like colorful Christmas lights diffused through frosted
glass. I felt jangled but ready for a fresh start.

For the previous five months, from September through January,
I'd lived with the Yada family. Most of the time, they dealt
with me at a distance. The Yadas owned a perfectly rectangular,
narrow four-story concrete building. The first floor was the
father's cosmetics store, where his wife and daughter worked.
The second floor was split between a hair salon in front, which
they leased to others, and their kitchen in back. The family slept
on the third floor, and I slept on the fourth, adjacent to rooms
where they stored their excess makeup inventory.

Each night, my host mother, Setsuko, would call me on an
intercom system.

Beep, beep, beep. "LOOO-LAAAAA! Dinnertime!"

I'd descend two short flights and eat my meals alone.

For months I blamed myself for their sometimes-cold,
sometimes-nasty behavior toward me. I told myself that they'd
sensed my dislike for them from the start. The Yadas had generously opened their home to me. I was a guest and also a stranger.
The onus was on me to be open, curious, and generous in return.
But I couldn't rewrite my emotions. I'd felt uneasy in their house
from the first week.

I can remember a night in early September, not long after I'd
arrived in Japan. It was just before nine, and I was sitting at the
dinner table under the fluorescent lights with my thick Japanese

dictionary open, translating a newspaper article for class. My host sister, Yukine, came up from the cosmetics shop for a cigarette break. Yukine was in her mid-thirties and lived at home. She'd graduated from college in 1991, when the Japanese economic bubble burst and her generation was left scrambling for the reliable jobs they'd been promised. She smoked constantly, even waking for a midnight cigarette, and her skin was pallid and reflective, like it was shining the concrete rooms back at me. There was a sparkle in her eyes that sometimes looked excitingly evil, but mostly she never looked at me, and I didn't get to feel the shiver her stare could bring.

Yukine grabbed her ashtray, sat down across from me, and pulled a cigarette from her pack. I tried to catch her eyes, but she stared at the plastic tablecloth, lit her cigarette, and began smoking. I looked back down at my dictionary. A few moments later, Taku, my host father, rushed in. In his late sixties, Taku dyed his hair a rich warm black tinted with mahogany. He wore small round glasses that seemed to sit on top of his lips, which were usually fixed in a chilly grin. In addition to owning the cosmetics shop, he'd been a hairstylist until his failing eyesight compelled him to retire. While I lived with him, Taku spent much of his time taking photographs around Kyoto and going to sculpture and ballroom dancing classes. The building was filled with his blurry black-and-white photographs of flowers and cityscapes.

Taku looked around and asked frantically, "*Doko?* Where's the remote control?"

Yukine pointed her elbow toward the top of the TV as she raised her cigarette to her mouth. A local news program was underway. It was a human-interest story about a ballroom dancing class for people who were disabled. A young reporter explained that volunteers visited the class each week and danced with the women and men in wheelchairs. The camera framed a man—round glasses, outsized grin, his hair gleaming at times purple, at times black—as he swiveled the wheelchair of a sour-faced woman in a glittering silver blouse around the waxy dance floor. Taku was on the screen! His televised smile seemed to eat his face.

The woman looked confused as TV Taku spun her wheelchair to the left and then the right, released one of her hands, twirled the chair away, and reeled it back. For a few moments the camera followed their movements. When the music ended, he swiveled her to a stop, and the reporter reentered the frame.

"Mariko-san, what does it feel like out there?" the reporter asked the woman. "It must be exhilarating."

The woman nodded in obvious discomfort. She looked away from the camera, toward someone out of sight. TV Taku's grin was eclipsing the screen as he stared at the reporter impatiently.

In our kitchen, Yukine kept her eyes on the table and lit another cigarette. The reporter gave up on Mariko and turned to TV Taku, in his black turtleneck and black jeans.

"Yada-san has been ballroom dancing since his mid-twenties. This is his second year coming to the Uzumasa Ballroom Center on Wednesday nights to volunteer with these disabled dancers. Yada-san, how is dancing with Mariko-san different from dancing with an able-bodied partner?"

TV Taku grinned, paused as though discovering a sudden calm, and then enunciated, "It's the same for me, but I have even more control."

laughed in horror later, wondering if I'd misunderstood. It gave me the shivers. How generous of him to volunteer, but who was he making happy? He was commandeering in his relationships with Setsuko and Yukine as well, fitting the stereotype of the mulish Japanese patriarch. Setsuko and Yukine both worked in his cosmetics shop from ten in the morning until ten at night, Monday through Saturday. The shop seemed like a makeup-filled hell.

Taku and Setsuko's marriage had been arranged when they were very young, and I suspected it wasn't what either had dreamed for themselves. They seemed to spend as little time together as possible. Setsuko had a high-strung vitality. A small and sharp woman, she used her own face as a makeup display to thrillingly ghostly effect: she powdered her pale skin to look even whiter and outlined her features in nacreous pastels. A wild inner monologue of harangues—of which I got to hear only a few—seemed to race constantly inside her head. It was like a runaway subway train that occasionally comes aboveground. Even she didn't seem to know when she'd emerge from a tunnel to air her thoughts out loud and when she'd plunge back into silent narration.

This was my first long-term exposure to living with a married couple, and it heightened the fears my mother had lodged in my head about marriage as a tool to restrict women's freedom and keep their labor hidden and devalued. Setsuko and Taku's relationship had become a series of constricting walls and obligations. It occurred to me that this boxy cement building was inseparable from their marriage. It had become its physical and metaphysical container.

Taku had found ways to sneak out of this gray space: his blurry photos, his ballroom dancing. I imagined that he had a secret life, perhaps a lover (I pictured a young man with bleached hair and blousy shirts who loved grilled squid). But Setsuko had no time for escapes. Perhaps I, a foreign exchange student, was intended as one, but she had no time for me either, and so instead I became another possibility that had died within this space, transforming from a mystery into a source of busywork.

Each night, I walked through the dim light of the closed cosmetics shop to reach the bath. The walls of the shop were lined in mirrors and posters of slim-figured Japanese and American women. I made my way past crowded displays of eye shadows, whitening and anti-wrinkle creams, and tubes of lipstick and mascara. While I tiptoed, I dreamed of toppling the displays of shimmering powders and glistening pastes, scrawling in lipstick on the mirrors, defacing the models, making a terrible mess of glittery substances, knowing that glitter messes are forever. But I never, in five months, managed to pause in the store. I always rushed past, eyes on the bathroom light, and hurried in for my bath. Each night, after I dried off and put on my pajamas, I meticulously picked my stray hairs from the shower floor. Setsuko had complained that I shed like a dog.

By the time I moved to Japan, I'd been studying Japanese for fifteen years. In kindergarten, my parents enrolled me in a fledgling Japanese-language immersion program in the Portland Public Schools. Neither parent was innately enthusiastic about Japanese—the Japanese committed gruesome atrocities in the Philippines during World War II, while my grandparents were living there—but my parents loved the concept of a bilingual public education. Every day we studied in both Japanese and English: we sang Japanese children's songs and celebrated Japanese holidays, studied kanji in the morning and cursive in the afternoon.

In the fifth grade, my class took our first trip to Japan. It was a sweaty and magical summer vacation that was just different enough from my life at home that all the memories have a magnified clarity—buying an ice cream push-pop from a vending machine, visiting an austere shrine tucked among bent pine trees, using a robotic toilet, seeing my first lightning bugs.

I remained in the Japanese-immersion program through my senior year of high school and traveled to Japan three more times before graduation, including spending a summer in Okinawa, near US military bases and the aquamarine tropical ocean. Japanese culture wasn't something I'd sought out, but it became part of my life. I loved the overarching quality of Japanese sensory attentiveness. I became awake to everyday objects: the pleasant uneven shape of a ceramic bowl in my hands; packaging that kept seaweed separate from a rice ball so it remained crispy until eaten; a single length of cloth that could be folded around an object and turned into a bag. Art and intention were embedded in unexpected places, making everything I saw more interesting to consider and appreciate, although most of the significance was lost on me.

When I went to college, I knew I wanted to continue studying Japanese cultural history. Months before leaving for my year in Kyoto, I'd pictured myself spending my days in temples and my nights singing karaoke and partying. I'd thought I wanted a family who'd be hands-off and let me stumble in after hours—I checked a box saying so on my application. But I was wrong about my needs. The Yadas were an easy scapegoat for

my unhappiness. My real problem was one of mismatched expectations. Even in a house filled with people, loneliness started to
overtake my life.

As November arrived, the maple trees I could see from my
little porch turned the most outlandish shade of red, like the
entire hillside was on fire. It was unspeakably beautiful and
unnerving to me, but I could rarely sit outside to gawk. A murder
of crows had moved onto my porch and cawed a dirge in my face
every morning. Then, while trying to stay warm one night, huddled against a little gas heater, I almost suffocated on carbon
monoxide. I clawed my way along the floor with the last of my
strength and consciousness to open the door for air. After that,
the winter grew even colder, but I was afraid to use the heater
and would get under my comforter as soon as darkness fell and
stay there until Setsuko intercommed me for my lonely dinner. I
finally knew I needed to go when I found a series of hash marks
carved into my desk, which I interpreted as a previous student's
desperate counting of their days, like a prisoner.

After waiting two months for my program to find a willing
family, in late January I moved in with the Yamaguchis, a
mother and her two grown daughters. The contrast was so stark
that for the first few days I couldn't sleep. I lay in bed with my
eyes wide open and tapped my feet. We lived in close quarters,
and I could hear my host sister Tomoko snoring lightly in the
room next door.

Every day after class I'd return home, rinse two cups of rice
until the water ran clear, and leave it to soak so that my host
mom, Junko, and I could immediately begin cooking the main
dinner dishes together once she came home at seven o'clock.

Born in 1944, during the war, Junko had a certain strength in her posture and dress that made her seem like the one you'd want at your side if everything started falling apart. In her early sixties, she wore cashmere turtlenecks that she kept impeccably clean and wide-wale-corduroy or wool skirts that fell to her mid-calf.

I loved to watch her make quick daikon pickles. First, she'd cut the tubular radish into two-inch lengths. Then she'd move the knife in a continuous circle around the perimeter of the radish, carving a perfectly even two-millimeter scroll. She'd slice the scroll into identical matchsticks, sprinkle them with salt, and press them under a rock to draw out moisture. Witnessing her mastery made me feel a little high. She'd let me try, and as I carved an uneven, nicked, and broken scroll, I marveled at how adept she was with a knife.

In contrast, I felt light and silly around her daughters, Nobuko and Tomoko. Nobuko was a violinist resting at home after a sequence of chemotherapy who affectionately teased everyone around her. Tomoko taught food science at a local women's university and had a project devoted to getting a new generation interested in traditional pickled heirloom vegetables. Like the Yadas, the Yamaguchis were a multigenerational household, which came without the social stigma so prevalent in the United States. It's traditional for grown children to live with their parents in Japan; modernization hasn't drastically changed that, a boon since the population is rapidly aging.

This was my first taste of adult friendship inside a home. It felt powerfully different from the Holman House, where I was a child among adults, and also from my college dorm experience, where my sense was that everyone was screaming their own song in profound disharmony—some louder than others, most seeking friends whose melodies fused with their own, everyone barely able to hear over the psychic din. In college, I found the cacophony at times thrilling and life-giving and at other times wholly oppressive. But here was a different kind of music making: more spacious, gentle, and collaborative.

Living in that small apartment, with a ledge where Junko collected pine cones from around the world and a balcony where she grew *sanshô* peppercorns, I learned to feel at home with the base flavor of dashi (broth made from kombu and *katsuobushi*—kelp and smoked, fermented skipjack tuna) and to ask after every ingredient, curious about its uses, spectrum of flavors, and unique story. The Yamaguchis exposed me to the depth of Japanese food culture, with its heightened place-based sensibility and keen focus on balance.

Kyoto homestyle cooking has striking precision. Dinners are composed of different foods presented on different plates so you can taste each thing in relation to the others. With each dish, Junko illuminated the simple, subtle flavor of the primary ingredient. I created the flow and dimensions of my meal by choosing each bite. Every dinner included pickles in shapes, colors, and flavors I'd never known. I decided I never wanted to eat a meal without a pickle again. I learned to scale and gut a fish and experienced how luxurious fresh unpressed tofu can taste.

Junko and her daughters gave me one of the most powerful gifts of all, companionship, and with it came many attending surprises. In school I'd learned about Japanese onomatopoeia, but it was divorced from life. Now, talking with me while we cooked and ate, Junko, Nobuko, and Tomoko taught me that there were words that described particular sensations I'd never tried to name. *Hoku hoku*: starchy foods like potatoes or sweet potatoes cooked so they are soft and can easily be split into pieces, still warm and steaming. *Shiko shiko*: the pleasant feeling of firm food, specifically the springiness of an udon noodle (and also, notably, the sound of masturbation). These words sometimes imitate a sound in the same way as English onomatopoeia. "Slurp" is *zu zu* for a liquid and *zuru zuru* for soba noodles. "Crunchy" has many translations: *shaki shaki* for a texture like biting into celery or daikon; *saku saku* for a crispy feeling on the teeth, like crunching on cookies or apples; *pari pari* for the crunch of something freshly fried. And there are more!

Just as often, these words assign a whimsical sound to something smelled, seen, touched, transformed, or even felt emotionally in a way that English rarely does. *Muku muku*: something soft that becomes big and fat, like whipping cream as it thickens, billowing clouds or smoke, or blossoms as they grow plump; also feelings that suddenly amass, like missing someone more and more, realizing you're in love, or having an idea take shape inside you.

The Japanese language provides more nuanced ways than English does to describe sensory experience. It's okay to reach across boundaries to capture your impressions. This lexicon created brand-new multisensory experiences for me, akin to synesthesia, so that when I saw a tightly packed suitcase, I'd hear *gyu gyu* and feel a constricting feeling in my chest, not unpleasantly. Even when I forgot the words, I remembered the distinctions.

One Saturday, Junko, Tomoko, Nobuko, and I went to a café called Moan (pronounced in two syllables, *moh-an*) tucked in the forested peak of Yoshida Hill in eastern Kyoto. We made tea bowls from gritty clay and then attended a formal tea ceremony, a ritual where every motion is considered. One person performs the ceremony and the others watch and drink tea. What seems

effortless is carefully planned and practiced. For us, the recipi-
ents, the ceremony began with a traditional sweet (*wagashi*), each
as beautiful as an ornament.

Following Nobuko's lead, I used a toothpick-length piece of
bamboo to slice my cake and to bring a bite to my mouth. The
sweet was too sweet, and the sugar made my mouth ache, but
then I drank the matcha—powdered green tea—which was
astringent and intense, and together they became perfect: tasting
both extremes and the place where they met. Sweet balances
bitter and bitter balances sweet.

I never told the Yamaguchis about dinner at the Yadas'—
about descending two flights of stairs to find a tray of food waiting for me, everything unnamed and losing heat in the empty
room. I luxuriated in our communal meals at the Yamaguchis',
especially hot pot on cold nights. Junko would lay out plates of
meats, fish, tofu, mushrooms, and vegetables, and we'd each add
ingredients to simmering broth in a small electric pot on the
table, watching as steam licked the surface and rose to our faces.
We'd pluck out what we wanted when it was fully cooked and
add more to the pot: sometimes our favorite ingredients—for me,
mushrooms—but just as often what we thought someone else
might want, nodding through the steam that *this* was for *them*.
What would start as a relatively plain broth became richer, fuller,
and more complex as we each contributed, and our bodies grew
warmer and warmer as we ate, like we were little hot pots too.

After dinner each night, we'd sit at the table and talk. I'd do
my homework and joke around with Nobuko about the ways I
misread things. Tomoko, who often arrived on a late train from
work, would share one of the new recipes her students had been
testing. Stoic Junko would transform into a playful toddler,
stretching and tumbling around on the floor with her feet in her

hands. At some point each night, I'd take the first bath. Even in the Yamaguchi house, I spent long minutes crouched on the shower floor, searching for my stray hairs.

When Zak visited in March, a few weeks after my birthday, I'd been living with the Yamaguchi women for two months. I was happier and calmer, but still fragile from months of loneliness. Zak has always looked youthful—people never imagine there are so many years between us—and seeing his boyish face lit me up. He's almost six feet tall, but he carries himself as though he were smaller, slouching a little in the shoulders. His hair is fine and his eyebrows almost nonexistent above dark eyes that usually have a faintly skeptical tilt to them. But when he saw me, his eyes shone with loving, protective care.

Zak stayed in the Yamaguchis' small apartment for a few days, and he and they came to adore one another. Everyone was always smiling, like we shared a joke that didn't need to be spoken aloud. When my spring break began, Zak and I took the bullet train to Kyûshû, the third-largest island of Japan. For a week, we traveled mostly by local train through the countryside. I told him about my chronic constipation. He told me about his relationship with his girlfriend, who highly recommended colonics. I told him horror stories of my months with the Yadas: of being woken in the middle of the night when Setsuko, drunk, began speaking into the intercom system: "LOOO-LAAAAA! *Ofuro—bath time!*" He read me a Haruki Murakami story about a brother and sister, the same age difference as us, who lived together. In one part of the story, the brother finds the sister sitting in the kitchen at night, crying uncontrollably. He sits with her in silence while she weeps for several hours.

On the third day of our trip, we arrived at Aso-Kuju National Park, where an enormous crater filled with green sulfurous water releases plumes of thick, fetid steam. We each had a small backpack and some water. Zak had part of a stale peanut butter cookie he'd brought from Portland. Reading the park map as best as I could, I mapped a route for us to hike from one visitor's center to the other. The ground was covered in black sand, and we hiked along wooden causeways that led to more stable, rocky ground. From there we walked wherever the ground seemed most used. We reached a steep hillside covered in boulders and picked our way up, looking for occasional splashes of yellow paint.

Zak told me about Christmas at home. Our mom had made sourdough donuts, as she always does, but they were far more delicious than ever before, he told me. "Light as air, crispy on the outside. A little sour from being double risen," he taunted, opening up a chasm of longing for things already past, which plumed their own fetid steam. We reached the top of the hill and followed a ridge that overlooked the crater.

"YADA!" I screamed at him, evoking both the Japanese expression *iyada*, for "No, I don't like it," and my first host family's name. "YADAAAAAA! YADAAAAAA! FUCK YOU AND YOUR CUNT DONUTS!"

I screamed "YADAAAAAA" and "FUCK YOU" over and over into the air, toward the pluming crater. There is so little open space in Japan to scream anything.

When we reached the far visitor's center, we discovered that it was out of commission. We were alone on the other side of the mountain, several hours from where we'd begun, in the middle of nowhere. We could see down toward the ocean and a small town along its shore. We decided to continue, hoping the road would lead to the town. We were starving and grumpy. My throat hurt from how many times I'd screamed into the crater. We walked mostly in silence for an hour, listening to our stomachs grumble, until suddenly a speedy red car containing a flashy-looking couple, both wearing dark sunglasses, drove past us toward the visitor's center. A few moments later, it came back our way. The couple pulled over, let us in, and, in what seemed like seconds, let us off in town at the train station.

It was late afternoon. We were too hungry to find out when the next train ran. Instead, we rushed into a big brown cement building that stood across from the station, made our way past a women's clothing shop, and entered a door that read, simply, "Restaurant." We sat at the nearest table. I opened the menu and began to read it aloud for Zak. The lunch special was *Kumamoto-gyû-don*, Kumamoto-variety beef over rice. This means something similar to Angus beef over rice, but that's misleading because Japanese beef (*wagyû*) is a far greater specialty item than an Angus steak. The Kumamoto breed, one of the *Akage wasshû*, or brown-haired Japanese cattle, descends from the Korean Hanwoo and Swiss Simmental breeds and is raised primarily on Kyûshû.

Japanese beef is the most highly marbled in the world. Fat runs through the muscles like a thousand rivulets of water through sand. For two to three years of their lives, *wagyû* stand in tightly confined spaces and are fed a grain diet. Rumors about bizarre rearing practices circulate the world. Many Americans have told me that *wagyû* (more commonly, although somewhat inaccurately, known as Kobe beef) is tender and well marbled because of the cattle's coddled treatment: they claim they're bottle-fed beer, which helps increase the appetite of animals who rarely move, especially during the humid summer months; vigorously massaged, which relaxes the otherwise inflexible, atrophying muscles produced by their inhumane confinement; and played soothing classical music. Japanese beef producers have told me that only a few operations perform these tricks and that they're not the primary reason the beef is so delicious. On a jingoistic note, they'll insist that the brilliance of pure Japanese genetics is the key. Both the US and Japanese accounts are misleading.

Because of Buddhist and Shinto prohibitions, most Japanese didn't eat beef at all until the mid-nineteenth century, when American gunboats forced the nation open. Japan began a rapid project of modernization, and not eating beef became a symbol of everything backward, small, and feeble about the nation— portrayed by its leaders as a body politic weak in spirit and flesh. A frenzied internal propaganda campaign to make Japan a nation of beef-eaters commenced. This included a focus on cattle breeding and production. Endemic breeds were crossbred with European ones in the decades before the turn of the twentieth century.

As Japan turned toward nationalism leading to World War II, they closed all cattle importation, rebranded their cattle as exclusively Japanese, and put in place a system of associations that carefully managed breeding programs to select for cattle with highly marbled muscles. It's a potent example of cooperation and determination, but toward a bizarre end that's inhumane to the animals, and a small reminder that collaborative effort isn't moral in and of itself, although its results can be astonishing.

'd never eaten Japanese beef before. It's too expensive to buy for a casual meal, and neither Setsuko nor Junko cooked it at home, but Zak and I hadn't eaten all day, apart from that stale peanut butter cookie, and we were in the heart of cattle country. I ordered two *Kumamoto-gyû-don* lunch sets, each twenty-five hundred yen (around twenty-two dollars at that time). When the waitress set the tray with the beef, a small cup of pickles, and a bowl of miso soup before me, the amount of food looked too modest to fill my empty stomach. Five bite-sized pieces of seared beef sat on top of a neat pile of rice in a small amount of rich, brown sauce. There were several slices of sautéed onion, three *sanshô* peppercorns, and a sprig of *sanshô* pepper leaves. It looked more aesthetic than filling, although the savory scent of the beef was making my mouth water.

Zak and I each picked up a piece of the Kumamoto beef. The flavor was rich and full, the meat as tender as a potato roasted in drippings. The beef melted in my mouth—*toro*. It was the most delicate meat I'd ever eaten. In my next bite, with rice, I tasted the fresh green flavor of a *sanshô* peppercorn, which I recognized from Junko's cooking. The leaf looked aesthetic, like a parsley sprig next to an omelet, but Junko had taught me that when you smack it between your palms, it releases a tropical aroma that enhances the taste of the food. The cook had done this before serving our meal, and a quiet scent sat around the bowl, strongest as you brought your face near.

Without speaking, I ate at a steady pace, choosing each bite carefully. Everything was perfectly, meticulously proportioned and considered. I interrupted rice and beef with bites of crisp pickle and sips of miso soup, and each item diminished at the same rate.

Zak was just as intent an eater as I was. When we both had only a small amount left, we paused and looked into each other's eyes. Zak said to me, "I feel so sad. Each bite is precious." I'd always hated the word *precious*—the result of too much Tolkien in my youth—but that was how I felt as well. I looked into my nearly empty bowl—two bites of rice, one peppercorn, a sliver of onion, one piece of beef—and assured myself that it was all right to mourn the passing of this meal and to long for the very moment I was in. I didn't want to take the last bite of meat, but I grabbed it with my chopsticks and placed it in my mouth. I felt sad and overwhelmed. When I looked back up at Zak while I chewed, I also felt a welling of gratitude and tenderness that he was with me. *Hokkori.* My heart felt like a steaming sweet potato, soft and warm.

After we finished and paid, we rushed to the train station and caught a local headed in the direction of Kirishima (Fog Mountain). During the ride, it became dark outside. We both bought Asahi Super Dry tall boys and drank them leisurely. I thought about the cattle drinking beer and whether it really stimulates the appetite and marbles your muscles. It was definitely working to relax me.

When we got off the train, only a few hours later, we ate again—this time, bowls of *shio* butter ramen. It's commonplace comfort food, cheap and delicious, made with simple, ingenious choices (a tab of butter plopped on top of the chicken broth, so you can pull your noodles through the daisy-yellow fat with each bite). We ate fast so the noodles wouldn't get soft and then raced to our hostel just in time to take a bath. For the first time in months, I felt completely at ease, which is how chicken noodle soup is supposed to make you feel.

Yuri's Miso Cod *Nabe* (Hot Pot)

Recipe by Yuri Baxter-Neal

MAKES 6 SERVINGS

When I first returned from Japan, I frequently made hot pot, known in Japan as *nabe*, but slowly fell out of the habit. My friend Yuri brought it back to me with this incredible miso cod version, which transports me to that early spring in the Yamaguchi household.

Hot pot is not to be confused with an Instant Pot. In Japan, hot pot simply means a pot held over a steady heat source, usually tableside, in which you cook food in simmering broth. Yuri makes this on the stovetop and brings it finished to the table. It's a very satisfying one-pot meal.

If you'd prefer, you can make this in a pot on the table—for example, over a butane burner. If that's your plan, you'll follow the first step, soaking the kombu, cutting it, and bringing the pot with the daikon and carrot to a boil. Then let people add items at their own pace from bowls on the table, plucking things out when they're cooked. Wait until the very end to add the miso (and skip the sesame oil and lime juice)—you can stir it into the broth that remains in the pot and drink it like miso soup!

If you go with the tableside approach, you'll want to make ponzu, a citrus-soy dipping sauce, for people to dunk their cooked items in. To make ponzu: Combine equal parts fresh citrus juice (lemon, lime, grapefruit, yuzu, or *sudachi* would be best), rice vinegar, and soy sauce or tamari. Add a spoonful of honey or sugar to taste. Give everyone their own bowl, containing around a half cup of dipping sauce.

I've made this dish like Yuri does, with rock cod and chicken, but I've also substituted heaps of mushrooms (to make it totally vegetarian) in place of both. This recipe is adaptable, so feel free to play, keeping in mind the basic steps.

2-by-6-inch piece kombu seaweed

¾ pound daikon radish, peeled and sliced

1 carrot, sliced

2 boneless, skinless chicken thighs, cut into bite-size pieces

½ pound shiitake mushrooms, stems thinly sliced, caps quartered

1 large leek, root end and raggedy top trimmed off, cut into 1-inch lengths, washed

1½ pounds Napa cabbage (about ½ large or 1 to 2 small heads), cut into 2-inch pieces, separating the white ribs from the leafy tops (but keeping both)

1 pound rock cod, cut into large bite-size pieces

1 package (about ¾ pound) soft or medium tofu, cut into large cubes

1 teaspoon salt

4 to 8 tablespoons miso (any type will work)

2 tablespoons toasted sesame oil

Juice from 2 limes

Put 6 cups water and kombu in a large stockpot or Dutch oven and let stand for 30 minutes. Using scissors, cut the kombu into skinny strips and return them to the pot.

Add the daikon and carrot to the cold water with the kombu. Bring the pot to a boil over medium-high heat with the lid on. Cook for several minutes. Reduce the heat to medium and add the chicken. Bring back to a boil and cook for about 3 minutes. Skim off any foam that rises to the surface. Add the shiitake, leek, and white Napa rib pieces and simmer for 3 to 4 minutes. Add the rock cod and tofu, pile the Napa leaves on top, and put the lid back on; this will steam the leaves. Simmer for a couple minutes, until the rock cod is tender.

Season with salt, 4 tablespoons miso, toasted sesame oil, and lime juice. Taste for salt, and if it needs more, add 1 tablespoon miso at a time until it's just the way you like it. Serve with rice, chili oil, and . . .

Junko's Daikon *Namasu* (Quick-Pickled Daikon, Carrot, and Ginger)

Recipe by Junko Yamaguchi

MAKES 1 HEAPING CUP OR 8 SERVINGS AS A SIDE

I reached out to Junko for her daikon quick-pickle recipe. She was fifteen years older than when I lived with her but was still adept with a knife. Her daughters sent me photos, and the memories came rushing back—the first time I saw Junko holding a daikon in her left hand and a knife in her right, turning the tubular radish into an elegant white scroll (a cutting technique called *katsura-muki*). Afterward, she laid the scroll on a cutting board, sliced it into pages, and then cut those pages into identical matchsticks (*sen-giri*). All of this precision was new and moving to me.

We always had some kind of pickle on the table to balance the heavier dishes of the meal. Junko often started making the pickles right after the rice but before cooking everything else, so the daikon and carrots had time to release their liquid and soak up the vinegar before we ate. I don't let myself stress about my clumsy knife skills—I have the rest of my life to practice. These pickles are great as a side and also in a sandwich à la banh mi. I've added fresh ginger because I love its sharpness.

This seems like a small quantity to make, but it's best to make an amount you can eat quickly, for the crunchiest texture.

⅓ pound (about a 4-inch segment or 6 ounces) daikon radish, peeled

1 carrot (1 to 2 ounces), peeled

1-inch knob ginger, peeled and julienned

Pinches of salt

AMAZU (SWEET VINEGAR)

¼ cup unseasoned rice vinegar

2 tablespoons sugar

1 teaspoon salt

2-inch strip lemon peel, minced

Cut the daikon radish into 2-inch segments. Cut each segment lengthwise in half so you can lay the flat side down. Thinly slice them and then lay the slices on top of one another like pages. Cut into thin matchsticks—as close to the size of real matchsticks as you can. Add a pinch of salt to the daikon matchsticks and mix. Let stand in a bowl for 10 minutes. Water should pool in the bowl. Meanwhile, cut the carrot into matchsticks the same length and width as the daikon. In a separate bowl, add the carrots and a pinch of salt, mix, and let stand for 10 minutes. (Keeping the two vegetables separate preserves the colors.) Squeeze out as much liquid as you can from both the daikon and carrot, discard the liquid from each, and combine them with the ginger.

Whisk together the *amazu*—vinegar, sugar, salt, and lemon peel—until the sugar is almost fully dissolved. Pour *amazu* over the daikon, carrot, and ginger and toss. Serve. Leftover pickles will keep in the fridge for several days.

TENDER

The communal dorm where I lived my sophomore and senior years at Amherst College felt pseudo-Greek in its grandiosity, at least from the outside. Inside, it was both sloppy and bare, filled with disintegrating furniture and body aroma. It was called the Zü, a joke mostly on us, the animals who lived inside. We didn't eat in the cafeteria; the Zü was the one dorm on campus where students cooked their own meals. Five nights a week, around twenty of us ate a vegetarian dinner together, and once every two weeks, a friend and I were responsible for making it. The first time, I was in such haste to chop a dozen onions that I almost cut off the tip of my thumb. By necessity, I learned about knife skills and cooking for a crowd, especially how to plan my time.

Food at the Zü was usually forgettable and occasionally disgusting. Everything had a questionable texture—too soft, too firm, never just right. And everyone was in a rush to go somewhere else: to finish studying, to meet up with a friend. We didn't have a shared commitment to one another and the place. We simply lived under the same roof and abided by the rules.

Some of my closest friends lived with me at the Zü, but there was also a real contingent of prestige bros in my dorm whom I distrusted profoundly. This whole raft of would-be Brett Kavanaughs might someday become Supreme Court justices. Certainly some would end up as investment bankers and consultants. In the meantime, they were egomaniacal banes in pastel khaki shorts who treated each other terribly. I was mostly outside their pranks, but they reminded me that living with someone without mutual care is worse than living alone.

My sophomore year, a senior tapped a maple tree in our front yard, collecting gallons of sap across several buckets. Maple sap is thin and clear and must be simmered for hours to concentrate its sugars into syrup, but the process didn't seem to work for him. For a few days, we watched him checking his pots, always with a puzzled look on his face. I later learned that his friends had sabotaged his efforts by pouring all the sap down the drain when he wasn't looking and replacing it with water, wasting days of his time making meaningless steam. Instead of concentrating sweetness, they trashed it. Witnessing this kind of hateful friendship depressed me.

My brother called me in the winter of my senior year. I was pacing outside the Zü, staring up through bare branches at a fortress of heavy gray clouds in the sky. A few months before, Zak had moved back into the Holman House. After my mom moved to Wisconsin full-time, my dad had lived there with transient roommates: a former Merry Prankster on the Ken Kesey bus; a bookstore owner the size of a giant; and, for a time, a man I was seeing long-distance who worked as a chef. My mom was the homeowner and eventually decided to kick out my dad, after helping him find a place to live, and to rent the house to Zak. She was ready for a change that made the house feel more accessible to her. My dad left behind bookshelves filled to the brim but mostly carted his trove of things to his new apartment a few miles away.

Zak moved into the Holman House with his friend Cynthia, who filled the gaps my dad left with her own oddities: a heap of broken bikes, a fleet of children's wooden desks, tubs of art supplies. The capacious Holman House could swallow collections whole. Tender Vittles, Cynthia's fluffy white magician's-rabbit-like cat, also moved in.

As I walked figure eights around the trees outside the Zü, Zak told me that Cynthia had invited her friend Chris, with whom she was working on a stop-motion animated film, to move in as well. Chris, he said, was an unreal cook. (Zak loves to inflict me with maddening envy.) Just the previous night, Chris had cooked a *tom kha* curry with galangal, lemongrass, and *makrut* lime leaves, filling the kitchen with what Zak called "the smell of grandma's perfume." Earlier that week, he'd made his mom's spicy and delicious pork *larb*, finished with the herb *rau ram*, at once fatty and fresh. I wanted to be in the kitchen with Zak, Chris, Cynthia, and their friends. I wanted to eat Chris's food, which sounded like it was *just right*, and also Zak's, who'd started life as the pickiest eater and slowly metabolized his pickiness into culinary acuity. I wanted to move to Portland, to my childhood home. I asked Zak if there was a room at the Holman House for me.

moved back to Portland in the summer of 2007. Chris and Cynthia didn't want work to drag them down, and at first, despite long hours at the stop-motion studio, they made a point to go out often and stay out late. But every time Chris stayed in and cooked Northern Thai foods from his childhood, Cynthia, Zak, and I encouraged him. Before long he was calling his mom more often, asking how to make his favorite dishes. I'd hear him talking with her on the phone in Thai, as he paced in and out of the dining room. His voice was pleading and then impatient, her muffled sounds squabbly and curt in response.

"What'd she say?" I'd ask when he hung up.

"She said, 'Why do you want to make that dish? You have no time. You have to go to work.'"

Or on another call: "What time is it? It's eight o'clock! Why are you doing that now? You're supposed to do that earlier!"

But his mom, Suda, shared her instructions and sometimes would call back later when she remembered a step or ingredient she'd forgotten. Chris's food got more and more delicious. The quality and intensity of the heat was inspiring, and I had many out-of-body moments while eating some perfect interplay of spicy, funky, salty, sweet, meaty, and bright flavors.

When Chris cooked, he was patient and precise. He rarely multitasked. Instead, he focused all his attention on the task at hand, not looking up or away but fully absorbed in one action: a chef's knife smashing garlic cloves or lemongrass, slender fingers pulling slimy strands of tendon from a chicken breast, a paring knife cutting the muddy intestine from a shrimp. At the stove, he'd wait to witness a transformation, his cues coming not from a cookbook but from the shifts in aroma, color, texture, and sound in front of him. He'd often start cooking at seven thirty, after work, and serve at nine—a time unthinkable to many but closer to what I remembered from my childhood in the same house.

Chris is tall and wire thin, so thin you wonder where the food he neatly but voluminously consumes goes. He has lustrous black hair, and his face is beautiful, with strong, angular features, round cheekbones, and full lips. He has a filthy mouth, a ribald sense of humor, and a loud, explosive laugh when he experiences disgusted disbelief. As a kid, he was so skinny his mom angrily called him *plait*, Thai for "hungry ghost." The name was a double-edged insult: first because these ghosts are freakishly tall and thin, and second because someone becomes a *plait* after they talk back or say bad things about their parents—when they die, their mouth becomes so tiny not even a grain of rice can fit inside. "You're too skinny," Suda would grumble as Chris grew. "What are people going to think? That I'm not feeding my kids enough?!"

Chris learned to cook at his mother's knee. Suda had moved from Thailand to Los Angeles on a student visa when she was in her twenties. In the seventies, she opened her own bar, the puzzlingly named Viking Thai, in what became the city's Koreatown. The bar closed, and she met Chris's dad, Precha, also a Thai immigrant. For several years, Suda worked at Montgomery Ward, tagging and packing clothes in the warehouse. After Chris and his brother were born, she began her own business making *nam*, Northern Thai fermented sausages, recreating the recipe from childhood memories. She worked from home, using a friend's restaurant's name. Chris loved the puckery, sour smell of the raw sausages, tightly wrapped in plastic and stored under the table in their kitchen. His mom would sell out as soon as she made her deliveries, and even decades after she stopped making them, people would waylay her in the street and say, "Suda, here's some money. Please make me some sausages."

By the time we met, Chris had been working on stop-motion animated TV shows for almost a decade. He painted puppets and worked in the "puppet hospital," fixing puppets and props that were broken on set. The precision he utilized in his job was evident in every aspect of his life—his elegant yet playful Goth clothes, his impeccable hair and nails, the meticulous way he used a fork and knife, and especially his preternatural cooking. Like Suda, he had vivid memories of flavors and the patience to iterate until he achieved them. Whenever he cooked, we'd pile around the kitchen's central island to help prep.

Cooking and eating with Chris transformed Thai food for me. It had always tasted delicious, but he began teaching my housemates and me to experience more nuance. Chris made foods that predated the arrival of chilis in Southeast Asia, foods his father loved, including a medicinal soup called *gaeng liang* spiced heavily with black pepper. He taught me about the culinary dishes of the Shan States, which repeat in subtle variations across Myanmar, Thailand, and Laos. I learned that pad thai had been invented in the 1930s as part of a government-sponsored contest to strengthen Thai nationalism with a unifying dish. "No way," I said, as he heated his wok until smoke curled from the surface, added a squeeze of oil, and then turned and nodded in my direction.

Zak was the first one to apprentice himself to Chris. He'd watch carefully, and when Chris was out with friends or on a date, Zak would try to replicate his favorite dishes: *tom kha* soup or *tam makuer*—charred eggplant, chopped and panfried with roasted garlic and chilis, and seasoned with fish sauce. Zak would

make small alterations, and I loved seeing in real time the way
recipes change through individual preference.

I hadn't lived with Zak since I was seven, when he moved
away to college, but across all those years he'd remained a central
part of my life. Zak is almost eleven years older than me, so much
older that he's had an outsize effect on my tastes. When I was a
baby, he changed my diaper and powdered my rashy butt. When
I was a toddler, he cooked me frozen peas with butter and made
sure I didn't fall to my death. When I was a little older, he took
me for my favorite after-school snack: jo jo potatoes with ranch
dressing from Pizza Plus.

Zak taught me to love coffee ice cream and hate cake, con-
vinced me to play basketball, steered me away from the saxo-
phone to the trumpet, showed me how to copy CDs from the
library, and shared his favorite movies, often either transgressive
dark comedy or hair-raising Hong Kong action: *Nuts in May*,
Swordsman II.

One Thanksgiving, when I was twelve, my parents decided
to send me to Zak instead of bringing him home. I spent a week
in his shared apartment in Rochester, New York, where he was
earning a graduate degree in computer animation. Zak gave me
his room and let me stay up until two in the morning reading
Love and Rockets comics, filled with adult content. We burned
copies of Sun Ra's *The Singles* and listened to them before wandering for hours around a nearby cemetery. We went to a
second-run theater and watched *Soldier*, a sci-fi movie in which
an emotionally vacant Kurt Russell stares blankly and silently
into the camera for minutes on end, as if a man without access to
his feelings is gripping or uncommon. Zak and I spent most of
the movie laughing under our breath, trying not to ruin it for
everyone else. Watching a movie with Zak is unlike watching

with anyone else. Moments of pure humor present themselves like fruits to pluck that no one else can see. When he really laughs, he snickers and snickers, his shoulders wiggling near his ears, his eyes almost closed and tearing up. That Thanksgiving, we skipped baking a turkey, which we both hate (or do I hate it because he hates it?), and instead made a pork loin, mashed potatoes, and coffee ice cream.

As a kid, Zak was so much in his imagination that he could be impenetrable. But his dad, Roger, and my dad cultivated his interest in making art that conveyed his acerbic, gross-out sense of humor. My dad recalls bringing *Zak's Book of Terrible Things*, a comic Zak made as a young teen, to a family reunion in rural Washington State, where one of his Norwegian Lutheran aunts proclaimed it the work of Satan. This, of course, my dad loved.

I felt like a little kid around Zak until I was in high school, when he moved back to Portland from graduate school and lived in various houses with roommates. He and his friends were surprisingly invested in exposing me to things they thought were cool, and I would pal around with them. I'm not certain that Zak ever articulated an agenda to make sure his little sister became someone he liked to hang out with, but he took my hand and let me walk with him wherever he went—to music shows, experimental movies, and parties; to his favorite spot to eat phở; and, in the summer, to "the river," which meant any river within an hour and a half of the city.

After college, our relationship changed again, albeit slowly. I was still a sidekick for a long time, and I felt grateful for the familiar role. He could put me in my place with a few words, shocked by all the adult social behaviors I *hadn't* learned from our parents or in college, especially about how to share space thoughtfully, how to keep a joke rolling, when to give someone space. I learned never to go to a party empty-handed, to always ask what I could contribute, to always bring beer. The space between our ages began to shrink. We were becoming more like siblings, less like babysitter and ward.

Living with Zak as a roommate, I discovered that he's a creature of habit. Zak often worked from home—he's a skilled digital animator—and every day had a set shape to it: a coffee from his tin-man percolator and a single piece of buttered toast in the morning; another coffee at three o'clock; an IPA at six, poured into his favorite ceramic cup; one bite of ice cream before bed. I found comfort in the regularity of his schedule, like a drumbeat I could march to occasionally, when I felt like it. I jumped into a few of his rituals. Every Tuesday, we played basketball with a group of his friends. Once a week, Zak and I would go out for lunch, always to the same place, until we befriended the owners and could tell them poop jokes.

At first, I didn't cook with Zak often; I just enjoyed the meals he made. Zak always prepares tortillas and salsa from scratch, pouring boiling water over the dried masa and roasting and peeling the chilis, garlic, and tomatoes or tomatillos. When he sautés vegetables, they taste better than anyone else's—at once greasy, clean, and more intensely themselves. He makes everyday food taste extraordinary, which seemed like a magic trick until I noticed how closely he pays attention to every ingredient.

Eventually, we all started cooking together, sous-chefing for whoever was taking the lead, tidying if the other jobs were taken. Zak and Chris could hum alongside each other in the kitchen, not needing to speak as they moved in sync to make a meal.

One day, when a bad smell appeared mysteriously in the house, Cynthia remembered that she hadn't finished eating a tuna fish sandwich the day before and had no idea where she'd left the remaining half. We searched high and low until we found a dead mouse smashed under a wine bottle. Cynthia recalled finishing the sandwich after all.

A few weeks later, groggy before work, Cynthia almost made a smoothie using a frozen chicken sausage instead of a banana. Zak caught her just in time.

Cynthia is more than a decade older than me. When I was in elementary school, she was working at a nearby pizza parlor called Oasis. Her parlor trick was something she called "Surprise Balls." She'd offer her coworkers a little ball of baked dough with a mystery ingredient inside: it might be some cheese or sausage; it might be a clove of raw garlic. *Surprise!*

Cynthia claims she loves balls—testicles, titties, and all things globular. She's beautiful, with pony-brown hair that falls in swoops, twinkly eyes, and a bubble butt. Those first years I knew her, she had several boyfriends who were handsome, fun-loving, and generally forgettable. Sometimes she hooked up with women, always casually. She joined the stop-motion-animation industry because she likes to manipulate physical objects. She feels magic in colorful consumer goods and natural items that mimic human ones, like stick guns, which she collects. She carries an enormous bag that seems to contain everything in the world: medicine, White Rabbit candies, a mini water bottle, loose change, tissues, colorful markers and pens, scrunchies, makeup, Lisa Frank spiral notebooks, sketchbooks containing half-finished nudes, chopsticks. I wouldn't have been surprised to see her pull her cat, Tender Vittles, from within its folds.

Whenever she was sick, Cynthia would wrap herself in all her crochet blankets and watch Eddie Murphy movies I'd never heard of. In *Meet Dave*, his body is a spaceship that lands on Earth. A tiny Eddie Murphy is also captain of the ship, navigating from inside the cranium. In one scene, after the aliens have realized they'll need cash during their mission, the spaceship goes into a dressing room, where it begins shitting out money. Bills and coins fall from Eddie Murphy's butt as he bears down, mouth in a grimace. Cynthia rewound the VHS, and we watched this scene over and over again. New meanings unfurled each time: Eddie Murphy is shitting out money. Eddie Murphy is a vehicle, a carapace. This movie is shit. This movie is money. Money is shit. Money is the most important thing in the world.

People love to be around Cynthia because she always shows you new things and a fun time. One year, she decided to knit all the organs and bones of a human body at size and assemble them into an anatomical whole, like the corpses on display in the controversial *Body Worlds* exhibit then traveling the country. She called it the Woolen Man. For months, her friends joined her in the project. They'd come to our house to knit kidneys, a spleen, a pelvic bone; to laugh, gossip, and snack. It felt like a gentle critique of art as the product of lone geniuses. Here, a group of women were enjoying each other's company as they worked, as women have for millennia. When it was done, the Woolen Man was disarmingly beautiful.

n high school, I felt I didn't live *in* the Holman House but *with* it. That sensation returned as soon as I moved back. The house was our fifth roommate, a chaotic, social, and demanding one, needing constant human attention. It never let people go—it was the kind of romantic who keeps marrying and remarrying, getting back together with exes, falling in love again. Zak pointed out that no one had properly moved out of the house since the nineties. "Take a core sample and you might end up with one of Uncle Paul's pubic hairs," he joked.

There was an accumulation of stuff everywhere, and nobody knew what belonged to whom. Every surface became a repository for magazines, books, receipts, little sculptures, rubber bands, hair bands, bags of cookies, jars of chili flakes. We'd clear the counters, and a week later, like snowfall in winter, the odds and ends would pile up anew.

My dad's books lined the upstairs hallway, making a dense library. My parents' cookbooks filled one kitchen wall, ceiling to floor. Low cupboards in the dining room held what my parents called "the people's dishes"—dozens of mismatched plates, bowls, forks, and spoons that allowed us to throw big parties and never need disposable dishes. Cynthia's art supplies, easels, and children's desks filled the corners of the basement, as did Uncle Paul's camping and fishing gear. Somehow other people's storage ended up there, too, so that we were never sure whose precious art and mementos we were boarding.

We kept the place mostly free of filth—we swept, occasionally mopped, scrubbed down the stove and the fridge—but the clutter was something else. I became mostly oblivious to it, the way one can acclimate to a bad smell with enough time. I couldn't see the clutter anymore; Zak could, however, and he'd frequently articulate the ways the house felt claustrophobic to him.

We never had a chore wheel. People only did what they wanted to and rarely anything more. That meant I was meticulous about keeping the fridge in order, but I never cleaned under the hood. Zak seemed especially bothered by the grout between the tiles on the kitchen counter, which shed bits of wet brown powder when he scrubbed it after dinner. I'd listen to him whine and shrug it off. What did I know about fixing grout? The scale of the house and yard and our laissez-faire attitude seeded a feeling of resigned acceptance in me, which wasn't altogether unpleasant. I gained so much from the company of my roommates. It was a trade I was willing to make.

One evening, alone with the Holman House while everyone else was out, I got high and watched *Grey Gardens* in Zak's office. This 1975 documentary brings you into the dilapidated East Hampton mansion of a mother and daughter, former socialites and cousins of Jackie Kennedy Onassis, who live in poverty, eat cat food and call it pâté, and feast on their delusional memories. It dawned on me that, like Big and Little Edie, Zak and I might one day live alone with the Holman House, surrounded by relics of our previous lives, with clutter piled to the ceiling, the grout between the tiles long gone and the alleys left behind filled with detritus—rancid sesame seeds, tomato stems, hair, chili flakes. Over time, ivy would engulf us.

The weed and this movie were a freaky combo. My breathing turned shallow and hoarse. I turned off the film and went downstairs: past my dad's books, which were leering toward me, threatening to fall; past my own desk, covered in letters and scrap paper; through the kitchen, toward the side porch, to breathe the night air. But as I reached the door, a flashlight beamed through the window. Paranoid, I dropped to the ground and started shim-mying along the floor, peering out through the glass porch doors as several police stalked in and out of our yard. I thought they were there to arrest me for smoking weed!

When the cops had gone, I hid under my blanket in my bed-room, still shaken. Cynthia found me there an hour later, brought me water, and told me about her night to help ease my anxiety. Afterward, I learned the cops had chased someone through our yard. I buried this moment of panic and continued to ignore the clutter.

I left college with an internship that became a job at a nonprofit, where my work focused on the economics of local farming. I spent a lot of my time trying to get more local food into school-lunch programs. Another portion of my time went into writing for a food magazine. I loved it. My parents had taught me a kind of values-based hedonism around food: they took overt pleasure in every meal, slurping, sucking their fingers clean, making loud smacking sounds of satisfaction. That pleasure amplified into delight when the food came with a backstory of human and ecological care.

I tried to write from that same hedonistic impulse: start with what tastes good to me, interrogate why, and then look at the people, culture, ecosystem, agronomics, mythologies, and poli-tics that brought it to this moment. I also started to develop my own systems for evaluating new food technologies, enterprises, and policies. In the face of complex issues, I asked: Who funds it, who owns it, and who profits? And the questions hidden on the flip side were equally important: Who doesn't own it? Who doesn't profit? I toured independently owned groceries and visited small-scale grain mills in rural Oregon, interviewed tribal members about huckleberries and prehistoric lamprey, and met immigrant farm workers turned farm owners. I also gravitated toward organic farmers.

I was becoming more passionate about food politics, but I knew that I didn't want to let that passion become moralistic. Being judgmental about what people eat is useless and nasty because food is a spiritual, intimate thing in our lives. My parents held many strong beliefs, but they—and my dad especially— tried not to moralize. He was so curious about what other people thought and where their ideas came from that he couldn't care less whether their politics matched his own. That seemed right to me. The most compelling way to share something is to *share* it, not to scold or whine or patronize. In return, you have to listen.

Chris later told me that he thought organic food was elitist. But even before he articulated his feelings to me, I sensed them and felt defensive. I'd heard this accusation about organic and local food often. I found it too prepackaged: in the United States, the whole food system—not just one component of it—is rigged and elitist, if in different ways. Mass-market products are significantly more affordable, are often the only choice at the grocery store, and can be delicious and nostalgic. But the companies that produce these products pay no attention to workers' rights, dump environmental remediation on taxpayers, rely on commodity-crop payments (which taxpayers also fund), and enrich owners and executives.

Rather than talking about food politics around the dinner table, I brought home food from farms and ranches I'd visited and told stories about the people I was meeting. We all cooked with it, and Chris started noting when ingredients tasted especially flavorful and describing them in words that felt new. He was honest when he liked something and when he didn't. In turn, Chris helped me experience food and flavor with more perception. Neither of us changed our preferences, but we both widened our appreciation. Our sharing often took shape in gestures of affection—when I knew Chris liked something, I'd stockpile it; when he knew what I liked, he'd make extra for my lunch.

Chris taught me to steam kabocha squash, which concentrates all its best characteristics, and at the end of every summer, when I amassed a pile of tomatoes, he'd make *nam prik ong*, a tomato and ground pork stew with shrimp paste. He'd pile our dining table with Filipino pork rinds (his favorite) and all the raw and steamed vegetables we had on hand—wedges of cabbage, lettuce leaves, sliced cucumbers, green beans—to dip into the thick stew. I'd eat until I floated above the table, hovering above the stained tablecloth, above the scatter of dripping candles, card decks, headlamps, and postcards, admiring my roommates seated in their usual spots with their favorite utensils, eating the last bites.

Over time, our household built a rhythm. Some iteration of the group ate dinner together four to six nights a week. We gradually created unspoken rules, guided by Chris and Cynthia, who shared the instinct to be exceptionally social and generous: If you cooked, you cooked for everyone, two people or ten. If you ate, you did your best to help prep and clean up afterward. We split larger costs like bulk products and a CSA share, but when one person cooked, they bought any extra ingredients they required, and if they needed others to chip in, they asked.

Zak, Chris, and I loved to cook, and we took turns taking the lead. Cynthia always set the mood with amazing decorations and odd party favors: a rubber stress banana to squeeze when someone was having a hard week; cocktail umbrellas; a bag of ice, which she invariably called "party ice"; silly straws. Who knew what might emerge from her voluminous bag!

While this arrangement might seem like a lot of work, it also brought me significant ease. I only made dinner two or three nights a week. I often had leftovers for lunch. Every time I made dinner, I was heartily thanked and cheered on. Every time someone else cooked, I felt awash in gratitude. Whenever dinner was ready, we'd serve ourselves from the rice cooker, sit down together at the dining table, and take food from the bowls laid around us, talking and catching up. After, we'd do dishes, wipe down counters, and sweep. This was decisively different from the tradition of women, frequently mothers, who find themselves underappreciated and burned-out, tasked with food preparation. It was also different from communal meals at the Zü, which were scheduled, were budgeted, and regularly went without gratitude. Instead, this was like a gift circle, a practice in giving and receiving without the burden of debt.

Years later, I'd find words for this kind of sharing in Lewis Hyde's book *The Gift: Imagination and the Erotic Life of Property*. Hyde, an artist and academic dwelling outside of academia, studied gift-giving cultures around the world and through time. He came upon common principles among them. "The gift must stay in motion," he emphasizes, which means you can't receive something and hoard it. You must participate in a cycle of giving. You don't have to give what you received, but you must pass along the spirit endowed in the gift. I noticed among our household that we didn't tally who cooked the most, who spent the most, whose dishes were the most difficult or involved. Instead, we cultivated a culture of thrill and thankfulness around dinner.

For me, it helped not to be part of a couple, taking turns. As Hyde explains, "gift exchange is more likely to turn into barter when it falls into the ego-of-two." When someone gives you something thoughtful or expensive, it can feel like it's about you and your worthiness. It can also be carefully tallied. Imbalances arise when one person feels unacknowledged or overexerted— when they feel that what they offer to the relationship is not equitably reciprocated. But when a gift moves beyond two people, the terms of the engagement change. In our household, we were not indebted to any one individual but to the community we helped build. This gave us the confidence to receive without guilt and to give without a sense of meagerness or competition.

There was an element of mystery to the whole thing. Our cycles of reciprocity created something with a life of its own. Mercifully, our group wasn't rooted in a named dogma. Instead, we were defined primarily by our commitment to one another, joined together in a marvelous little anarchy.

After a few months of having only my roommates and childhood friends as company, I began befriending people my own age. One night, I joined my friend Gary on his second date with a man named Jordan. The three of us biked into industrial North Portland to a karaoke bar called Chopsticks III: How Can Be Lounge. We drank whiskey gingers and Jordan sang "Hurdy Gurdy Man" by Donovan in a voice so low and sexy I couldn't blink. Gary sang Guided by Voices' "My Valuable Hunting Knife" in a sweet and childlike voice that seemed barely to belong to the irreverent Gary I thought I knew. I watched them fall in love, drunk on tender, desirous feelings. And I fell in love with both of them under the shimmer of metallic streamers in that windowless bar.

I came home at two thirty in the morning, and Cynthia was still awake in her chaotic bedroom. I lay down on the bed next to Tender Vittles and told her I'd watched two people fall in love. I felt inside the experience, a participant in someone else's story. She stroked my hair and shared her own memories. She helped my heartbeat and energy slow and let me drift off to sleep amid bits of fabric and yarn.

Cynthia, Zak, Chris, and my friends began to heal something broken inside me. I had what I considered standard young-woman self-loathing, an unending discomfort of the self that manifested as disgust with my body and with my mind, which I blamed for my body. I took this feeling to be normal for women my age, an initiation into living inside an adult female body, which would now and forever be the disappointing home for my spirit. Falling in love with my friends and roommates—with their intellect, humor, quirks, style, expressions, and even issues—was the first step toward something that felt new. The second step was feeling loved in return. The knowledge that someone I was so wild for was also in love with me—not because we wanted to bone or felt excessively needy, but because we adored each other's company—changed how I perceived my worth. My friends and I shined love on each other like mirrors building heat.

I felt a profound commitment to my friends and roommates—a feeling as strong and unyielding as the love I saw between couples, and perhaps less challenging because we weren't so individually beholden to fulfilling each other's needs. We were as appreciative of one another as we were amused to be so different.

This community expanded the geography of my love. They also helped me invite myself onto the map I was drawing.

Underneath these memories is the thrum of the financial recession that began in 2007, the year I graduated from college. I wouldn't have put these words to it then, but I experienced the Great Recession as an erupting Mount Saint Helens, in the distance until it wasn't—until, suddenly, the skies were blackened all around me and ash was raining down. It didn't kill my generation; it simply froze us in place and changed the stability of the landscape we thought we knew. We felt unsure what to do next, given the scarcity of jobs, and were shocked that something we'd never heard of—subprime mortgages—and a bunch of greedy bankers three thousand miles away were immobilizing us. We could look and scream, but we couldn't move forward.

I stayed put in my job and my home. This had a concentrating effect on my personality—I was like a broth simmering on the stove, becoming more condensed. Many of my friends also stayed put, lived in group houses, and shared rent. These friends became incredibly close to one another in those shared spaces, even if they didn't participate in the kumbaya meal throwdowns happening at my house. Their gift languages took other forms.

I was acutely aware of the hypocrisy of our government bailing out corrupt banks while everyday people were being crushed by debt. A few of my friends frequently received threatening phone calls about student loans. Almost none of us had money, and our economic futures felt increasingly precarious, but in a strange way, I found it easier to share when we all had very little—to cover the dinner bill when someone was short on cash, to loan your car or offer your time, to buy someone clothes when you saw something they'd like.

In Hyde's writing, there is a clear critique of capitalism. He quotes a common Indigenous precept: "One man's gift . . . must not be another man's capital." He continues, "property is plagued by entropy and wealth can become scarce even as it increases." I knew this intuitively. If my friends and I stopped being generous with one another, we'd start counting and hoarding the meager things we had, because in this economy they were unlikely to replenish. The only thing that made us feel abundant was each other.

C hris was born with a disease that has similarities to sickle cell anemia. He had his spleen removed at a young age. His blood doesn't flush iron effectively, and during high school, he received a transfusion every month.

He'd been slowly weakening, with acute pain in his muscles— this was nothing new for him; he'd experienced cyclical declines throughout his childhood—but one day his pain level increased significantly and he asked me to take him to the hospital. I drove him to Legacy Good Samaritan in northwest Portland. He looked so scrawny in his hospital gown, which floated around his limbs like curtains, but his attitude was stoic and resolved. After we got him settled, he told me to leave and come back later that night. He knew he'd be there for a few days and gave me a list of things to gather.

I had several hours to burn. Instinctively, I went to the place I often go when I want to process heavy feelings: Kelley Point Park, where the Columbia and Willamette Rivers meet. It was an uncommonly hot spring day, and I was overdressed in jeans and a long-sleeved shirt. I sat on a big piece of driftwood in the brutal sunshine, feeling sweaty and uncomfortable, and soon found myself crying in a lumpy way—not passionate or steady but in hiccups. Then something warm and wet splashed onto my fore-head. I reached up, felt a sticky liquid splattered across my face, and realized I was covered in bird shit. I screamed and, just as abruptly, burst into disbelieving laughter. *Of course a bird took a dump on me today*, I thought. *I feel like a toilet.*

Somehow, this bird poop was the medicine I needed. My mood lightened. I dunked my forehead in the Willamette and scrubbed some of the white goop from my hair. I kept laughing as I went home to take a shower and gather the things for Chris. I'd ask him to be honest with me, I decided, to tell me if he wasn't going to be all right, rather than assuming everything was about to end. I'd try to be loving and present instead of self-pitying and overdramatic.

A week later, he was released with new medication and new strength, and we returned to our rhythm. Freshly reminded of how fragile he was, I felt more amazed than ever at his forceful personality, generosity, and sharp presence of mind.

I was going through my own medical challenge around the same time. One day, when I was twenty-four, I noticed a ceaseless buzzing in my left ear, like a swarm of mosquitoes humming into a microphone. Shortly after, I realized I also couldn't hear well from that side. I was constantly having to ask people to repeat themselves. I went to an ear, nose, and throat doctor, who decided to give me a hearing test. I was placed in a small sound booth with headphones and a little clicker in my hand. I had to listen for beeps. *Beep*, I'd hear. Click. *Beep, beep*. Click.

Toward the end, a woman read me words, and I was instructed to repeat them. Although she began speaking at a normal volume, the words became sequentially quieter.

"Say the word *rubber band*," she read.

"Rubber band," I answered.

"Say the word *beach house*," she read at a quieter volume.

"Beach house," I answered.

"Say the word *dickwad*," she read in a muted voice.

"Dickwad," I answered.

"Say the word *dickwad*," she repeated.

"Dickwad," I answered.

What was she saying? It definitely wasn't "dickwad," was it? Was this a Rorschach test? Had she said "dickwad" twice? Should I repeat it a third time if asked? I couldn't wait to tell my household about my dirty pubescent mind, even as I feared what it meant that I couldn't make out these words.

A few weeks later I returned to the doctor's office for an MRI of my head, and a few weeks after that I learned that I had a genetic disease called otosclerosis. Calcium was accumulating in my middle ear and preventing the three little jangly bones from jangling and sending sound to my inner ear. I could have surgery, but the long-term prognosis was that I'd go deaf early—the doctor couldn't say when, but sooner than many other people—and that pregnancy would exacerbate the disease.

I was growing deaf, and I was growing up. I was not all right, and I was fine. I ignored this diagnosis, which wasn't going anywhere, and went on a trip to Japan to spend five weeks with friends and the Yamaguchi family. When I returned home, I felt more certain about how I liked to spend my time. I saw myself as acutely vulnerable, even a little pathetic, so as a counterweight, I decided to care more intensely for my friends in this unpredictable and often brutal world.

Chris and Zak's *Tom Kha Gai* (Chicken Coconut Curry Soup)

Recipe by Christopher Rabilwongse and Zak Margolis

MAKES 4 TO 6 SERVINGS

Chris and Zak make this soup whenever anyone feels sick. It's surprisingly simple and quick, and the results are rich, aromatic, rib-sticking, and delicious. The coconut milk, lime leaves, galangal, and lemongrass create a perfume that cuts through a stuffy nose and never fails to make me feel taken care of.

Tom kha gai was the first of Chris's dishes I remember Zak riffing on. Chris showed him how to make a simple broth by poaching chicken breasts, which are then added to the soup—a step Zak now regards as essential, although today Chris usually opts for the faster method of using premade broth. Zak always adds maitake mushrooms for their aroma, and Chris only sometimes does. The recipe has diverged in two, which I love.

I'm sharing my hybrid between Chris's and Zak's recipes, but if you want to make the chicken broth yourself, put 2 bone-in chicken breasts or 4 bone-in chicken thighs in 8 cups water in a medium saucepan. Bring to a rapid simmer (do not let it boil), reduce heat to low, cover, and cook for 50 minutes. Transfer chicken to a cutting board. Once the chicken is cool, remove and discard the bones and skin and chop or shred the meat. You'll have two quarts of broth. Save one in the fridge or freezer to use later. Proceed with this recipe, ignoring the raw chicken and adding the cooked chicken when you add the mushrooms.

Chris insists that for a real Thai taste (and a sweet and shrimpy note), you should add 1 tablespoon of the roasted-chili paste known as *nam prik pao* at the end, but we typically use our own chili oil (in which case, Chris will also add a teaspoon of sugar). The final soup should be sour, spicy, and salty, with a hint of sweetness. Lime leaves, galangal, and lemongrass often come in large quantities, so cut up the galangal and lemongrass and freeze any extra to make this again. (You can use the extra lime leaves in *khao tod*; recipe on page 190.) Don't eat the galangal, lemongrass, or lime leaves from your bowl—pluck these odds and ends out as you eat.

4 cups unsweetened full-fat coconut milk*

2½-inch piece galangal, cut into ½-inch-thick slices

2 to 3 whole stalks lemongrass, very bottom trimmed off, cut at a diagonal into 2-inch lengths, smashed

6 to 8 *makrut* lime leaves, veins removed

⅓ bunch cilantro, washed

5 to 6 cloves garlic, smashed

10 to 12 Thai chilis, stems removed, with a thin slit cut into the pepper lengthwise (don't skip this step, and don't slice the pepper in half!)

1 pound boneless, skinless chicken thighs, cut into bite-size pieces

1 pound fresh shiitake and maitake mushrooms or wild mushrooms like chanterelles in season, sliced

4 cups chicken stock, homemade or store-bought

4 tablespoons fish sauce, plus more to taste

Juice of 2 limes, plus 1 lime cut into wedges for serving

Optional: 1 teaspoon sugar or 1 tablespoon *nam prik pao* (see headnote)

Chili oil to taste

In a large stockpot or Dutch oven, bring coconut milk, galangal, lemongrass, and half of the *makrut* lime leaves to a boil over high heat. Cut the cilantro where the leaves end, throw the stems in the pot (you'll fish them out later, but they add flavor), and set aside the remaining leaves. Reduce heat to medium-low and simmer for 30 minutes. Don't leave unattended or it will overflow. Remove the cilantro stems from the pot and discard. Add smashed garlic cloves, chilis, and chicken. Simmer until chicken is cooked, about 8 minutes.

Add mushrooms, the remaining lime leaves, and 4 cups chicken stock. Turn heat to medium-high and bring back to a simmer. Cook until mushrooms are done, about 4 minutes. Turn off the heat. Chop up the reserved cilantro. Season soup with fish sauce, lime juice, and optional sugar or *nam prik pao*. Add the chopped cilantro. Serve with a side of rice and offer lime wedges and chili oil for people to add to taste.

*Chris recommends Aroy-D brand coconut milk. Any brand that lists coconut milk as its only ingredient will work. Avoid anything with gums or sweeteners.

DRIFTLESS

When I visit my mom in the Driftless region of southwest Wisconsin, we bike together. She'll pull out the old road bike her brother Paul built from parts when he lived with us in Portland. It's in the shed that sits between her little year-round greenhouse and the outhouse that serves as the only loo on the property. We cycle up her one-mile gravel driveway, out to roads that twist and turn through hilly farmland, past Amish kids in overalls and sturdy full-length dresses working with horses and hanging up laundry. From the ridgetops, the hills in every direction look like bubbles on pizza dough.

In the fall, the hillsides change color every day. The basswood leaves turn a daisy yellow, and the oak leaves become the orange-red of a Firecracker ice pop. The Amish on Wolf Valley Road will be harvesting corn. Their two-horse team pulls a metal scythe through the stalks, leaving behind a flat field of roughage like a pile of cut hair.

My mom sets her bike seat high—she claims it keeps her left foot from cramping. As she pedals, her butt swishes across the saddle, side to side, so she can reach each pedal at its lowest point. I bike a little ways behind and watch her whole body swinging left, right, left, right, like a pendulum. The Amish in their fields and buggies wave at us.

What I love most about biking with my mom is watching her fly downhill. She's now in her seventies and still loves to go fast. She dresses like a hard-core cyclist: ass-tight shiny black shorts, gloves, clip-in sandals, a fanny pack slung on her left hip that I know has a half-smoked joint in it. Hay Valley Road descends steeply from the get-go. I watch her speed up, stand on her pedals like a jockey, and lean into the wind.

"Hoohooooo!" she calls out, like an owl.

"Hoohooooo!" I reply.

I imprint this image of my mom in my memory: leading the way, a bit stoned and giddy, speeding down a road toward the Kickapoo River as fast as she can.

When I was nine, perched tentatively between my inner world and the whale mouth of pop culture, my mom started freelancing for a dairy cooperative, Organic Valley. After a while, they hired her as marketing director, and for the next nine years, she traveled from Portland to their headquarters in southwest Wisconsin for part of every month. For the first few years, she stayed in a plywood one-room cabin called the Belvie (or Belvedere), which was an outbuilding of a larger house called the Kettle Lodge.

An old man named Jerome—who remained forever old and, therefore, mysteriously eternal—lived in the Kettle Lodge at that time. Jerome looked like a wizened goat god, an ancient mischievous Pan. He was without an inch of fat, his skin stretched over small muscles, his cheeks hollow beneath round cheekbones, many of his teeth missing, his beard long, white, and fluffy, like mohair. He was shoeless, always. In the summer, he was shirtless and wore tiny swim trunks. His ribcage protruded beneath his skin like the prow of a little boat. I could often see his testicles hanging out of one side of his shorts. This didn't shock me—I was familiar with saggy testicles from nude beaches and hot springs, the little ETs men kept hidden in their pants that would loll out on hot days. My mom told me Jerome had suffered from polio as a child, although I didn't have any idea what that meant.

Jerome was the most engrossing conversationalist I'd ever met. I'd carefully choose when to start a conversation with him because even when I was age ten or twelve or fourteen, we'd end up talking for hours. He treated me like I was fascinating and wise. His conversations had a rhythm—his inquiry, my reply, his response, my reply, a new inquiry—that felt like a train you couldn't disembark from. His voice also had a rhythmic rise and fall.

"*Tell* me, *Lola*, what *do* you *think* about *China's* Five-Year *Plans?*"

Because I was a try-hard, I'd make up answers to hear him reply and expound. A former high-level accountant at Sinclair Oil, Jerome had dropped out of corporate life and, in 1974, found himself in the Driftless region of Wisconsin. He helped build the Kettle, honed his astrology and numerology practices, and made a living as a canny tax accountant. "I *like* that *number,*" he'd say, his voice rolling, as he talked clients through their worksheets.

Jerome's reclusive brother, Mick, lived in another outbuilding and appeared very occasionally—maybe once a week—with the suddenness of remembering a forgotten word. *Mick!* Mick was also agelessly old, with stringy white hair and deep-set eyes.

He wrote in his books, over the printed words, in red and blue ink so that you couldn't read what was beneath—all meaning was hoarded and obscured. He was always kind to me, mumbling questions and leaving without the answers, which I was glad not to give. My mom told me that it wasn't too many drugs or Vietnam that had led to Mick's hermetic lifestyle but something in his nature.

When I visited in the summers as a kid, their mom, Geneva, would also be staying there. I could hardly believe that these biblical old men had a sweet, loving mother who was even older than they were, who made fruit salads and devotedly tended her flower beds. Other people lived at the Kettle too, sometimes for years, but the overall social makeup of the community felt transitory.

The Kettle Lodge is part of the Kettle Land Trust. When Jerome and his friends bought the land in 1977, they decided to use an atypical ownership structure that centers on a shared long-term vision for the land. Land trusts are nonprofits that take legal ownership or stewardship of a piece of property at the behest of the owner and hold it in trust. They have a board of directors that enforce a land-use management plan. The goal is not to sell at the highest price or to increase the property value but to help secure affordable housing within cities, preserve farmland, practice environmental conservation, or implement historic preservation. Land trusts are often tools in the movement to decommodify land and remove the profit motive.

The word *trust* here exists in multiple planes. It's a legal agreement: a contract that makes certain requirements of the landowners. It's also an emotional bond established between people and the land, and a promise for future generations. Land trusts have an extensive history both of deceit and of visionary goodness, from English noblemen trying to hide ownership to civil rights leaders in Georgia founding the 5,735-acre New Communities land trust to provide Black farmers with long-term stability. The point is to enable something bigger than the individual, to acknowledge that people live and die but places continue. Conservation easements, for example, are recorded with the deed and exist in perpetuity, following the property no matter who owns it. A land trust says: landowners have the power to nurture or extinguish life; maybe we should keep that power in check.

The Kettle Trust property is 150 acres contiguous with the 8,600-acre Kickapoo Valley Reserve, which is jointly owned by the state of Wisconsin and the Ho-Chunk Nation. The seven members of the Kettle Trust are allotted private home sites, which include discrete deeds. Collectively, they manage the extensive common lands. Some of the members rarely interact. Not everyone lives onsite. Their meetings can be bureaucratic, contentious, and time-consuming. But the members try to make decisions based on the longevity of the place. They trust that the land will outlast them.

Eventually, my mom bought membership shares of the Kettle Trust and partial ownership in the Kettle Lodge from people who'd helped found it but subsequently left. She moved into her own room. Now, when I visited, I stayed in the lodge. When I graduated from high school, the Kettle became her full-time home.

The lodge is built into a slope. When you arrive down the driveway from the north, you can only see the upper story, a blackened teapot overlooking a large wooded bowl. The lodge is twelve-sided, for the twelve houses of the zodiac, with an enormous stone fireplace at its center. A two-story bank of windows faces south, toward the view. The texture of the Kettle is handmade and utilitarian, with an amazing hippie high-low aesthetic: Tiffany lamps, cracked pottery, pencil plants, handwoven baskets, and Metro racks.

My mom seemed right at home. She was always puttering, always hanging laundry. There were clean tablecloths and a basket with clean, mismatched napkins. She gardened like a small-scale farmer, planting twenty- and forty-foot rows of garlic, onions, and potatoes, and she loved to cook from her garden throughout the year and feed whoever was around.

From the front door of the Kettle Lodge, you can walk downhill through the Kettle Trust and into the Kickapoo Valley Reserve, hiking for miles along the Kickapoo River, past sheer cliffs; up forested bluffs; through sedge meadows, thickets, and swamps; through white pine, hemlock, sugar maple, elm, silver maple, and green ash. My mom knows which old white oak trees sprout maitake mushrooms in the fall. If I visit in the spring, she takes me to an open forest at the edge of a meadow where ramps—wild onions with the broad, green leaves of a tulip—carpet the ground.

"Hoohooooo!" she'll call out to her partner, after hours of gathering. "Geo-orge!"

"Smoke break," he'll reply, and they'll cuddle on a downed log, sharing a joint, beaming at our filled baskets.

When I first realized my mom loved Wisconsin, I was mystified. Growing up in Oregon, I was oblivious to the beauty of other places. Growing up in a city, I couldn't imagine life without a movie theater or dim sum. But she had her own rhythms in Wisconsin. Her roommates, coworkers, and neighbors were becoming her best friends, and her connection to the land was deepening.

She and her friends would often canoe the Kickapoo River in summer. Sometimes, she did it alone. Before work, she'd lift her canoe onto her car and load her bike onto the rack hanging from the trunk. After work, she'd drop her bike at Bridge 14, drive upstream to Bridge 7 with some beers and a joint, launch her canoe, and paddle leisurely down the river—then stash her canoe, bike back to the car, return to retrieve the canoe, and head home to cook dinner. It all seemed like so many onerous steps to me. But there was that middle part, floating down the river, cutting loose, staring up at Cambrian limestone cliffs that were 510 million years old and feeling awe, taking a swim in the pools beneath them. It was exactly like my mom to do everything intensely and athletically, even relaxation.

I n Portland, we are bound on the north by the Columbia River, a massive body of water that springs from the high Canadian Rockies and builds volume as it courses south, then west, toward the Pacific Ocean. We learn about ice ages at school because the Columbia was formed by their repeating advance and retreat. Over several million years, glaciers periodically melted and water burst violently forth from an immense frozen lake, carving this river gorge through the rock.

The Driftless region was also formed by ice ages, but through negation: repeatedly, the advancing and retreating glaciers skipped this twenty-four thousand square mile area, moving around it like a stream around a boulder. (*Drift* is another word for *glacial deposits*.) The pounding water of the melting glaciers had a scouring effect on the land around the Driftless but not in the Driftless. Within its bounds, the land continued its slow progression from before the ice ages, small rivers cutting deeper and deeper gullies.

The Driftless extends through parts of Wisconsin, Minnesota, Iowa, and northwest Illinois. The Mississippi River sluices through its center. It's like nothing around it, and its strangeness has attracted equally odd residents. All farms are small farms because the land doesn't allow for mile after mile of flat plantings and standard machinery. It demands owners who know its contours intimately, who are devoted to their little valleys and hills. The eccentrics who live in the Driftless are united by their connection to this distinctive landscape.

The Driftless nurtured Organic Valley, the cooperative where my mom worked. The co-op formed in response to the brutal agricultural crisis of the 1980s in the United States—a perfect storm of record production and demand alongside federal policies encouraging farmers to take on debt to grow, followed swiftly by declining exports, high interest rates and oil prices, sinking cost of farmland, and increasing consolidation and competition from bigger farms. It was "the most severe financial stress for the U.S. farm sector since the Great Depression," according to the USDA. Farm debt doubled from 1978 to 1984. Within the Driftless, many farmers hadn't begun using chemical fertilizers, pesticides and herbicides, or antibiotics and growth hormones. In some cases, this decision was founded in an environmental ethos; just as often it was because it represented too much change.

Organic Valley started with a group of fifty traditional and Amish farmers and back-to-the-land hippies. They banded together, hoping the new market for organic might help them escape the impossible financial squeeze they were in. It was one of those unlikely, life-saving alliances born from necessity that creates something larger than the sum of its parts. The dire situation kept everyone's self-righteousness in check and helped them find their shared mission: keeping family farmers in business for generations.

The centerpiece of their business plan was a complete reversal of the way the standard commodity pricing system works. Instead of letting the market dictate what they received, they decided to establish and demand a price based on their actual farming costs. It seems obvious that farmers should be paid relative to their costs, but commodity rates aren't based on the humans who produce food; they're based on supply and demand. The only thing that made this reversal possible was customers' willingness to pay more for organic foods. The co-op wanted to grow and invite more farmers to join. It was a perfect fit for my mom, who had a businessperson's ravenous appetite for growth tied to an environmental activist's devotion to the cause.

When my mom was hired in 1994, her job was enormous. Organic Valley wanted to expand the co-op to a new region. Her assignment was to find farmers in the Pacific Northwest who were ready to convert to organic. Then she was tasked with finding partners in this new geography who'd mirror the ones Organic Valley had in the Midwest. She had to convince conventional milk processors, the co-op's competition, to bottle organic milk as the first run of the day; find distributors to haul their milk; convince groceries to carry it and customers to buy it; and advocate for the burgeoning organic market at the policy level.

She was ferocious in her commitment to the work, an honest-to-god powerhouse. I have a faint memory of her getting dressed for a food trade show. She's putting on a pumpkin-colored silk pantsuit, pulling her dark hair half back, tying a dapper little floral silk scarf around her neck, and applying purple lipstick, under-eyeliner, and a spritz of Le Baiser du Dragon on her wrists and under her chin. She looks beautiful, urban, and intense. This is the mid-nineties, and this is her version of a power suit.

The relationship between her work and home was fraught. Everyone at the Kettle was also involved with the co-op in some way or another. Jerome had been its first chief financial officer, walking barefoot into banking meetings and blowing them away with his financial acumen. George, her partner, who often stayed at the Kettle, was also her boss. He'd become CEO of Organic Valley as a young, long-haired, back-to-the-land pragmatist. As he grew older, George began to look more and more like Benjamin Franklin, with shoulder-length hair that was a little thin on top and a placid smile. George and my mom had a complex relationship, not least because she reported to him at work, but they loved each other a lot and both liked exploring the Driftless and tending the Kettle.

By 2013, the year after my mom stepped out of her role as chief marketing executive after eighteen years working for the co-op, there were more than eighteen hundred farmer members and six hundred employees, and the business was approaching one billion dollars in gross annual sales. Her intensity had ratcheted down with age, but she was still a fireball, racing into the twilight on her bike, her butt swishing back and forth as she pedaled.

In my late twenties, I realized that my mom had moved from one group house to another when she left Portland for Wisconsin. She was modeling something I was exploring—living with roommates—and I hadn't noticed. I didn't know any other people her age who were doing that, although my uncle Doug and aunt Nancy lived in a related arrangement called cohousing.

Once, when she was visiting me in Portland and we were working in the garden together, I asked in half jest why she'd never joined the Rajneeshees. In the eighties, an Indian guru named Rajneesh moved to rural Oregon, and hippies and pseudo-intellectuals flocked by the thousands. In some ways, it made perfect sense that my mom would've joined: she loves cooking for big crowds; they had group sex, which I assumed she'd be into; they got high all kinds of ways, drugs and otherwise; and they were wildly productive and built an entire town from the ground up.

She was plunging a tall steel spade into the earth, pushing it deeper with her foot and turning the soil to rebuild a raised bed. As she worked, eyes on the dirt, she gave a quick, casual response: "I don't like chanting. I'm not into gurus. I don't like being told what to do."

Then I asked why she always chooses communal living. She stopped digging, looked at me, and answered more tentatively. "My parents fought a lot. My brothers and sisters and I were each other's havens. We'd hide out together."

This answer didn't seem complete—her seven other siblings, after all, weren't living in communal lodges and working for co-ops—but I thought I understood what she meant. She seems magnetically drawn to recreating the sensation of a large family wherever she goes: raucous dinners, extra food on the stove, clothes hanging on the line. She has excess energy and finds release in small expressions of affection. Her words implied safety in numbers and comfort in having someone to care for when so much is out of your control.

I think there's also an element of honoring her mother in her actions. Franny was the daughter of Polish immigrants. She married in her teens and became the mother of eight kids. She and my mom were incredibly close. (Franny's nickname for my mom was Cheepka, Polish for *vagina*!) Franny had an oppressive husband, my grandpa Gregorio, whom we called Goyo. She found sanctuary in the household domains that she controlled: her kitchen and garden.

I never knew Franny, who died when I was young, but I knew my grandpa well. When I was nine, Goyo moved in with us. He stayed for the spring and then lived with my aunt Gloria for the remainder of the year. In the years that followed, he repeated this seasonal migration between his younger daughters. He was five foot five, trim, with patches of white hair in wisps and occasional lonely whiskers. His full bottom lip protruded in the loveliest pout, which he pursed in and out like a drawer opening and closing, a gesture that looked like *thinking* but actually meant *being*. He almost never spoke. About his childhood in the Philippines, his raving jealousy toward Franny, his unreal knack for fixing cars and bowling strikes—all these details came from my mom. In answer to my endless questions, all Goyo would ever say was an equivocal "could be."

My mom was filled with pent-up anger at him for his mistreatment of her mother and years of cruel dominion, but by the time I met him he was sapped of cruelty and energy in general.

He never did anything intentionally sweet, but I didn't care; he always let me eat his Popeyes biscuit, which was enough.

Goyo never spoke about the three-year Philippine-American War just before his birth, when US troops killed more than twenty thousand Filipino soldiers and more than two hundred thousand (and possibly up to one million) civilians died—some murdered, others felled by famine and disease. He never mentioned the four-decade-plus American occupation of the Philippines that began in his childhood, the effects of neocolonialism on his psyche, or the US propaganda that described Filipinos as infantile and subhuman. He never complained about the disregard and open racism he experienced from his Italian American neighbors and General Electric coworkers in Schenectady, New York. Instead, he was cruel to those less powerful than himself. The "could be" answers he gave so often later in life seem to me, now, less an expression of possibility and more the residue of unending uncertainty and dislocation.

For years, my mom's life was shaped by anger at her dad. She has a "fuck men" attitude that encompasses all possible meanings of that phrase: she likes to fuck men; she distrusts, resents, and disregards men. My mom calls herself a "disinheritor." She refused the gender roles foisted on her: she threw away her bras and girdles and stopped teasing her hair, pursued a career, had children out of wedlock, and declined to be subservient to a man. She worked to exorcize her Catholic guilt and corresponding sexual repression. She discovered drugs, and with them a joyful wonder and connection to nature.

Not long after our conversation, we were back at our freshly turned raised bed to plant seed garlic she'd brought me from Wisconsin. I found myself asking my mom if she considered herself Fil Am—Filipina American—or white. It's a question I've asked myself in the past, too, although Zak and I both describe ourselves as white because we appear white. In the United States, identity is often perceived in stark terms, and it's felt important to acknowledge the position of power and literal safety from law enforcement that comes with looking the way I do. But, in truth, I experience my identity in a messier way.

I wasn't raised in a larger Filipino community. The first time I visited my family in Manila, when I was eleven, everyone—and I mean *everyone*—laughed at me. My mom had intended to name me for her grandmother, but instead she named me the Tagalog word for *grandmother*. "Well, hello, little *lola*, little granny," my cousins, aunties, and uncles teased. My name was proof of good intentions and clumsy misunderstandings.

Yet I'd had one eye across the Pacific since I began studying Japanese at five. I marked the year with Japanese holidays, starting with the Japanese New Year and followed promptly by my favorite, Setsubun, the first of spring, when we threw soybeans out our door, calling out *"oni wa soto, fuku wa uchi"*—devil out, happiness in—and ate an uncut roll of sushi, standing up, all in one go. Visiting the Philippines, I felt embarrassed that I was studying the language and culture of a people who'd violently taken that country during World War II instead of the language of my family.

When I'd speak Japanese around Portland, people would ask, head cocked to one side, "But you're not Japanese, are you?" I wanted to answer, "No, but I *am* part Filipino." Yet that felt defensive and misleading too. I don't identify as Asian American. If anything—and this still feels confusing—I identify as the child of hippies who hold very idealistic notions about multiculturalism, ones I got swept up in and am still untangling myself from.

I see my identity as irreducibly bound up with countries and cultures that I don't claim as my own.

Hippies went searching for alternatives to the mainstream. Some appropriated from Asian and Indigenous cultures and spirituality to create their own systems of meaning, taking only the pieces that suited them, sometimes to exploitive ends. My parents' antidote to this blatant appropriation was immersion. They made sure my education was thorough, from a direct source, and infused with complexity. They introduced me to a foreign language at a young age and sent me to Japan and the Philippines. Whenever I got too starry-eyed about Japan, my mom would remind me of the Bataan Death March. My dad would add, "Don't forget the Rape of Nanjing."

Despite my muddle, I felt clear that my mom is *hapa*, a Hawaiian term that many East Asian Americans of my generation define as "half-Asian." (The Filipino slang for it is *tisay*, a Tagalog riff on *mestiza*.) Yet when she answered my question, her knobby fingers busy shoving garlic cloves into the soil in even rows, her voice was halting. She told me that she thought of herself as white, just as I do, acknowledging her own power as someone who "passes" as white as well as the disconnection she feels from Filipino identity. I was surprised.

My mom is small, with thick black hair and full lips that purse like her Filipino father's, but her eyes are round and hazel like her Polish mother's. Over the course of the year her skin moves from pale to deep brown, making the photos I take of her look like I'm toying with saturation. She never travels without bringing home *pasalubong*—small presents—and always adds four times more garlic than any recipe calls for. So many Filipino Americans are multiracial—in the Philippines, Indigenous cultures mixed with Spanish, Chinese, Mexican, and American ones, the result of a long history of exploitative colonialism and trade. But my mom doesn't experience her identity in polychrome.

She clarified that when she was growing up, no one saw her as white. She and her siblings were taunted as Japanese enemies. But her family was so set on assimilating in post–World War II America that she doesn't know any other identity. My mom, the fifth of the eight kids, was the first baby boomer in her family, born after the war concluded. Her family never spoke Tagalog at home. The only words that came down to me are *puki* ("vagina"), *puwit* ("butt"), *sabaw* ("meat drippings"), *kuskus balungos* ("too much fuss, and for what?"), and *mati gás ang ulo* ("stubborn"). This is the vocabulary of a child—and of a mother to her children, who are undoubtedly a pain in her *puwit*.

When she left home, my mom felt she had to reject everything connected to the culture of her upbringing, the good with the bad, because it all smelled of patriarchal rot. I think my mom's involvement in the hippie movement in Los Angeles and San Francisco in the sixties and early seventies had an obliterating, deracinating effect on her. The psychedelics of that era were undeniably freeing, allowing a generation to heave off the stultifying cultural expectations of an unambiguously racist, classist, sexist, homophobic country. But trying to erase your past can be poisonous. The dismantling philosophy of hippie culture was itself a form of assimilation, and I am a product of that process.

I don't have to do the heavy labor of heaving off that my mom did. My parents made sure I don't feel forced to obey a fearsome God, salute the flag, or sit mute while men speak. This freedom of thought is empowering. Yet I'm left a little unmoored, one of so many hippie kids, descended from two and three generations of assimilation, who are one-quarter this, one-quarter that, adrift in our supposed freedom, trying to figure out where and when we should drop anchor.

Neither my mom nor dad situated themselves in spiritual practices. My mom was devoted to rejecting the Catholicism of her youth and, with it, the power of her father. And yet she felt at sea without the systems she'd been raised within—a big family, a church—because it's lonely to grow old outside a multigenerational community and difficult to face disaster when you live a solitary life. Communal living provided an alternative, allowing her to reject patriarchal society while embracing matriarchal care and connection. And when she brought her orientation toward group living into her career, she found a sense of belonging and purpose others might find in religion.

Co-ops and land trusts aren't inherently good; they depend on human will and vision and the profound complexity of collaboration. But they give human texture to the otherwise exploitive corporate free market economy. They give equity a fighting chance. My mom channeled her ambition toward something animated by hope, something that felt larger than herself, which is what she was looking for.

Food remains a tether to her identity and her past. While Goyo lived with us, despite her residual anger, my mom started cooking more Filipino dishes: pork chops with garlic fried rice and chopped green onion and tomato, fried chicken, chicken adobo, *buko* pie, avocado ice cream. Sometimes she'd bring down the *kudkuran*, a device that looked like a child's wooden rocking horse, and my ninety-two-, then ninety-three-, then ninety-four-year-old grandpa would sit astride it and grate fresh coconut on a serrated knife where the horse's head should have been. I learned through osmosis—my mom would make foods he loved, and the comfort they both felt would flow into me.

Jerome moved out of the Kettle when his childhood polio caught up with him and he became too weak to go up and down the spiral staircase. He joined his son and daughter-in-law in nearby Viroqua. New roommates, some of whom had been old roommates, moved into the Kettle.

One of them, Eddy, was like a younger brother to my mom. He'd taken over a massive empty tobacco warehouse in Viroqua and filled every inch of it with books. Most people call it Driftless Books, but he named it the Forgotten Works Warehouse after one of the settings of Richard Brautigan's *In Watermelon Sugar*, the quintessential commune novel. It's like a child's fantasy of a bookstore. The space is cavernous, with books stacked to the ceiling. There are a thousand secret corners, hidden shelves, and mysterious rooms. Literally or figuratively, you can pull a book from a stack and get swallowed into another dimension.

My mom's friend Lisa moved in after leaving her partner of decades. The low rent made the Kettle an affordable way station. Lisa has an innate understanding of physical objects and their uses and can fix almost anything. My mom is already a creature of systems—"everything needs a place," she loves to remind me—but Lisa ratchets it to new levels. George lives at the Kettle part-time. And then, wait: *Mick!* Mick is still in his outbuilding behind the greenhouse and still appears and disappears at irregular junctures. My mom often narrates the hours she and others spend cleaning his small place of rotting food and garbage, but I love knowing that this recluse has security, shelter, and people checking in to make sure he's safe.

These friends and roommates have their heartbreaks, melt-downs, and spats that sometimes fester into resentment. My mom will occasionally rant over the phone about the most mundane things, like someone's tea bags piling up in the sink. I imagine her sounding off in a voice I know so well, tinny and cruel, and I picture her roommates rolling their eyes or, worse, feeling belittled.

For all its twelve-sided glory, the Kettle can feel small, confined, with few spaces that don't open into the center, as though it wants its residents to face one another. The lodge has a way of being insistent, even a little needy; someone must cut the wood and feed the fire. I view it as both confrontational and generous, and I can't tell if I see these qualities in the building because I see them in my mom or if she chose this place because it fits her nature.

Like the Driftless region itself, the Kettle is a collection of unique people sharing a cultural terrain unlike anything around them. The Driftless region, this place made up of a thousand special places, makes me think of our relationships to the land and to each other. Our curiosity and care inform the work of our lives.

When I was a little girl, my dad would tuck me into bed, turn out the lights, and whisper that my mom would be up soon. I'd stay awake until her footsteps came pitter-pattering into the dark room. She'd sit on the lip of my bed, lean in, and whisper, "What's your last little secret?" She asked me this question every night, and every night I saved an answer for her. "My last little secret is . . ."

Franny's Chicken Adobo

Recipe by Francis Marquez

MAKES 8 TO 10 SERVINGS

My grandma Franny would cook dishes for Goyo that she learned while they lived in the Philippines during World War II, when the country was occupied by the Imperial Japanese Army. After Franny and Goyo moved to Schenectady, New York, in 1945, they tried to appear like a cookie-cutter American family, but Franny held on to Filipino foods. Hidden in the home, she adapted her favorite dishes into a mash-up of Filipino, Polish, and midcentury-Americana cooking.

When I visited the Philippines, I learned that her playful interpretations are in keeping with the history of Filipino food, which has been shaped by Indigenous, Spanish, Chinese, Mexican, Japanese, and American influences. Generations of cooks have navigated complex identities, heaped and collaged. Hers is one scrap of paper in a boundless papier-mâché creature whose shape I'm still trying to perceive.

Franny's chicken adobo, which includes nontraditional apples and sherry, is beloved by her kids. My mom makes it whenever she wants to conjure her mom. We have Franny's copy of the recipe, mysteriously written in three different pens and a pencil. She scrawled this anecdote to the side:

> Legend has it that the coconut was named by trad-
> ers from Spain and Portugal who apparently thought
> that the shell's three "eyes" resembled the face of a

clown: loosely translated, the Spanish word *coco*
means "grinning face."

This is a very saucy dish, or, as you'd say in Tagalog, rich in
sabaw, the meaty drippings. You must eat it over rice. Be sure to
pour extra sauce in your bowl! Blasphemously, I like to drizzle
Zak's chili oil (page xxi) over the top. Like all curries, it tastes
better a day or two after it's made.

¼ cup high-heat oil (like sunflower)

2 chickens, cut up, or 8 pounds mixed chicken pieces,
bone in, skin on

2 medium onions, chopped

2 apples, cored and roughly chopped

10 cloves garlic, minced

4-inch knob fresh ginger, peeled and minced

1 cup apple cider vinegar

1 bay leaf

1 tablespoon curry powder

1 tablespoon salt

1 teaspoon freshly ground black pepper

2 tablespoons lemon juice

2 cups full-fat coconut milk*

Heat oil in a large enamel or cast-iron pan over medium heat
until it shimmers. Add chicken pieces in a single layer. Don't crowd
the pan. You'll have to work in batches. Brown the chicken on both
sides. Test each piece by prodding. If it sticks to the bottom, it's
not ready to be flipped. When it releases with a gentle nudge, flip

it. Remove browned chicken pieces to a bowl and repeat until all pieces are seared.

In the same pan, add the onion and apple and sauté until the onion has a little color on its edges, about 3 minutes. Add the garlic and ginger and cook until fragrant and just starting to color, about 30 seconds. Add the chicken back to the pan and toss everything together. Pour in the apple cider vinegar and scrape the bottom to loosen any deliciously browned bits. Add the bay leaf, curry powder, salt, black pepper, lemon juice, and 1 cup coconut milk, which should cover the meat halfway. Turn the heat to low and cook for about 20 minutes, until the chicken is fully cooked but still succulent and firm. Add the remaining 1 cup coconut milk and cook for an additional 15 minutes. Serve with rice and chili oil.

*Any brand of coconut milk that lists coconut milk as its only ingredient will work. Avoid anything with gums or sweeteners.

OFFER ME S'MORE

t was 2010, and I was pushing the furniture to the edges of our living room to make a dance floor for our first Halloween party at the Holman House when our neighbor Leona approached me. She and her two kids had recently moved in with her grandma across the street.

"Hey, Lola! Do me a favor?" She peered at me with sly eyes.

"Sure, Leona," I said, setting down our small coffee table. "What is it?"

"Take a hit of my special blunt."

Afterward, I hallucinated that I smelled gas and spent the better part of the party believing that everyone was going to die in an inferno, even after I checked every possible source. But once my paranoia subsided, I had an amazing time and felt spectacularly free! Friends were deejaying, and I danced for hours. Chris and Cynthia's coworkers—painters, seamstresses, fabricators, and carpenters at Laika, the stop-motion studio where they both worked—constructed the most elaborate and inspired costumes I'd ever seen. My closest friends appeared in twos and threes, forming bubbles that I traveled among.

The Holman House contained discrete spaces—the kitchen, the living room, the side porch, the yard—so I felt like I was in an intimate nightclub, bouncing from dance floor to bar to chill-out lounge. The pink-orange walls of the kitchen glowed like the inside of a lit-up pumpkin. Every once in a while I'd catch a glimpse of Leona in a red-and-white tracksuit, dressed as herself, asking for a lap dance. The house was soaking up electrical currents as the chemistry between strangers, soon to be friends, sparked.

The Holman House had its own agenda and needs. It would speak to me in a wordless language, the way dark earth hums, and demand a party. It was always an imperative, and we'd oblige. For how chaotic the house could feel, it was also capacious, asking to be filled. Some of these parties were for other people: baby showers and birthday parties for friends. On Christmas mornings, I invited people over, taking up my mom's tradition of making sourdough donuts. Many of our friends lived in apartments, and my parents' unspoken philosophy about the house echoed in my ears: *We only deserve it if we share it.* Our large house was meant to be well-used. I often told myself it wasn't us saying yes to people's requests but the house itself, speaking through us.

In a reverse migration from my childhood, my mom began visiting more often. She'd come for a week every season or two and integrate seamlessly into our lives, making dinner, scouring the sink, recycling magazines, sorting through and tossing bits of clutter but leaving her own residue of weed ashtrays and magazines behind, helping in the garden, taking long bike rides along the Columbia River, showing me secret routes she'd discovered. My dad came over all the time—to plant things, weed his succulent patch, prune his marionberries, watch Blazers games, and borrow his own books. The Holman House never let people go.

I met Corey playing basketball with Zak at a weekly pickup game. A few of us would go out for beers after we played, and Corey often joined. I thought he was *so* funny and good-looking, tall and sporty, with green-yellow eyes like a reptile's and curly, soft hair. As we all joked around, I'd stare into Corey's light eyes and feel my crush brewing.

On the Fourth of July when I was twenty-four, Zak invited me to Corey's house for a party. Corey's next-door neighbors set off illegal fireworks, which shot up between Douglas fir trees into the canopy of sky. After midnight, Corey built a small bonfire in his backyard, next to an orange canoe he was trying to patch with resin. A group of us sat around it, telling stories. When I was totally spent, I got up to leave, and Corey followed me to my bike.

"Could we hang out sometime?" he asked. "Without your brother?"

Over the following month, we went on a few dates, and I stayed over at his place a couple times. In August, I invited Corey to the Holman House for my friend Gary's birthday. In honor of the occasion, I was making racks of lamb arranged in a crown, stuffed with homemade sausage, and decorated with miniature paper chef hats.

"I didn't know you could cook," Corey told me afterward, and I wondered: *Seriously? Do we know anything about each other?*

I'd figured out quickly that he wasn't focused on cooking. Early on, he made me a dinner of tacos served with corn tortillas still cold from the fridge. The brittle tortillas cracked in half as I tried to fold them around the beans. *Never again*, I swore to myself. *I will never again let him serve me cold tortillas from the fridge.*

Corey and I started dating more seriously that fall. He's a multitalented visual artist who works primarily in illustration and painting. Sometimes I'd find little jokes Corey had drawn for himself on scraps of paper—doodles of a fish shooting out eggs or caricatures of powerful men, like his portraits of US senators. "Mike Crapo, Idaho," one said, and above it, he'd drawn a weaselly man with intense, glowering eyes. I stole these to keep forever.

Corey never ate breakfast, but at lunch and dinner he'd become a boa constrictor, swallowing entire meals in one gulp and then starting on a second. He drank too much and spent some of his weekends hungover, watching one movie after the next, recuperating. He didn't have a top sheet on his bed, just a comforter, which I found disturbing. He'd get lost in his thoughts and seem entirely absent, then comment on some small detail of the scenery I hadn't noticed. Unexpected ideas seemed to emerge from his subconscious like grand little ships exiting a tunnel, custom-made to delight me.

Corey loved music and was curious about what I liked. He'd buy records he thought I'd appreciate: dancehall, rocksteady, dub, soul. There was nothing more peaceful in the world than being on road trips with him, sitting in the passenger seat and listening to music as we made our way through the desert. Sometimes he challenged me—"I want you to be a better listener," he told me one day—but he also treated me like I was infinitely intelligent, and I felt loved for my whole self.

For many years, Corey and his best friends lived and made art and music together in a warehouse they'd built out illegally.

A management company gradually raised the rent to untenable levels, essentially evicting them, but even as it dissolved physically, the Warehouse, as they called it, held an adhesive form. Corey and his former housemates got together all the time at their friend's bar, Tiga, through art projects and bands, and around backyard bonfires. Every summer they camped together along the high rivers and lakes of Mount Hood. They texted constantly, like sweethearts. His closeness with his friends moved me.

From the beginning, I was clear that I wouldn't prioritize my partner at the expense of time to myself and with friends and that I expected the same of him.

"I'm never going to get married," I told him, probably too early in our relationship. I was surprised to find that this shocked Corey, who I'd thought of as fairly nontraditional. But I'd known since I was a girl that marriage was something I didn't want, and though I often reexamined my decision, my firmness didn't waver. Whenever I thought about it, I'd recall a day when I was ten years old and my cousin Jessica described her dream wedding to me: she'd wear a white bikini and her soon-to-be husband would wear black swim trunks. They'd stand on the end of a dock. I was going to be one of her bridesmaids, she told me, and would wear a one-piece swimsuit in navy-and-white stripes. All the guests would float in inner tubes.

"And when we kiss, the minister's gonna shove us in the water," she told me in breathless excitement.

She asked me about my dream wedding, and I confessed I'd never thought about it before. My parents had never married. This explained, literally, why they never divorced, but for me, it also explained why their eventual separation was relatively peaceful instead of contentious. In fact, although they weren't a romantic couple anymore, they still spent time together and shared each other's families. None of my friends' parents who had divorced did that.

Hours later, when I tried to conjure my own dream wedding, I kept imagining myself in a bikini being shoved off a dock. Water shoots up my nose, and I surface, heaving, as everyone I know looks on from their inner tubes, shivering and purple-lipped. (Lakes in Oregon are freezing cold.) The bikini, the shove, the sense of drowning: forevermore, these remained my images of a wedding.

Weddings inaugurate marriages, and I could never separate the two in my mind. I didn't tell Corey about my vision of water-bound matrimony, but I was honest about where it had landed me: I didn't want to marry. I'd fallen in love with Corey, but I didn't know how I'd feel ten, twenty, thirty years in the future, and I didn't believe in promises I couldn't keep. I also knew I didn't want to be defined by a single relationship in my life, as though it were the biggest accomplishment, the most deserving of a banquet. Lots of things deserve parties and banquets. Lots of relationships are sacred. Why not celebrate them all?

This, it turns out, was the season of love. Cynthia fell for a carpenter and handyman named Andy who'd wander our backyard shirtless, exposing his muscular back, which was covered—top to bottom, side to side—in a dragon tattoo. They had loud sex and filled our garbage cans with used condoms. Zak was dating a woman named Erin who was half a foot taller than him, worked in fashion, and was so different that it seemed to crack open buried components of his personality, namely a latent fascination with pop culture.

Chris met a strapping man, also named Erin, also a builder and carpenter. Erin the man was incredibly fit, always fresh and pert from the gym, his skin wet and glistening like he was daily reborn. Erin was in his mid-forties, but he seemed younger. He told me about older women ogling him at the public pool and at his dad's assisted-living facility. On one visit, a woman in her eighties had cornered him and demanded, "Kiss me!"

"Why don't we start with a hug?" he replied, and they hugged for a while before he continued on his way.

Some nights, our house was overflowing with people and we had to add leaves to the dining table; on other nights, it was quiet. The waxing and waning were familiar to me, but I was a tyrant about asking for people's plans. I loved camaraderie yet disliked surprises. I wanted to know about guests at least a few hours in advance.

Not a day went by when I didn't text the group: "Who's around tonight? Anyone wanna cook?" Miraculously, someone always volunteered, and no one disregarded the texts. I hated the occasional instances when we each made separate dinners. It didn't bother me if someone didn't come home for dinner or asked us to save them a plate, but I couldn't stand being in the kitchen as each person cooked their own meal, vying for space and cleaning only what they considered their individual mess. It made me feel lonely. I didn't know when we'd so firmly established our rule that if you volunteered to cook dinner, you cooked for everyone. I did know that it was important to me, and I enforced it zealously.

Our Halloween parties grew bigger every year. Chris outdid himself annually with outrageous, grotesque, and spectacular costumes. He was a Pussy Cat with an eighteen-inch-long anatomical fabric vulva running the length of his torso, sewn onto his furry onesie. He was the Human Centipede, as in the horrific eponymous Dutch film that had just been released, dragging two life-sized dolls behind him, attached mouth to butthole. He was Donatella Versace, with massive puffy lips, so convincing I wondered if he should put on a variety show.

I was never one for dressing up, so I winged it, drawing the mouth of a lamprey on a piece of cardboard the day of the party and strapping it to my head with a shoelace, wearing a borrowed sailor suit, or simply painting my face ghostly white with fake blood dripping from my ears—which hit a little too close to home when I really thought about it.

The parties were for us, but they were also bigger than us. Over time, I sensed that many of our guests didn't know their hosts, but they had strong feelings for the Holman House anyway. It had given them a space to cut loose, to flirt, to feel connected. Multiple friends met at the party and later fell in love, married, and had babies. Sometimes, I'd meet a friend of a friend—a stranger to me—for the first time, and they'd say, "I've been to your house for Halloween. What a house!" and I'd imagine some hidden landscape of memories they were glimpsing in their mind's eye.

f I don't leave now, I'll never leave," Cynthia joked to me when she decided to move with Tender Vittles into a new home with Andy. They hauled out vanloads of her stuff, but some items remained because none of us were sure whether they were hers or not—the Holman House had claimed them for itself. Soon, she and Andy had a son, Ozwald. I moved into Cynthia's bedroom on the first floor, Chris moved into my old room, and we had one extra space to share.

Cynthia later confessed to Zak that she'd thought he hated her because of all his grumbling about the clutter in the house. I was shocked—how could she feel something that brutal and never say a word?

"Our household is more fragile than you think," Zak told me at the kitchen island one night while he drank his icy IPA and I snacked on an orange. "We get along because we have to. In some ways, I feel stuck here because I've chosen the path of being destitute."

Zak worked with public artists, doing the computer animation for their installations to help fund his own animations. He never made a lot of money, and although he could have moved out, he wouldn't have been able to afford anything as nice as the Holman House. It was all part of what I perceived as an uneasy compromise for him. He was introverted and inclined to spend time alone. Our household forced him to regularly socialize, which could be positive or negative, oppressive or pleasurable. If he didn't remind me of his feelings, I could regularly overlook them, content in what felt like happy chaos to me.

In Cynthia's absence, various friends came to live with us for short durations. Our home became a stable landing pad for people who needed somewhere to go during transitional moments in their lives. We welcomed a friend after his divorce, as he navigated his next move. He and his son shared Chris's old bedroom, and some mornings I'd find them in the kitchen playing chess together before school. His son, who was struggling with all the changes, called our house "Porkville" due to the aroma of Chris's many ground-pork dishes. I knew it was a pejorative, a way to dismiss this place that was not the home his parents had shared, but I loved the gross nickname anyway.

My mom, with Andy's help, turned my dad's former basement office into an apartment. She purged most of his storage
items, which pained him greatly. The basement didn't have its
own kitchen, but it was spacious. She'd stay there whenever she
visited, which made it impossible for us to rent the apartment
long-term. Zak and I refused to rent it short-term on Airbnb,
claiming it was a principled political decision. This was not
untrue, but it was also not the whole truth. I didn't want to deal
with people coming and going or manage their needs. Our rent
was based on my mom's mortgage. The cost was stable and
affordable for our group, so while the money would've been nice,
it wasn't a necessity.

Our decision provided an unexpected benefit: we frequently
had a nice place for far-flung friends to stay. We all took advan-
tage, and summers were filled with visitors. We took up the habit
of throwing a low-key party whenever someone stayed with us so
our friends could gather and linger. Everyone took on different
roles: minding the barbecue, washing the dishes, tidying the living room. There was something unspeakably moving about
watching my whole community care for the Holman House and
give back to it.

Later, one of Chris's coworkers moved into the basement
apartment after her partner beat her violently and she needed
distance and safety. I'd never met her before. The day she arrived,
her mouth was so swollen and disfigured from being hit that I
struggled to look her in the face. She hardly spoke for the pain,
but the longer she stayed with us, the more at ease she became,
her face and composure healing in parallel. She was British, and
she thought my love for dark chocolate was ridiculous.

"Candy is supposed to taste good," she'd laugh.

She stayed with us for several months, and one evening, before she returned to England, Corey and I were watching Anthony Bourdain's TV show *Parts Unknown*. She joined, having never seen the show or heard of him before, and immediately excused herself.

"I can't watch this; that man seems suicidal," she said as she left.

Years later I discovered that she'd seen what I had not, that she could see a whole world that I could not.

In a strange way, because none of us had kids and because we all stayed put, this period of our lives has a blurry quality in my memory, one year to the next distinguished primarily by the news of the moment. Our life was steady; the world felt off-kilter. Nightmare politicians arrived in and departed from the spotlight like malignant infections. And the body politic was unwell, so infections were constant.

To distract myself, I became obsessed with the anticipation and reward of seasonal change: in late March, when the magnolias bloomed at the Hoyt Arboretum, and a few weeks later, when the dogwood trees along Ainsworth Avenue sprouted a thousand pink tongues; in August, when the huckleberries ripened in the fields on Mount Adams, and in September, when the golden chanterelles began mushrooming in the second-growth forests. I knew Halloween was near when Zak made his first chanterelle *tom kha* soup of the year. I experienced time not as moving forward but as cyclical, never the same and always renewed.

My boss at the nonprofit took a different job, and for a few years, I was without steady oversight at work. I started doing whatever I wanted, which seemed like a surefire way to get fired but worked out for reasons I never understood. Following my own whims, I hosted a community festival focused on mushroom foraging and their life cycles. I helped organize an event to introduce locals to CSA farmers. I found I really liked planning interactive events and collaborating with artists.

Once, I got caught napping under my desk and made no apology. Another time I walked into an important meeting with chocolate Magic Shell unknowingly smeared on my face. I didn't have a very serious, committed relationship to my workplace. In so many ways it was a dream job—I had freedom and kind coworkers—but I felt a sense of impending doom. Where was this going? Wouldn't someone realize, at some point, how many liberties I was taking?

Every year I waited to be fired. Every year they seemed to barely notice my transgressions.

At Halloween in 2012, only an hour into the party, the cops arrived. *Crap*, I thought, *it's too early*. At this point I was semi-pro at dealing with the cops for noise complaints—each time originating from the same neighboring couple, who were always invited. First visit: the cops issued a warning. Second visit: you received a steep fine. If their first visit happened late enough, they'd be too busy with other noise complaints to return, and we'd only get the first warning. But it was barely ten thirty.

I went outside, underneath the rhododendron Chris had so nicely pruned and shaped, bare of flowers now, and found a single cop waiting for me. On our side porch, someone was revving a fake chainsaw and someone else was playing the snare drums like they were in a marching band.

"Offer me s'mores," the cop said, over the din.

"Excuse me, would you say that again, please?"

"Offer me s'mores," she repeated tersely.

"Um, I don't think I have any graham crackers or marshmallows," I said, befuddled.

She leaned in close. "I'm Officer Samora. We received a noise complaint."

Was this party so loud that I couldn't hear a woman only two feet from me, or had my hearing deteriorated further than I'd realized?

"I'm so sorry, officer. I'm sure we can lower the sound."

She explained their process—the first warning, the subsequent fine—and then she left. I begged the men on my porch to quiet down. By some miracle, the cops didn't come back that night. I told this story often. "Offer me s'mores," I'd laugh as I told it, hiding the fact that I believed I was going completely deaf.

By then, in my late twenties, my hearing loss had become so severe in both ears that I was considering hearing aids. I'd had the ear surgery that was recommended, something called a stapedotomy, which was explained in detail but left me with only the image of a cat door inserted inside my ear. This little flap transformed the sound in my left ear into something harsh, without any of the roundness I'd always taken for granted. The surgery helped me hear, but my comprehension was limited.

Misunderstandings like my encounter with the cop were becoming more frequent. But after she left, I still danced all night long, enjoying Halloween with my friends, bobbing and hopping to soul, R & B, and Chris's beloved house music, which would shake the foundation of the Holman House like earth tremors.

At the end of that night, Zak was the last one awake, trying to herd out the stragglers. Around four in the morning, one man remained on the side porch. He pulled a twenty-dollar bill from his pocket, looked Zak in the eyes, and lit it on fire, letting the ash dissipate into the sky.

Around this time, a thought had come to me that I found unspeakably painful: that someday, when I was fully deaf, I wouldn't be able to hear music. I imagined my future self. There'd be a song I wanted to remember—some jagged, unfinished piece of melody looping in my mind—but I'd never be able to figure out how the rest of it went. It would remain broken, forever unresolved. I believed the depth of my experience of joy would diminish at the same steady drip as my perception of sound. This thought was so corrosive that when it would surface, I'd sit and cry. Then I'd shove this thought into the dungeon of my head and try to lock the door and throw away the key.

Corey was living in a rundown apartment off Thirty-Fourth and Belmont. Beneath him was a coffee shop and, next to that, a bar. I was so hard of hearing that the music never kept me awake when I stayed over, although I could feel it rattle the bed. The owner of the building died, and his son decided to jack up the rent. Corey was making very little money, despite scrambling for and finding regular jobs.

"I want to move in together," Corey told me. We'd only been dating for, oh, five years at this point.

"Am I ready?" I asked aloud. I did not feel ready.

"Don't you ever want to live on our own?" he asked me.

I answered honestly: "Not really. I like living with a group of people."

The next day we fought over the phone. In the middle of our fight, my teeth started chattering so hard I thought they'd crack, a physiological response I couldn't have predicted. When I looked ahead, I knew I wanted to stay with Corey. He was my transcendent match. What he was asking for was so plainly reasonable. I also knew I wanted to keep living communally. A familiar voice inside my head told me that if I really loved him, we'd find our own place together. This was the next step in relationships as serious as ours. But this omniscient narrator knew nothing about me. Why was this the test of our love? Did I truly think my married friends loved each other more than Corey and I did? No, I didn't. Was I stuck in childhood, unable to grow up? Maybe. I'd never lived alone or with a single partner. Was I afraid of solitude? Dependence? These surging, open-ended questions made me seasick.

I knew that Corey and I couldn't afford a nice place of our own even if we wanted to. At this point, Portland had become so expensive and we both were making so little that even staying at his crummy spot together as the rent rose would've been difficult. But even though my choice to live collectively was less a choice than an economic necessity, could I still own it? The idea of living with only one person, even someone I loved, didn't sound right to me. Would we have to make each other dinner every single night, back and forth, back and forth, like a perpetual motion machine?

I invited Corey to move into my room in the Holman House without initiating a robust conversation with Zak and Chris because I couldn't bear to hear a no. I didn't thoroughly consider how my decision would affect them. None of my roommates had invited their partners to move in. It seemed like one of our unspoken rules. Zak and Erin had separated, but Cynthia simply left when she fell for Andy. Chris and Erin had made the decision not to move in together. They had a schedule that allowed them both time together and time apart, independence and closeness. It seemed like a good model.

When Corey moved into the Holman House, something shifted that made our relationship easier. I liked not having to make regular plans but simply coming home to him. Corey was very attuned to the news and would get keyed up by something he read and not be able to calm his anger or sorrow. His politics were becoming increasingly radical and Marxist. He was deeply concerned that our society was so committed to its own perpetuation that it couldn't and wouldn't make changes to drastically improve people's lives: with things like universal health care, affordable housing, or an empowered labor movement. He saw workers becoming as atomized as nuclear families, a million independent contractors without systems for solidarity and organizing.

Sometimes his fears would make me feel disconsolate. We'd unpack our thoughts together, but I found great relief in watching Corey, Zak, and Chris processing their feelings around the kitchen island as well. Zak wheedled humor from bleakness. Chris rarely entertained the battering of the news, and his fun-loving energy was a needed palate cleanser. It had a positive effect on Corey, and, later, he told me that he loved living in our community too.

Our household adopted our friend Adam's tuxedo cat, Wendy, when Adam moved in with a woman who was allergic. Ten years old and a real sack of bones, Wendy didn't meow so much as talk. Corey would translate her sounds into words that, afterward, sounded like exactly what she was saying. "Marco Ruuuubio,"

Wendy would say as she walked through the kitchen toward her food, echoing the radio reporting on the senator, then running for president. "Papa Balloon," she mewled, trotting back to the bedroom.

Mornings in the Holman House followed a consistent pattern. Wendy was the first one up, and she'd yap for someone to feed her. Corey woke up not long after, between six and seven o'clock, energetic and alert, like a dog who'd just pooped. He'd feed Wendy and then make pour-over coffee into a glass quart jar. In summer he'd water the hanging baskets and low pots he planted with what I called "grandma flowers": zinnias, geraniums, impatiens, fuchsias, begonias, and petunias. He didn't eat anything. Sometimes he'd put on a record and sit and listen. He needed a full hour or two of milling around the house before he could go to work.

I'd wake up next, sometime before eight. I'd drink the last of Corey's coffee and make Earl Grey with milk. I'd eat something hearty, like a feral kefir I made accompanied with fruit, nuts, and toast. I'd sit, eat, drink, and stare into space, grumpy, easing into my mind, barely able to interact. This took maybe thirty minutes. Corey would poke at me, kiss me, ask me too many questions, and overall enjoy tormenting me. And then he'd go to work around eight thirty, and usually I would too.

On weekends, after I finished my coffee, I'd putter around the kitchen for a while, washing ziplock bags, unloading the dishwasher, feeding my sourdough. Zak emerged next. A night person, he rarely fell asleep before one. When he came downstairs, he'd be wearing soft pink slippers an ex-girlfriend had given him that were disintegrating on his feet, old pants he'd patched at the crotch or knee, and a T-shirt from some long-lost Portland business. He'd walk with slow, heavy steps, like the memory of sleep was weighing his body down. I learned not to say anything until he made his coffee in the percolator and ate his piece of toast. Once the coffee hit, he'd brighten, and we'd talk about the day ahead.

Sometime after ten, Chris would come downstairs, his footsteps light and steady. "Good morning, Lola Bear!" he'd call out sweetly.

He'd heat up our wok over the highest flame, add half an inch of oil, wait until it was smoking, and then cook beaten eggs with fish sauce and a pinch of sugar. When the eggs hit the oil, they poufed dramatically, expanding like cotton candy. Sometimes he'd reheat some rice and splash the eggs with salty Maggi sauce. Other times he'd warm a big flour tortilla over an open flame, cook a piece of bacon and a few loose hash browns, and wrap the eggs and everything else into a neat bundle—a calorific, filling breakfast burrito for an improbably thin man. He poured extra half-and-half in his PG Tips tea and headed out the door, to Erin's or a friend's.

On Saturday mornings, an evangelical group would gather above the auto body shop on the other side of the alley and sing together. Their voices arrived not in words but like chimes on the wind, high, tinkling, and ethereal. One day, I couldn't hear their singing anymore, but I sensed their voices were still there, as surely as busy Martin Luther King Jr. Boulevard, the cat door in my ear, and the stars in the daytime sky.

In theorist Roland Barthes's *How to Live Together*, he describes his ideal living situation as "idiorrhythmy." It's a word, he writes, that he'd been searching for his whole life. When he finally found it—in the monastic tradition—it brought together a collection of desires and beliefs he'd longed to name. When I encountered his book, the word fulfilled a similar role for me. *Idiorrhythmy* describes the lifestyle of monks on Mount Athos, who were both isolated and in contact with one another. "Each subject lives according to his own rhythm," Barthes writes. He called it "something like solitude with regular interruptions . . . the utopia of a socialism of distance."

What that meant to me was individuals living their own lives, respecting their own needs and patterns, and bumping into one another within common spaces and shared concerns. Because they weren't overly prescribed, each interaction was dynamic instead of stagnant.

Our household was made up of strong personalities. We each had our own projects and fascinations and, importantly, personal rooms. Yet we often met in the kitchen, around the TV, and in the garden. We didn't institute a strict dinner schedule—Zak cooks on Mondays, Lola on Tuesdays, etc.—but we did eat together many nights. We still didn't have a chore wheel and only tended the things we each cared about most.

That didn't always work out, as when Zak had to scold me for eating his leftovers, or when Corey left records strewn on the dining room table and I simultaneously found his stray socks under all the couches, or when Chris's semi-ironic religious statues began to accumulate on a table in the kitchen. But I didn't think forced interaction and schedules would work. I liked something more anarchic—a set shape that allowed for maximum freedom. Using Barthes's language, we were an idiorrhythmic cluster. No one person was in charge. There were power dynamics, but they were in a constant state of flux. None of us were easily perturbed, and when our tempers did rear up they quickly flamed out, rarely agonistically.

Barthes criticized couples, nuclear family units, and especially larger communes "because their structure is based on an architecture of power." His interest was in small groups cultivating "a zone that falls between two excessive forms": solitude and assimilation. I felt like he was describing my home. I loved how our dinners felt spontaneous, even though, I suppose, they were predictable. I had my own space and a lot of alone time. I also had access to shared space. My interactions with my housemates frequently surprised me. For me, this combination was just right.

The housing crisis was worsening. Rent was unaffordable for anyone without a high-paying job or family wealth. Zak's new girlfriend, Sarah, a postal worker, could barely afford an apartment in the supposedly affordable urban neighborhood where she delivered mail, which seemed like a sick joke. Most of the local workforce stood no chance of buying a home. Many of my neighbors moved to the margins of the city—places like Gresham and Vancouver, Washington—where they could afford rent. None of the kids I'd grown up with, except Leona, stayed in the neighborhood. Only on the Fourth of July did the neighborhood feel like itself again, with people returning to visit their grandparents and aunties and uncles, partying in the streets and setting off illegal fireworks, which was misery-inducing for animals and veterans and a potential fire starter and also one of my greatest joys.

Racist housing policy had laid the tracks for gentrification for decades. The city disinvested in its historically Black neighborhoods and literally removed residents from their homes to build the I-5 freeway, Legacy Emanuel hospital, and basketball arena. Black community leaders had planted cherry trees along the avenues of the greater Albina neighborhood, tending its spirit just as carefully, but over time, more affluent, mostly white residents displaced many of the working-class people who called these communities home. Housing prices rose and rose. Decades later than needed, Portlanders passed bonds to create more permanent, affordable housing. Yet the housing crisis was destined to get worse because the problem was mammoth and knotted. It was enmeshed with our entire financial structure and the racist, classist roots of our culture.

It wasn't lost on me that I still lived in my childhood home, which was rising in value every single year, a boon for my mom. I was a recipient of intergenerational wealth, the kind I wouldn't have been able to attain for myself. I was extremely fortunate to have a secure foundation and roommates to help pay rent. I didn't take for granted my low costs and safe, warm bed, nor the ways in which they safeguarded my mental health.

In 2015, after years of floundering at work doing various projects but unsure what they added up to, I decided to start a business. I had the initial idea when I realized all the noodles I bought were made in Japan using US wheat. I called them "boomerang noodles"—grains flung across an ocean and noodles whipped back. Why not make a noodle here, using flours from some of the farmers I knew? As someone who doesn't identify as Asian American, I felt self-conscious and uncertain about the endeavor, but eventually, with encouragement from my mom and my Japanese American friends, I started making organic ramen noodles. I committed myself to making sure the business served and was deeply involved in Portland's Japanese American community. I called the business Umi Organic—*umi* meaning "ocean," the body of water shared by Japan and the United States. While this gave me a great deal of power over my time, it was also all-consuming and financially stressful.

I wanted Umi to be a co-op, but co-ops arise from mutual vision and need, and I'd come up with this concept with my mom and a friend. I loved our business—it occupied the bulk of my thoughts—but from the very beginning, I distrusted the role of heroic entrepreneur and girl boss that I felt projected onto me by the media, customers, and even friends. There was nothing self-made about me. My mom had worked in the natural-foods industry for decades and had shown me the ropes. I resolved that my business wouldn't be about personal enrichment; I'd work to create something that provided meaningful living wages, even as the cost of living rose, and would attempt to support organic farmers, moving money from urban to rural areas. I dreamed of someday becoming a co-op and was filled with purpose.

I loved the work and the friends I worked with. I especially loved the farmers market—that famous symbol of elitism that I found to be more complex. We launched Umi at the Hollywood Farmers Market in the summer of 2016. Our booth featured a custom wooden counter my friend Peter built, where I dreamed people would pull up to slurp noodles; signage Gary designed; cloth napkins Cynthia had sewn; a menu that changed every week; and a single product to take home: organic ramen noodles.

Twice, I burned my bangs while trying to light our massive propane turkey fryer. We'd arrive at the market hours early to boil the largest pot of water I'd ever filled, and it would take us just as long to pack up, waiting for the now-gelatinous water, thickened by the tapioca starch that coats our noodles, to cool. At Hollywood, a couple ran a sausage booth called Buns on the Run, and after the market closed, they'd pull out camping chairs and sit for a while before packing. Those first markets, even after sitting for half an hour or more, Buns on the Run would manage to leave before us. I vowed that one day we'd beat Buns on the Run. It was months before I looked out the rearview window of the van and saw Buns on the Run still placidly sitting, resting their buns.

When I got home after those first markets, after washing dishes at our commissary kitchen and then unloading Peter's impossibly heavy table into the garage, I'd drink an entire milk-shake and fall into bed for the kind of nap that left me feeling like wet, threadbare fabric. But I loved the work—I felt proud of the food we made and excited about the community we were entering.

The following season we joined King Market, in my neighborhood. I fell for it immediately. There were always parades of dogs and little kids stumbling over those dogs. We started to make miso sesame and *bibim* sauces, and sometimes a pesto made with *shiso* or cilantro or wasabi leaves. We refined our menu, making it a direct expression of the market, using whatever vegetables we could buy—pickling them, roasting them, putting them on top of our noodles tossed in our new sauces—to show customers that, honest to god, any vegetable cooked almost any way would be tasty with our noodles. Once, we roasted small Nantes carrots and they came out looking like cocktail wieners, but the point remained: these, too, tasted good (even if they didn't look that way) on top of Umi noodles.

The market began to feel like home. My dad helped portion noodles and set up in the morning. He brought our staff hot pancakes with bits of butter still melting on them from his apartment one block away. I listened to the NBA playoffs on a little radio at market with my friend Elan, a mushroom forager, as CJ McCollum hit the shot to beat Denver and advance to the Western Conference finals. The barter economy at the markets made me feel like the richest person in the world, carrying home boxes emptied of noodles and filled with the most beautiful produce: melons, tomatoes, lettuce, nectarines, romanesco, radicchio!

There were many days that were murkier and harder. I remember hefting heavy coolers of unsold noodles into the van after a day with few sales, the weight of disappointment turned into a physical load I had to lift. I recall standing in the brutal sun because the tent wasn't providing any shade and, a few months later, standing in the very center of the tent because the rain was somehow blowing in from every side. There were quiet, cold days when I worked the market alone, and no one was shopping, and time didn't make any sense. I'd clean up in the kitchen afterward, so physically tired the only thing to do was drink a milkshake and sleep.

Our fellow vendors started their mornings the same as us, loading vans with their tired bodies, only to unload them and build a temporary home for their business—the same as us but sometimes earlier, farther away, heavier, more. I loved the markets. I didn't love how physical and emotional the work could be, but I loved the way I was part of something larger than myself. I was feeding into an ecosystem and felt a shared heartbeat. Those of us who felt this would look one another in the

eyes and feel that thump-thump together. Your life gives me life.
Thump-thump. My life gives you life.

Umi began making organic whole-grain yakisoba noodles for
public school lunches, and this, too, felt aligned with my
vision for the business. I felt pride in Umi and power in learning,
in minute detail, how food makes its way to market at different
scales. But over the course of four years, these feelings collided
with a growing cynicism about our industry. I felt the squeeze of
an impossible bind: How could I pay someone a living wage and
keep our food affordable?

To make a profit often requires scaling up, and that frequently involves investors. So many of my peers dreamed of
embarking on the modern hero's journey: starting a business,
attracting investors, growing rapidly, selling to a conglomerate,
striking it rich. People rarely achieved this, but when they did,
nothing changed about the system, which continued to underpay
workers and pollute water and soil. I wanted to run a business
that defied the profit-first capitalist system. But I operated within
it, and I was a small fry.

Umi could be wrenching because even when I did things I
felt proud of, we still struggled financially, only eking by. The
business always felt precarious, even after big wins with new
customers and new products. *What a terrible businessperson I am*,
I'd think to myself, dismayed. *I have no fire in my belly to close the
sale and reach the top.* Or—wait—was that a good thing? Was business too dominated by people scrambling over each other, burning themselves and others alive with their rapaciousness? What
did success on my terms look like? Was it even possible? Could I

achieve financial stability and hold on to my ethics? When was I too complicit within systems I should be helping to dismantle? The problems of inequity and environmental devastation within the food industry as a whole overwhelmed me. They felt as intractable as the housing crisis.

I'd bike to Kelley Point Park to tease apart my feelings, pedaling through my changing neighborhood, past the Nabisco factory— where Nilla Wafers filled the air with an overpowering scent of vanilla—and families subsistence fishing on the Columbia Slough, along a Superfund site called Smith and Bybee Lakes, to the place where the Willamette and Columbia Rivers converge. It was easy to get riled up and harder to know what to do, harder to feel anything besides ground-down.

One day in mid-October, an acquaintance invited me to a Halloween party. "It's the Laika party," she told me, naming the studio where Chris and Cynthia worked.

"Excuse me?" I asked. "Laika throws a party?" This was news to me.

"Yeah, they fund this amazing costume party at somebody's house in Northeast."

No, they do not fund it, I wanted to scream in response. *That is my and my roommates' house*, our *money that pays for the DJ and the keg*, our *time spent cleaning up for a full day or two afterward!* This was bad news. I wasn't supposed to be invited to my own party. If guests believed a corporation was footing the bill, I realized, they'd have no problem trashing our place.

That year, a group of people dressed as raccoons did trash our house, perfectly in character. The next morning, I awoke before everyone else and began cleaning. I felt dejected. I tiptoed through the kitchen, surveying the scene, trying to avoid wet splashes of beer and wine. My hangover lived inside my skin, hot and stinky, pressing on my organs. I knew the Holman House demanded parties, but this was taking too great a toll.

After gathering all the cans, bottles, and cups, but before dealing with the bigger messes, I left to get a burrito. I asked for a veggie burrito, ordered food for my housemates, and brought it home just as they were waking up. I bit into my burrito and discovered it was a tube of plain rice. That's an exaggeration but barely. I started to cry.

"I can't do this party anymore," I told everyone later.

It felt selfish and especially unfair to Chris, who loved Halloween so much. But I needed a break. I was being inflexible again, having a conversation that wasn't a conversation at all. Everyone was understanding, though, even Chris, who'd also noticed a change in the party's tenor over the years. In the past, Halloween had been our gift; now it felt like an obligation. I promised the Holman House, in the silent language we spoke, that we'd still party, but noted that we were going to ratchet down the intensity.

Corey realized I was losing my shiny optimism and felt partly responsible. To cheer me up, we'd go to the forest to hunt mushrooms. For a little while, I'd think about nothing besides spying splotches of gold and racing from one chanterelle to the next, chasing riches that felt real.

Corey's Usual Bullshit
(Spicy Ground Pork, Tofu, Mushrooms, and Greens)

Recipe by Corey Lunn

MAKES 6 TO 8 SERVINGS

When Corey first moved into the Holman House, he wanted to cook dinner for us, but he didn't have many dishes he felt confident making for others. He started asking Zak, Chris, and me for recipes, and slowly he found his own style in the kitchen. His cuisine was inspired by the household—our fixation on rice, greens, mushrooms, and pork—and also entirely his own, inflected with a comfort food base note that never left. He disparaged his own cooking by giving it funny names. He called the first dish that became a regular fixture "Corey's Usual Bullshit." It's his take on *mapo* tofu, with sautéed garlic, ground pork, large cubes of tofu, green onions, and plenty of chili. Corey adds lots of mushrooms and sometimes greens. Corey's Usual Bullshit provides many levels of satisfaction.

When I make Corey's Usual Bullshit, sometimes I add miso in place of oyster sauce and Sichuan peppercorns, chili flakes, or sambal in place of Thai chilis. It's a very adaptable recipe. Make your pork, mushrooms, and greens a bit too salty. The unseasoned tofu will act as a counterbalance. Serve it over rice.

    2 tablespoons high-heat oil (like sunflower)

    8 cloves garlic, minced

    2-inch knob fresh ginger, peeled and minced

    1 pound ground pork

1 pound chanterelle, hedgehog, shiitake, or cremini mushrooms, thinly sliced

Salt to taste

2 bunches kale, chard, or collards, washed, tough stems removed, and sliced

¼ cup soy sauce or tamari

1 tablespoon oyster sauce or miso

5 to 10 Thai chilis, stems removed, thinly sliced

1 package medium tofu, cut into 1-inch cubes

1 tablespoon toasted sesame oil (optional)

5 stalks green onion, trimmed and sliced

In a large skillet or Dutch oven, heat the oil over medium heat until it shimmers. Add the garlic and ginger and cook until aromatic, before the garlic darkens, about 30 seconds. Add the ground pork and stir to combine. Cook, stirring occasionally and breaking up pieces as you go, until the pork is fully cooked and beginning to brown. Fold the mushrooms into the pork and cook until the mushrooms are tender and any liquid has boiled off. Season with a big pinch of salt. Fold in the greens, add a lid, and continue to cook until the greens are tender, stirring occasionally.

Add the soy sauce, oyster sauce, and Thai chilis, and stir well. After a few minutes, fold in the tofu, being careful not to mash it, and cook until heated through, about 2 minutes. Drizzle with optional toasted sesame oil, top with green onions, and serve with rice.

RIGID LIQUID

As I entered my thirties, I didn't consider moving out of the Holman House. I saw myself aging there. My roommates had been in their thirties when I moved in, so it didn't seem wholly unusual to me, although as the years went by, I watched many of my friends leave communal houses for single-occupancy apartments or homes with their partners.

I was happy for my friends who had their own places, where they felt calm and comfortable. Many of them had active social lives and consistently showed up for the things they cared about. And even when they didn't, I was struck by how wonderfully rebellious living alone can be, especially for women. Domestic labor—cooking, cleaning, laundry; caring for children, aging relatives, and partners—is still often unpaid, compulsory, and gendered. Women are measured by their service, their smiles, their appeasements. Living alone bucks all of that righteously.

But I started to feel more uneasy for my friends when they partnered and had kids. US culture has created a storyline that compels middle-class couples to move toward isolation. This seems like the worst possible place to be in if you have children.

Some of my friends disappeared into their overextended lives. When I talked to them, they sounded exhausted and confided that their needs felt unacknowledged. One friend joked about the amount of laundry she did: "How could I still be a medieval peasant?"

If we'd been under the same roof, it would've been easier for me to lend a hand. My housemates helped me with laundry, grocery shopping, and errands when I asked, and I did the same for them. I offered help to several friends, but it proved difficult to leave my own rhythms and merge into theirs, and for them to accept support. Group living wasn't easy, but the alternative wasn't either. Why was group living considered so uncouth? It seemed very practical.

Sometimes I felt like my friends were growing up, and I was stuck in youth. *Is this adulthood?* I'd ask myself. *Is this* legitimate *adulthood? What is legitimate adulthood?* I'd cycle into defensiveness, constructing convincing arguments for why, in my thirties, I still lived with roommates in my childhood home, why I hadn't had children or gotten married, and why my savings account had five dollars in it, just enough so the bank wouldn't close it. But my friends understood how tenuous all our lives were, and the judgment wasn't coming from them; it was coming primarily from the voice inside my head.

Yet I knew that single-family homes weren't how most people in the world lived. They weren't even how many Americans lived. In fact, just shy of one-third of US adults live with an adult roommate who isn't their romantic partner or an eighteen-to-twenty-four-year-old student—usually they live with another family member, like Zak and I do.

The nuclear family is a surprisingly recent formula, cemented in the second half of the twentieth century, mapping neatly

---

alongside the rise of post–World War II consumerism. If everyone owns their own home, they also need their own car, their own tools, their own washing machine and dryer. Racist housing policy during this same period prioritized single-family homes in the suburbs and set limits on where anyone who wasn't white could live, excluding them from the newly minted American dream.

US culture has internalized these policies as though they represent a universal ideal, when their origins show that well-being was never the aim of the design. In turn, isolation has the power to feed alienation, loneliness, apathy, and myopia. If a nuclear family ruptures, its members can find themselves radically alone. Yet isolation is still held up as an important marker of advancement.

How many people enjoy living communally in middle and older age? I began to wonder. Was my household bound to fail? I found myself interested in the older people in my life who'd maintained a commitment to group living as they aged. There was my mom—a whirlwind who compulsively collected eccentrics all around her. And there were my dad's brother Doug and his wife, Nancy, a few hours north of me in Port Townsend, Washington, who'd continued living communally while raising kids and in older age.

What was their journey toward group living? Was there something in their structured approach, which had withstood the decades, that was relevant for my home and its future? And on a personal level, could I learn something from my aunt and uncle about durability, imagination, delusion, and hope? In 2019, I started visiting Doug and Nancy every few months and asking them about their lives.

To get from Portland to Port Townsend, I drive north along the west side of Hood Canal. Port Townsend sits on the Olympic Peninsula, a thumb of land jutting from the far-northwestern corner of the continental United States. To the west of the peninsula, the Pacific Ocean rolls uninterrupted to Japan. To the north, the Strait of Juan de Fuca separates Washington State from Canada's Vancouver Island. And to the east, Hood Canal, one of the fjords of the Puget Sound, separates the peninsula from islands that are one more leap from greater Seattle.

After passing through Olympia, the state capital, and curling west onto the 101, I enter the base of the thumb. I pass tribal casinos (there are eight Indigenous tribes living on the Olympic Peninsula), half a dozen tribal-run firework stands (my favorite is The Ill Eagle), state parks, oyster farms, and small towns at junctures where streams enter the canal: Potlatch, Hoodsport, Lilliwaup, Ayock, Hamma Hamma. The canal sparkles to my right. The Olympic Mountains of Olympic National Park, which comprise almost half the land area of the peninsula, tower to my left, their glacier-covered peaks sharp and jagged like molars.

Leaving the 101 at Quilcene, I head toward Port Townsend, through evergreen forest, clear-cut, and farmland; past RV parks, small-town cafés, and shops that reveal the intermingling of two white rural Americas, those of hippies and rednecks: Stoken Arms & Outdoors, Bead-Witching Baubles, Calvary Community Church, The Snarky Quilter.

I crest a hill, the dense trees thin out, and as the road descends I see Port Townsend before me—a Victorian village on an adjacent hill, the bay shimmering around it, Mount Baker and white-capped volcanoes in the distance. The setting is breathtaking.

Continuing north, a few miles from downtown, I arrive at Doug and Nancy's house. Their place is always a little unkempt, with piles of paper, books, and dishes on all the surfaces. The wooden floors and tables have a pale roughness, but Doug frequently brings Nancy big bouquets of flowers that light up the room with color. When they wither and fade, Nancy takes them outside, to a place she saves only for dead flowers, where she offers thanks to the farmers for growing something for beauty, bugs, and birds, and to the flowers themselves for bringing her joy.

On one of my visits, in spring 2019, I arrived at my aunt and uncle's home and let myself in without knocking. Doug lumbered in and asked me if I wanted "gruel," his name for multigrain porridge.

"Why not call it *hot cereal* or *porridge*?" I asked. "Both sound way more appetizing."

He smiled, his bright blue eyes glinting like a glacier seen up close, and he said nothing. Calling it *gruel* was a Doug-style joke. It wasn't especially funny, and for a moment his deadpan delivery made me question whether it was a joke at all, but I recognized its form: he was teasing himself—of course his food would be gruel—and he was teasing me, for dressing up my meals in language.

Doug ground whole dried corn kernels in his Vitamix. He couldn't find the lid, so he placed his enormous hand over the top, and bits of cornmeal leapt between his fingers onto the shelf above, falling in a perfect cinder cone next to the mugs. I was surprised that his palm wasn't as large as the blender lid and unsurprised that he didn't clean up the mess.

I always fixate on Doug's large, powerful hands, which remind me so much of my grandfather Del's. In addition to being a high school principal, Del was a carpenter, and his hands had the callused strength of a woodworker's. Each finger was individually huge, with a broad square nail and thick, hardened skin around the fingertip. Del's and Doug's fingers seemed impossibly giant to me, like five little arms attached to a palm.

Like his father, Doug has big hands, big shoulders, big hairy ears, and the inclination to talk as if to an audience, even when you're the only other person in the room. Like his mother, he has clear blue eyes and a love for reading. When we're together, he likes to recite his own poems. They're always political, always about the human destruction of nature, and he often recites them in something approximating song, which feels incongruous with the angry content. I can't remember the last time I spent a day with Doug when he didn't describe human violence as an existential danger, nor when he didn't demand—to no one; to everyone; to me, his audience of one—a massive cultural shift away from it.

I feel somewhat passive sitting across from him. Our conversations are one-directional—I receive his orations—but I don't mind because I find him fascinating. How can one person be such a muddle of righteousness and goofiness? Typically, ranters suck all the energy out of a room, but I feel good around Doug. From my earliest memories on, I've felt a distinct energizing sensation in his presence, like standing near a waterfall, the crashing water inside him charging the air with cool, electric ions.

ittle Dougie was born in Akron, Colorado, in 1949. When he was one, the family moved to Lakeview, a small town near Oregon's border with Nevada. Lakeview sits about a mile above sea level, in the sparsely populated high desert. Many people think that Oregon mildews under a perpetual rain cloud, but most of the state is arid and vast, unlike the deserts of the Southwest in terms of flora and fauna but just as dry and moonlike.

Lakeview has no lake view, but the landscape holds the memory of water—an expansive bygone lake left its dry, sunken bed behind. Nearby are geothermal geysers; an antelope refuge; the Paisley Caves, which house poop that's twelve thousand years old (among the oldest known human remains on the American continent); pictographs made by Northern Paiute peoples; and fields of wild grasses that turn the most beautiful shade of honey yellow in the fall. My grandpa Del became the Lakeview High School principal in 1950.

Eleven years later, he moved the family north to Moses Lake in Central Washington, east of the Cascades, a larger but equally arid town on one of the country's major arteries, I-90. This time, they actually lived on a lake. Del was once again high school principal, and my grandma Alice taught ESL and poetry at the local community college.

Sitting at Doug and Nancy's dining table, finishing up my porridge, I asked Doug about his life after he left the family home in Moses Lake. I knew he'd dropped out of college in 1968, built a catamaran with a friend by strapping two kayaks together, and floated down the Missouri River toward New Orleans. Soon after, he'd traveled through the South with a carnival, which my dad has always described in sinister, thrilling tones. But what happened after the carnival?

In his early twenties, Doug moved to Seattle, trading the deserts of his childhood for a life never far from salt water. He swapped a landscaping dump truck for a friend's derelict twenty-eight-foot cabin cruiser and taught himself to repair the oak ribs, install an engine, build a crude interior for living, and equip the vessel for diving. Doug became a commercial diver for geoducks, sea urchin, herring roe on kelp, and abalone, working around the Puget Sound and Alaska for almost a decade.

Doug launched into a story, jabbing his meaty fingers in the air as he spoke. On one abalone diving job in Alaska, the boat he was aboard caught fire in the night. When he emerged from the living quarters below deck, he saw flames leaping from fifty-five-gallon drums of gasoline not far from forty scuba tanks filled with compressed air. He could hear the captain screaming, "Mayday! Mayday!" Doug was the last person off the burning boat, which sank with fifteen thousand pounds of abalone onboard. They paddled in lifeboats to a small island in the middle of the bay and were miraculously saved by the *Pacific Princess*— the actual Love Boat, famous from TV—then cruising by.

This was Doug's third workplace mishap that ended up squandering piles of seafood and his third near-death experience on the ocean. He took it as a sign and quit commercial diving. The next year, the area where he dove, the Prince William Sound, was poisoned by the *Exxon Valdez* oil spill.

So much marine life wasted and his life almost extinguished. This story should have felt grave to me—but instead, I got snagged on that detail about the Love Boat, which is classic Doug. His emphases and anomalies in tone perplex me. This ever-solemn man loves to say words pulled straight from cartoons: *Boink! Splat! Boom! Kapow!* Even his political comments have an odd lightness. He once invited me to an anti-nuclear picket line at the offices of Washington senators with the words, "When we come together in defense of our only home, Lifegiving, Fragile Earth, we align with the energies of Mama Gaia and Macho Papa that flow in our veins. *Woah!!*"

After breakfast, Doug poured me a glass of his homemade hemp milk, also blended in his Vitamix, and I asked him about his first foray into group living. In 1977, Doug visited an intentional community called Findhorn in Scotland.

"I had an awareness of the fragility of culture for a long time," he told me, looking off into the distance, a bouquet of hyacinths on the table between us. The flowers smelled strongly of seaweed and mulled wine. "I wanted to explore something that touches mystery."

Today, Findhorn is famous as an "ecovillage"—best known for its pioneering environmental experimentation, from wastewater reclamation to wind farming—but it was founded in the early sixties by a group who called themselves the "channellers" and sought telepathic communication with extraterrestrials. They built a landing strip for flying saucers. They also started a hugely productive organic farm, turned a castle into a hotel, and erected a trailer park to live in.

At the time, they were funding their community through a kind of fee-based voyeurism, where tourists could stay in the castle hotel for a week, observing or participating in the goings-on as they saw fit. Doug arrived before his week was set to begin, and they told him to return in a few days, but when he offered his skills as a builder, they let him stay. He was assigned to help another American finish the centerpiece in what Doug called "a vortex for a building itself designed to lift off if the space brothers ever decided to lift us up."

Doug knew the leaders within a week. One day, after meditating on Clooney Hill, site of the flying-saucer landing strip, he recalled, "I found myself in front of a sacred well of living intelligent water." In that moment, water came newly alive for him, as sentient as an animal, forever the element that connects him to mysticism and wonder.

Findhorn had loomed large in my understanding of Doug's past. Years ago, the first time he mentioned it, I remember feeling envious that he could walk into a situation and be so immediately useful, helping build something of value. I'd imagined that thing was a house or a lodge. I didn't realize it was the centerpiece for a spaceship, although I suppose that didn't make it less useful to *this* community. I knew he was only at Findhorn for two months, but that can be a long time, and this moment in his life seemed like a hinge that shifted him toward communalism. From that period on, he always, in one form or another, undertook projects that demanded shared effort.

When I asked Doug what the most lasting remnant from this experience was, he thought for a second and then answered, "Marmite! I really liked it."

For Doug, Findhorn was just one moment when his curiosities were bumped along by others on their own explorations—an encounter that didn't ricochet him in an entirely new direction or conjoin him to a group but nudged him down his own mysterious waterway.

Doug was invited to stay at Findhorn indefinitely, free of charge, but home was calling.

"I lived in the northwest of the United States," he told me. "If I wanted some transpersonal meditative whatchamacallit, I realized I'd rather be in Washington State than in Scotland."

On my next visit to Port Townsend, I brought my parents along. As we crawled up Hood Canal, past spindly magenta foxgloves crowding the roadside and bald patches of clear-cut, I asked them about their visit to Doug at the Polarity Institute, his next stop after Findhorn.

"So delightful," my mom giggled from the back seat, where she'd lit a joint.

It was 1978. My parents hadn't been dating for long when they decided to bicycle from Portland to Orcas Island, due north of Port Townsend in the Puget Sound. It was a very difficult ride, extending over several days and hundreds of miles. They camped along the way and took a ferry for the final leg. At the end, they met up with Doug, twenty-nine years old and living in an intentional community that also served as a training center for something called Polarity Therapy.

"Everyone drank what they called Polarity Tea, which was heavy with fenugreek, a laxative," my mom said. "Everyone was eliminating constantly." She relished this detail.

Upon their arrival, my dad heard screaming coming from a room in a nearby building. There, he discovered people standing barefoot on the edge of a low wooden box, trying to grind "crystals" out of their feet. Never one to miss an experience, he joined and described the sensation as pure, raw pain, like standing on a knife's edge.

"The men had to carry everything, including the vacuum," my mom continued. Gender roles were sharply delineated, and one day my mom was scolded for carrying a pot of potatoes. Instead, a very slender man in ill health was called over. She could barely stop herself from grabbing the pot back. As they reminisced, I recognized my parents' mutual delight in bizarre, singular experiences. Anything to shake up routine and shock the system. The gender roles at the Polarity Institute were unacceptable to them, but their stay was brief; like visitors in a foreign land, they were tickled to see the local customs.

Soon, we arrived at Doug and Nancy's house. Doug was cooking white turnips and black cod in miso sauce. Nancy had made a big salad dressed with red wine vinegar and dried oregano, as she always does. My parents were both wearing their long hair down, uncombed and wizardly. The last rays of the sun poured through the window and illuminated their frizzy manes.

Doug and Nancy's first floor is an apartment occupied by Marlow and Leslie, their gray-haired and gentle in-laws—the parents of their son Danny's wife—who walked up the stairs with a platter of weed brownies. Everyone dug in like old hands. *Where am I*, I laughed to myself, *a college dorm for the elderly?* As night fell, we continued to talk by candlelight. I brought up the Polarity Institute again.

After Findhorn, Doug had heard about a group who trained students in an "eclectic healing modality" called Polarity Therapy, a chiropractic practice that went beyond the physical to the mind-body connection—"chiropractics for the soul," he called it.

"I paid a fee and then was invited to stay on as a technician and help them build the place." In exchange for his labor, he received room, board, and training in Polarity Therapy with the idea that he might someday bring it to others.

He described breakfast at the Institute: "No coffee. Take ten oranges' worth of juice, then half a cup of olive oil and cayenne pepper. Shake it up and drink it with a quart of water. Go away and throw it all up. Then eat rice gruel. No protein sources." He shook with laughter.

"That's actually a good way to cleanse your gallbladder," my mom piped up.

"HA!" my dad shouted.

Nancy rolled her eyes.

"In one of our classes, we were instructed to insert our fingers in other peoples' noses. It was quite unpleasant. People were saying, '*Oh god!*'" Doug screeched in imitation of their protest. "You should have seen a whole room doing this."

"Truly a mindfuck!" my dad called out, pleased with himself.

The room had become pitch-black except for the pool of candlelight we sat in, our faces distorted by shadows.

"I was a strong 220 pounds as a commercial diver. I weighed 150 pounds after Polarity." The diet of rice gruel and vomiting took its toll. Doug said that he'd wanted to move his grandmother Agnes, then in the last years of her life, to the island. He pictured the community members doting on her, a beloved grandma to all. But her daughter, his aunt, refused to let Agnes join him because he was so emaciated that she worried for his sanity and health.

The Polarity Institute fits perfectly my image of a 1970s intentional community: dogmatic, esoteric, remote, with tasteless food, strict gender roles, and foot crystals. But to my surprise, Doug shared these stories with perverse, self-flagellating delight, making fun of himself most of all—because he *would* be the one to join this carnival, this self-help maelstrom. I heard the same tone from my mom's earlier giggle, this sense of a past life that's so baldly absurd it can't be taken seriously.

Doug is a searcher, attracted to the ridiculous because it sits at the edge of the unknown, a place of possibility. In a world where he sees little reason for optimism, he seeks out confrontations with the bizarre because he isn't afraid to be extreme and outlandish in pursuit of something that surprises him into hope. He can lurch into conspiracy—crop circles are among his favorites—and reel it back in before he alienates the person he's talking to.

From the outside, Doug appears to be filled with contradictions. He's solemn; he's goofy. He's earnest and absurdist. His outrage necessitates believing he's right. His openness allows him to learn that he's wrong. He seems serious about everything except himself. He transforms despair into comedy, not to erase discomfort but to invite it in.

One of the underlying mechanisms of the Polarity Institute was that it acted as a matchmaking club for heterosexual singles. There was a strict celibacy-until-marriage policy, enforced, Doug tells me, by a man named Grandpa Gooch. Doug had already fallen in love with Nancy when he moved to the island, although they hadn't made commitments to each other. He invited her to visit, but she was totally put off and left as quickly as she'd come.

"I was at Polarity for two years," Doug continued. "I didn't develop close bonds with friends. At some point I decided, *I am not called to this vocation.*" He laughed.

But even unpleasant experiences are never one-dimensional. He hated the Institute's rigidity but enjoyed living on the water of the San Juan Islands, being part of a multigenerational community, and creating a built environment with others. It was a place he wanted to move his grandma, after all.

My parents remembered their last morning on Orcas Island. They asked Doug to give them a boat ride to the mainland, but there were no men in leadership roles around to grant permission for fuel. My dad went from door to door asking, and at each residence he was greeted by a woman whose husband was absent and who claimed she was powerless to grant his request. Frustrated by this bizarre predicament, he was walking back to the dock when he found Doug, who'd stolen a gallon of fuel and told my parents to jump aboard his inflatable boat. They putt-putted across the sparkling water with their bikes, and on the other shore, free from the island, Doug bought himself a cup of coffee.

One morning, during one of my solo visits, Doug was out helping a neighbor patch her fence and Nancy came down the hallway to greet me. She wasn't moving well. With every other step she careened to one side before righting herself. I embraced her gently and gave her a kiss on the cheek. Nancy is the physical opposite of her husband—not much taller than five feet, with delicate bones and thin limbs—and the intellectual equal, although her passions and outrage surpass his. Doug fell in love with Nancy in his late twenties. Five years his senior, she had a gravitas and independence he found irresistible. She was an anchor to keep his goofball tendencies moored.

During my visits to Doug and Nancy's home, I usually sat down with one or the other at their dining room table, snacked, and listened to their stories. When Nancy spoke, she took a lot of time between thoughts to gather her words. She held my gaze, though, and I found the silences riveting. Her eyes are quick and expressive, her muscles sinewy, and her shoulder-length hair a wolfish silvery-gray. In her late seventies, she walks with a cane, and my instinct is to help her through every transition, from sitting to standing, standing to sitting, up and down stairs. Sometimes she wants help, but just as often she's self-sufficient, surprisingly deft given her limited mobility. She's quick to laugh with unrestrained joy.

I was a teenager when I learned that Nancy's mom had died by suicide when her daughter was nine. Nancy has such intensity and reaches heartbreak so easily. Was this the reason? When I asked Nancy about her mom during one of my visits, however, she most vividly recalled her generous spirit. Her mother often volunteered at a clinic for people with multiple sclerosis, which had caused one of Nancy's uncle's deaths. Her mom was a socialist and activist with a big, loving family. They sang together in a Cleveland choir, which Nancy loved.

In the mid-sixties, after Nancy graduated from the University of Chicago with an art degree, she spent over a year teaching in Chicago and then traveled to Florida and began a solo road trip up the East Coast, visiting friends along the way. She'd fallen into despondency, unsure what to do next and overcome by the weight of a world she perceived as ruthless, violent, and off course.

"One day, a bird flew into my windshield and broke it," she told me. Glass shattered. Her road trip continued, but the memory of the broken window remained. As she drove from New York to Boston, she suddenly broke down in the car, crying. "In that moment, my grandma appeared to me as a living presence—smiling, beaming. I realized how much a smile meant. It liberated me."

Her grandma's presence emboldened her to reject the buttoned-up reality set before her—marriage, domesticity, a private life in a private space where men determined her course.

For the first time, Nancy felt safe to drift, protected by maternal ancestors who were not alive but were nonetheless present.

Nancy returned to Chicago and then followed some friends from the Midwest to California, where she lived in group houses organized around the macrobiotic movement. In Los Angeles, she began Sufi dancing, a kind of ecstatic whirling that helps people release their grip on reality, get high without drugs, and experience religious euphoria. When she moved to Port Townsend, she hustled for work, and her father, an electrical engineer, gave her a few thousand dollars—enough money to buy five acres with a friend. She built her own cabin on Egg and I Road.

The Nancy I knew as a child was very different from the woman I was encountering now. She'd been a fearsome woman, a fire-and-brimstone hippie who saw all consumer choices for their human and environmental toll and felt sincere anguish about others' suffering. The news of the day never failed to make her livid with self-righteous anger. Even though I believed Nancy's choices were morally right, I found her rigidity unsettling. My parents had taught me that being rigid makes it hard to talk to people.

As a kid, I paid little attention to the reasons behind Nancy's rules and focused primarily on the rules themselves: no shoes or clothes made overseas by companies that exploited child labor, which meant she reamed Doug when he bought synthetic sneakers for my cousin Danny; no refined grains; and, worst of all, no refined sugar. Nancy seemed easily flustered and more easily enraged. "She's stubborn as shit," my mom whined one Thanksgiving when Nancy wouldn't let her serve the Martinelli's

Sparkling Apple Cider she'd brought, because it was made with conventional apples and added sugar.

I took perverse pleasure in breaking Nancy's rules. In middle school, I'd bring money on visits to Port Townsend so I could buy my cousins illicit coffee ice cream, which would turn them into sugar- and caffeine-crazed demons. I'd cackle and heckle and race alongside Amanda and Danny as we sprinted up and down the public stairs leading from downtown to uptown Port Townsend before they both passed out in a triumphant sweat in the grass. I'd swear them to secrecy before we plodded back to their home, where Nancy would pile our plates high with brown rice, curried lentils, and winter squash wedges, everything low in fat and salt and made extra bland by the coating of sugar inside our mouths. As we reluctantly poked our food, Nancy would scrunch her lips into a tight knot.

In 2004, moments after Nancy read a headline announcing that George W. Bush had been reelected, she had a brain aneurysm. She was on the Edmonds Ferry, going to pick up Doug from the airport, and was struck by a gyre of rage and disbelief that short-circuited her mind. It took years for her to recover, and she's never fully regained mobility. I was nineteen years old at the time, and I took Nancy's aneurysm as a lesson in cultivating dispassion. It was dangerous to feel too much anger.

For a long time, Nancy seemed at once brittle and strong to me, an oxymoron of personal chemistry that reminded me of glass. In nature, glass is made when sand or rock, high in silica, becomes molten and then rapidly cools—something solid and determined is set ablaze, perhaps in a volcanic eruption, and then quenched so fast that a crystalline structure can't form. Glass is neither solid nor liquid, neither fixed nor flowing. Scientists call it both a rigid liquid and an amorphous solid.

Nancy's fragile solidity was formed through the volcanic eruptions of her rage and heartbreak, cooled too quickly by the necessities of life and left in what resembled a fixed form. When glass shatters—a cup slipping from a drunken hand, the bottom of a canning jar cracking—my hair stands on end, every follicle alert in goose pimples, my heart quavering like a stricken animal. Being near Nancy inspired a similar fear. *What if the glass shatters?* And then it did.

But as in Nancy's story of seeing her grandmother's ghost, when glass shatters, something is set free. I'd taken for granted what was required for women in the sixties to reimagine their lives and cut against the cultural grain, but it wasn't a subtle shift. It was a cataclysm. Rejecting cultural norms took a strength of conviction fierce enough to oppose the status quo. Nancy hardened herself around this conviction even as she embraced a sense of softness from her grandma's smile and her inner world. Empathy and outrage forged a tenuous solidity in her that was both tough and delicate. These states coexisted in uneasy harmony: the ability to break, the vulnerability to be broken.

Once, several years after her aneurysm and recovery, Doug and Nancy came to visit us during a week that overlapped with our Halloween party. In the deep hours of the night, I went to the basement to find out how badly the stomping feet and thumping bass overhead were affecting my aunt and uncle. I found Doug sound asleep, snoring, and Nancy, shoes off, eyes closed, dancing uninhibitedly through the room to the quaking sounds overhead, her movements loose and emotive, a body at once possessed and free.

D oug is one of the first people I met in Port Townsend," Nancy
   recalled, occasionally taking a bite of bread with chimichurri
sauce, her favorite. While she talked, I was cracking hazelnuts
with a miniature cracker I'd found on the floor beneath my chair.
"We'd been friends, and we made love once. When we made
love, I thought, 'I could marry this man.'"

When he landed at the Polarity Institute, Nancy's affections
withered. But Doug persisted. After he left Polarity, he coaxed
her to Panama, where he'd taken work as a maritime carpenter.
Soon they were married, and Nancy became pregnant with my
cousin Amanda. They made their way north, eventually living
with my parents in Portland. Amanda was born in my parents'
rented house off East Burnside Street in 1982.

Doug and Nancy decided to move back to Port Townsend,
where they found the community they sought, one deeply committed to radical politics and countercultural experimentation.
Doug joined a dozen men and one woman—each bringing their
skills as architects, engineers, woodworkers, and builders—in
forming a cooperative construction business called Blue Heron.
The members of Blue Heron dreamed of someday being part of
a network of co-ops throughout Port Townsend, modeled after
the Basque region, where a federation of more than 250 co-ops
known as Mondragon runs everything from banking to buses.
Blue Heron became specialists in green building, and Doug and
the others built the first permitted load-bearing straw-bale structure in Washington State.

Doug joined us and offered to make me lunch—a cup of
homemade hemp milk and a corn tortilla blistered over an open
flame, with a smear of spicy mayo, one slice of smoked salmon,

and one pimento-stuffed green olive. I could only imagine being served this odd tostada in one other place in the world: my own father's apartment. After we ate, Doug and Nancy brought out manila file folders of old brochures, newsletters, and postcards and spread them across the table.

After moving back to Port Townsend, they became more intensely involved in peace activism, especially in Nicaragua. At the time, the United States had been funding and providing military support to a collection of the country's right-wing groups, known as the Contras—shorthand for *counterrevolutionaries*—in their efforts to prevent the democratically elected socialist government, the Sandinistas, from maintaining power. On the news, Doug and Nancy heard the Reagan administration downplaying the human rights violations being committed by the Contras, but examples of terrorist attacks on civilians made it through the veil of propaganda.

Nancy showed me a postcard that featured two Nicaraguan girls, one staring boldly into the camera, the other tucked behind her sister, peering out shyly.

"They remind me of my cousin and me," she told me, thumbing the postcard affectionately. "She was shy and would hide behind me." Suddenly switching from tenderness to gravity, she added, with fresh alarm, "The US was not letting this young democracy thrive."

In 1983, when Amanda was one, Doug joined a national Quaker-led group called Witness for Peace, which put American civilians where the fighting was the worst to bring attention to the conflict. Before he left, he, Nancy, and their local Quaker group gathered about fifty people at the nearby recreation center. Doug asked them if he could go as a representative of the community, to try to find a sister city. The group that gathered, Port Townsend's mayor, and the city council gave their blessing.

In Nicaragua, Doug was brought to Jalapa, an agricultural town on the Honduran border and one of the first targets of the Contras. In the streets, he could hear the deep, throaty rattle of nearby fifty-caliber machine guns. Doug asked the local elected leadership for their town to become sister cities with Port Townsend, and they agreed.

Back in the United States, Nancy took the lead organizing marathon dances to fundraise for Jalapa. "TWENTY FOUR HOUR NON STOP CELEBRATION FOR BODY & SOUL," one invite read. "LIVE MUSIC, FOOD FOR ENERGY TO BURN, HEAPS OF PRIZES, REJUVENATING MASSAGE."

The idea was that teams of people would be sponsored to dance for twenty-four hours—one member of each team was required to be on the dance floor at all times, and pledges came through each hour. Their first year, Doug recalled, it wasn't until midnight that they earned enough to pay for the dance hall, much less anything else. Over time, however, the marathon dances earned thousands of dollars for the People-to-People Sister City organization and raised awareness throughout town about life under siege for everyday Nicaraguans. Nancy was reviving her love of Sufi dancing, of whirling and twirling for hours in a state of prolonged ecstasy and escape. But now the dancing was in pursuit of connection and hope.

My cousin Danny and I were born in 1985, in the midst of the Iran-Contra Affair. Between 1981 and 1986, Oliver North had diverted a portion of money the United States earned from illegally selling weapons to the Khomeini government in Iran, which was under an arms embargo, to the Contras in Nicaragua. Doug and Nancy followed along closely and impatiently as Congress banned the continued funding of the Contras in 1982 and 1984, but President Reagan was determined to upend the socialist Sandinistas and covertly continued this wild and tangled plot to illegally sell weapons on one side of the Atlantic to illegally fund militias on the other. The extent of the operation emerged in 1987. The United States had been playing a Bond-style supervillain.

Over the course of five years, the People-to-People Sister City organization fulfilled their promise to leaders in Jalapa, who'd asked them to send a diesel generator to provide backup electricity for their water supply and to build a children's park, a tender request made to create a space where kids could be kids, free of thoughts of war.

"We broke the US embargo under Reagan," Nancy recalled proudly. Their large freight truck was filled with supplies, from medical equipment to sewing machines to the components for a hand-carved, brightly painted carousel made by a Port Townsend woodworker, a whimsical addition not thought up by Doug but urged on by his enthusiasm.

"We set up a swing," Doug added. "From first to last light, the swing never stopped moving. We put in a slide, a jungle gym, and the carousel in the center of the park."

As the years went on, however, Nancy and Doug became exhausted trying to focus people's attention on a situation that had subsided from public view. Nancy was at her breaking point, caring full-time for two young kids while Doug worked in construction. The effort had taken an emotional toll, too, with Nancy thinking about the war—about young boys beheaded or stolen from their families to fight for the Contras against their will—as her own son spoke his first words and lost his first teeth. She'd lost some of her hair and her period had stopped. The Jalapa project was like a marathon dance itself; at some point, they had to turn on the house lights and call the party to a stop. While both cities remained formally in relationship, the ferocity of connection diminished.

Nancy offered me the manila folders with all their sister city artifacts and stood up to stretch. A device sent electric pulses to her leg to help her walk, and a few weeks before, it had malfunctioned, repeatedly shocking her. I knew she was in pain, but aside from her lilting gait, she didn't show it. She flashed me a loving yet inscrutable smile and went outside to offer a prayer to her dead flowers.

Lola's Radicchio Salad for Nancy with Spicy Cilantro Dressing

Inspired by Althea Potter, recipe by Lola Milholland

MAKES 1 CUP OF SALAD DRESSING AND 4 TO 6 SERVINGS OF SALAD

When I think of a rigid liquid, my first thought isn't glass; it's mayonnaise. Poet, critic, and theorist Fred Moten (who isn't a mayo fan) said about mayonnaise specifically, and emulsions generally, "It's something about that intermediary—I don't know—place, between being solid and being a liquid, that has a weird relation to the sublime, in the sense that the sublimity of it is in the indefinable nature of it."

In honor of in-between places, contradictions of matter, sublimity, and the cilantro-heavy chimichurri sauce Nancy always keeps in the fridge, here is one of my all-time favorite emulsified salad dressings and a suggestion for a great winter salad.

I started playing around with the idea for this dressing after tasting an unreal salad my friend Althea Potter made. The idea of a spicy salad had never crossed my mind, but the addition of a serrano chili is a revelation. The dressing is also the most beautiful shade of light electric green. It's versatile—great on a salad and really nice with tacos.

Prepare to have your mind blown: you can remove the bitterness in radicchio by soaking it in ice water. In fact, this works for all chicories (and rabes) because the bitter compounds are water-soluble. Be sure to soak your radicchio for a minimum of thirty minutes and up to an hour. A bonus of the ice bath: the leaves become crispier!

SPICY CILANTRO DRESSING

½ bunch cilantro, washed and spun dry

Juice from ½ lime (or 1 tablespoon lime juice)

1 tablespoon apple cider vinegar

2 cloves garlic, smashed and peeled

1 fresh serrano chili, stem and seeds removed, cut into big pieces

1 tablespoon yogurt or sour cream

½ teaspoon salt

¼ cup olive oil

Chop off the very bottom of the cilantro stems but keep most of the stems and all the leaves. Add everything except the olive oil to a blender or food processor and blend until smooth. A little at a time, add the olive oil and blend, stopping and starting until all the olive oil is incorporated. Pour into a jar and keep refrigerated. Use within 2 days.

RADICCHIO SALAD

2 heads radicchio

½ cup grated Parmigiano Reggiano

2 tablespoons raw pumpkin seeds, toasted in a dry skillet until aromatic and a few seeds have turned golden brown and puffed

Freshly ground black pepper

Fill a large bowl with ice and water. Separate the radicchio heads into leaves, tear the leaves into pieces, and plunge them in the ice bath. Let stand for at least 30 minutes. Pull out the leaves and spin or pat them dry. This step mellows out the bitterness. If you do this in advance, store radicchio in a plastic bag in the fridge until ready to eat.

Put radicchio in a large bowl. Pour ¾ of the spicy cilantro dressing over the top and toss. Taste a leaf and add more dressing or salt if needed. Add most of the Parmesan and most of the toasted pumpkin seeds and toss lightly. Top with freshly ground black pepper, plus the remaining cheese and pumpkin seeds. Serve.

IN THE THICKET

Port Townsend is webbed by an elaborate series of public trails that connect residential corridors. There are no way-finding signs, just tall thickets of primrose or blackberry on either side and a sharp curve always barring the view of wherever you're going. Throughout the summer, the trails are lush with flowers. Locals know where these trails lead, and visitors wander as if in a dream.

Not quite population ten thousand, Port Townsend sits on the end of a peninsula. No major freeways slice through its streets. There is none of the low, rumbling drone I recognize as the base note of city life. The barrier between urbanity and wilderness is fuzzy: deer are everywhere, residents in their own right. Port Townsend is habitat for visionaries, dreamers, tinkers, and clowns. Half-finished boats sit in side yards next to piles of lumber and trailers on blocks. Houses are handmade and whimsical—spiraling staircases, fairy-tale towers, colorful ceramic-tile murals, glassed-in porches made of windows and doors. Port Townsend is the home of the Wooden Boat Festival, nearing its fiftieth anniversary, as well as people who build and love wooden boats, make things with their hands, and experience the ecstasy within the repetition of creative craftwork.

Two centuries ago, Port Townsend was a place where the S'Klallam people lived and harvested food from the sea. Sheltered from the slamming of the harsh Pacific waves, the town is still near enough to the ocean to receive its abundant marine life and the smell of brine on the breeze. The first white settlers were men of means. They founded the town on a series of dreams—none of them involving the S'Klallam people, whose land they took. The first dream was that Port Townsend would be a gateway to British Columbia, the newest destination of the gold rush. The second dream: that it would be the entrance to Washington State from the ocean, before overland travel was easy. The third: that it would be a strategic military post worthy of a full-scale fort. And the fourth: that it would be the terminus of the Union Pacific Railroad—a prize that went, instead, to Seattle.

Each dream roared and then subsided, swelling like a tide before retreating into the Salish Sea. What was left was an overbuilt town with formidable city buildings, elaborate Victorian houses, a nineteenth-century army base, castles, and a population that never uncoupled grandiose delusions from the actual grandeur of the natural setting. In Port Townsend, the dreamers are still dreaming.

After stepping down from the sister city organization, both Doug and Nancy were ready for a project closer to home. They understood how to work with people toward a common goal. And since Nancy also wanted more land for their kids to grow up on, they began to discuss a new idea being batted around the peninsula: cohousing.

Cohousing is, of course, *not* a new idea. The S'Klallam people lived in communal longhouses on this same land for centuries. But I trace the iteration my aunt and uncle were exploring in the late eighties through a peculiar lineage: a game of telephone played across the Atlantic Ocean, beginning with a French philosopher named Charles Fourier, who was born in 1772. Fourier's most famous vision was for what he called the *phalanstery*. Fourier combined the word *phalanx*—a military unit moving in close formation—with *monastery*—a home for monks—to express the idea of a cohesive group living peacefully in sync. The phalanstery he conceived was a self-contained utopian socialist community that would reside in one massive building. Based on his social calculus, this earthbound ship should house exactly 1,620 people inside. Families would live in individual residences, all contained within the larger structure, and share domestic resources like childcare.

Fourier designed the structure toward optimal human productivity, believing that if everyone could choose their own work based on their passions and had their basic needs (including sexual desire) met, there would be social harmony. He was anti-Semitic, pro women's and gay rights, and a prolific fantasist who, some say, believed that humans would develop long, functional tails. He'd wanted to be an architect and imagined that a physical structure could embody a social structure, that his design itself would encourage cooperation and concern for fellow residents. Writ large, this basic concept is called architectural determinism.

Fourier never saw his vision realized, but he profoundly influenced American Utopianists (and the infamous French architect Le Corbusier). In the nineteenth century, the Industrial

Revolution and the birth of mechanized factory work was transforming society inside out. Within this dramatic transfiguration,
as many as one hundred documented intentional communities
sprang up in the United States. Two Utopianists, Albert Brisbane
and Victor Considerant, seeded Fourier's ideas here, spurring a
wave of intentional communities that were distinctly nonreli-
gious when compared to their contemporaries like the Shakers or
the Mormons. Most famous among the thirty-plus Fourierist
communities are Utopia, Ohio; La Réunion in Texas; North
American Phalanx in Colts Neck, New Jersey; Brook Farm in
West Roxbury, Massachusetts (Nathaniel Hawthorne was a
founding member); and Wisconsin Phalanx in Ceresco, Wisconsin.

Most of the Fourierist communities went belly-up within a
year—a 1,620-person arc proved too ambitious to populate or
maneuver. Many of the buildings that housed them burned to
ash or were torn apart for salvage. Some were repurposed by
other communities with their own ideologies. Still, the movement of American phalanxes influenced the experimental communes to come, which held on to the earlier idealism and vision
of a better way to live than mainstream culture had plopped on
their lunch trays.

In 1964, a Danish architect named Jan Gudmand-Høyer and
his wife, Angels, gathered friends together to dream up a new
housing structure that would provide a greater sense of community. The milieu was different, but the larger context was similar:
urban planning was failing to provide interactive, supportive
community life, and people felt disconnected from their neighbors and underserved by their governments. Taking inspiration
from experimental intentional communities in the United States,
Gudmand-Høyer encapsulated a piece of Fourierist Utopianism

into what became known as *bofællesskab* (Danish for "living community"). In 1967, fifty families created the first "living community," and from their model, hundreds of variations sprang up across Scandinavia. The idea was brought back across the Atlantic by two American architects, Kathryn McCamant and Charles Durrett, whose book, *Cohousing*, first published in 1988, reframed and renamed an old idea.

From Lyon, France, to Red Bank, New Jersey—and from Hillerød, Denmark, to Port Townsend, Washington—each leap across the Atlantic shifted the idea of communal living, stripping it of its utopian tail but retaining a commitment to architecture as destiny.

D oug, Nancy, and their friends were enamored with the idea of building a community that shared resources and space. They wanted to bring their activist spirit into how they created their home. The same year they heard about Danish cohousing, they began planning their own iteration.

Cohousing is very different from a phalanstery—it's not organized in a single massive building, and the idea of shared economics is largely absent. But it retains key features, namely the belief that how we design the spaces where we live will transform us into more caring, fulfilled people.

The Danish version of cohousing is different from what people call *co-living*, sharing a single residence. It bridges the American dream of single-family home ownership with communalism, creating a neighborhood of private residences that share things like laundry facilities, community gardens, green spaces, and a common house where people gather and share meals. (The community may also share tools, like a lawnmower, or an event and holiday calendar.) Residents are intended to see themselves as a collective, and the layout of the space encourages interaction.

Doug and Nancy's friend Bjorn found land for sale, with open meadows and wild roses, within Port Townsend city limits. Doug, Nancy, Bjorn, and another friend, David, bought one acre as a starting place.

"There was no road, just tire tracks on the grass," Doug recalled over our usual bowls of gruel and glasses of hemp milk. "There were thickets in places, which we wanted to keep."

When it came time to construct their home, Doug used his skills as both a builder and a master salvager. A friend informed him that a defunct one-story bingo parlor at the Jefferson County Fairgrounds was available for free if he'd pay to move it. Doug and his friend Jim sliced it in half to make two standard-sized buildings. They each paid three thousand dollars to move their halves.

"I excavated for a foundation before my half arrived and cast a concrete foundation for it while the half building was temporarily suspended on wooden timber cribbing. What fun!" he said.

Per his friend Niels's advice, Doug built walls and lifted his half of the bingo parlor on top to create a two-story home. Jim and Doug worked together on each other's homes for a year, until both buildings' exteriors were finished in cedar shingles. The family moved in in 1992, when Amanda was ten and Danny was seven. Just to the southwest, they left a large thicket of brambles and vines as a corridor and shelter for wildlife. In his deadpan hyperbolic style, Doug called it the Sacred Thicket.

A group of families met for two to three hours a week, every week for around five years, to plan the future cohousing community. This was another marathon dance. In meeting after meeting, Doug and Nancy learned about facilitation, nonviolent communication, and consensus building.

"One of the greatest mistakes in communication is to believe that it has occurred," Doug told me, a lesson from hundreds of hours of process-oriented meetings—just because you say something out loud doesn't mean anyone hears or understands you. "It took a lot of work to get the city to accept what we were asking. We wanted to do it all ourselves. We did not want to have a developer onboard. The city had never done a cohousing land unit development, and it was difficult for them. 'You cannot design your own city streets,' they told us. 'If you want to put in your own septic, your own electricity, your own water supply, you have to hire out.' But we wanted to do as much as we could. We wanted to experience some kind of joy, a feeling of coming together."

Over the course of a decade, they were able to collectively purchase six additional acres at around thirty-five thousand dollars an acre and a separate one-acre homesite. They called their community "RoseWind," for the blooming thickets of native Nootka roses at the windy site. It became the first formal cohousing community in Jefferson County.

The original group agreed on specific design guidelines. Roads scarcely penetrate the edges of the land, leaving the large interior common area accessible only by trail. The houses couldn't be too tall or too close together: "We agreed that on the shortest day of the year, sun should be able to enter everyone's first-story windows,"

Doug told me. Today, RoseWind includes twenty houses, many built by Blue Heron. Half have mother-in-law apartments, including Doug and Nancy's bingo parlor, which are rented out to provide affordable housing. Each house is independently owned, and its owner pays their own taxes as well as one-twentieth of the commons. Individually they couldn't afford the substantial green spaces, but collectively it's possible.

"There's some suzerainty to what happens here," Doug said, "but we ask people to check with the group: 'We'd like to do this, how does that sound?'"

The first sight of RoseWind is the common house, a one-story beige stucco building fronted in a tall lilac bush and hollyhocks. In 2001, more than twelve years after they began the cohousing project, the community finished building the structure, which includes a large common room, an industrial kitchen, and a game room with a Ping-Pong table. I've never visited without running into someone using the space. Around the building is a field containing a bonfire pit, benches, a massive garden, and a small orchard.

A city trail runs past the common house, along the field, past the garden, uphill between cedar-shingled and pastel-painted homes with solar panels on their roofs, behind a wooden geodesic dome, beneath and between flowering hedges, and up to a gravel road where Doug and Nancy's house sits, before passing onward to somewhere else. Along the way, you might spy a few sculptures of people in conversation, painted in mute colors, labeled "RoseWind Conversation IV" or "RoseWind Conversation II"— the heroes the community wants to memorialize are the unnamed ones, committed to process.

RoseWind became something like a village. The common house serves as the town hall, where regular meetings are held. Members take turns making a shared meal there every Monday night. When someone wants to organize around political and environmental issues, they reserve the space and convene there to strategize. My cousin Amanda held her wedding after-party there, and the extended Milholland family gathers there on the day after Thanksgiving to press cider and plan a scavenger hunt. The common house makes it affordable to throw a big party.

When Nancy had the brain aneurysm, the RoseWind community raised funds to help. As Doug and Nancy grow older and Nancy's mobility continues to decrease, it's a gift to be surrounded by neighbors they know intimately. Doug helps neighbors with home repairs and continues to attend regular meetings. They're part of a sustained community and have put in the time and energy to build a framework of trust.

Unlike many older people I know, Doug and Nancy aren't isolated; cohousing has largely worked as promised for them. They know their neighbors and keep tabs on one another. They don't have to travel far for meaningful conversation. Their singing group meets half a block from their home. They share in the everyday details of their friends' lives. This kind of knowledge makes it easier to ask for help and to appear when needed. Isn't that what we all want when we grow old? Many elders end up in congregate homes, but they're often alone, even in proximity to others. I don't worry that my aunt and uncle are forgotten. They live too close to friends, physically and emotionally, to slip by unnoticed.

B ut RoseWind also developed holes where they'd expected cohesion. Doug and Nancy had, for example, envisioned accessory buildings that would provide more lower-income housing.

"We wanted multifamily units and had designs for an eight-plex apartment building for low-income residents," Doug said. "The apartment complex could've been built. We still have the design, and we had a friend to finance it. But the residents said, 'Why do we want this? We like this open field.'"

I was reminded of a story my dad once told me about his childhood home on Moses Lake. A lawn sloped down from my grandparents' ranch house, past three abundant apricot trees and poky quack grass, to the marshy shore of the lake, dotted in cattails. When the family first moved there, all the yards heading north were continuous, without any fencing, and kids ran freely through the shared space, playing and flying kites. Then one day around 1970, someone built a fence, severing the open land. Immediately, others followed. Soon the entire shoreline transformed from one vast park into a series of skinny private lawns. That lawn hemmed in by fencing is what I remember from my own childhood.

RoseWind was designed to work against the American idea of fences and make private yards into a shared park. But who was this park for?

One evening, as I was wandering the grassy commons and talking on my phone, a woman interrupted me, a startlingly false smile on her face. She was wearing a gardening hat and holding a trowel.

"This is private property," she said through her frozen smile. "Do you know someone who lives here?"

I was unable to speak. The field was large and empty; no one else was in sight. From the garden, she probably couldn't have heard me speaking, only watched as I meandered to and fro. I wanted to tell her how selfish it was that she didn't want others to enjoy this space. Yes, it was private property, but it was also unused. In Austria, the Czech Republic, Estonia, Finland, Iceland, Latvia, Norway, Scotland, Sweden, and Switzerland, there's an agreed-upon principle, sometimes codified as law, called the "Right to Roam," "Freedom to Roam," or "Everyman's Right." So long as you're not harming the natural environment or landowner, you can access any lands, private or public. That is, I grant, one of the least American things I've ever heard of. In the United States, worth is measured by what we own and how we control it. But RoseWind was based on a Danish design, and I thought the point was to create an alternative to American ideas about private property. This place was supposed to play by different rules.

"I'm Doug and Nancy's niece," I finally answered. "I'm sorry, was I bothering you?"

Her face remained unchanged. "Was I not nice enough," she responded.

Then, because there was no answer to this question that wasn't a question, we both turned and walked away.

Later, Doug and Nancy told me that this woman, a longtime resident of RoseWind, had, in fact, called the cops multiple times on her fellow residents because she felt threatened by them. She was widely reviled, but she owned her home, and though many had asked her to leave, they couldn't force her to.

Everyone wondered why she wanted to live in the community, but I didn't doubt she enjoyed the common spaces she lorded over. I loved them too.

Port Townsend faces the same rising prices that plague the rest of the West Coast and leave so many people without housing or crushed under the burden of rent. When they began in the nineties, the cost of building RoseWind was more modest, but today, joining is unaffordable for anyone who hasn't just cashed out a home elsewhere or isn't already wealthy. When one person leaves, they sell their house at market rate. As a result, RoseWind has, in effect, become an exclusive retirement community for well-to-do hippies.

Doug and Nancy brought idealistic hopes to RoseWind. They sought to create something like the phalanstery—a separate world within our world, operating by a different logic. Except RoseWind does still exist in the real world and in the speculative housing market; it uses its broken tools and is subject to outside forces.

Architectural determinism is a half-baked idea. How spaces are designed does matter, but nothing is determined by a single environmental factor. Houses and people and neighborhoods and people form reciprocal relationships. We create our homes, and our homes create us. We exist together within a society with its own structures that bend and mutate us both. Doug and Nancy could no more control rising home prices in their town than they could a belligerent coresident.

Like RoseWind, Blue Heron did not end in the triumphant vision of its original members: a co-op among many. Doug got to work with some of his best friends, making buildings he was proud of, but he became less and less involved after an accident in which he fell off a building and fractured his back. He fully recovered but eventually left Blue Heron entirely. Over four decades, membership shrank from thirteen all the way down to one man—cooperating, I suppose, with himself.

Over and over, Doug and Nancy had attempted to move their communities toward collectivity: marching determinedly upstream, against the current, hand in hand with as many people as they could find. Over and over, they were pushed back downstream. They'd lost people along the way. They might not have been returned to exactly where they began, but they were closer to it than their efforts warranted. What had begun as an exercise in inclusiveness became something muddier. I began to wonder whether any version of nonexclusive communal living was possible within the current capitalist structure. Could the initial visionary spirit survive the powerful stream pushing against it? Was disappointment inevitable?

Sometimes, before I entered the bingo parlor, I'd wander into the Sacred Thicket. In 2004, as Nancy recovered in the hospital after her aneurysm, my cousin Danny began to clear the brambles. He was overwhelmed by feelings of helplessness and wanted to make his mom happy when she returned home. Doug was furious—how had he failed to teach his own son the value of this messy, chaotic refuge for little creatures? Danny stopped partway. In the clearing left behind, Doug placed a child-sized picnic table.

When I was very little, I used to come to the thicket and hide in the tangled vines, building an imaginary world where my favorite dolls were alive, where we rode rainbow slides together, and where everything was made of sugar. Visiting the Sacred Thicket as an adult, looking down at the tiny picnic table Doug hid there, I wondered, not for the first time, if my aunt and uncle were living in a false utopia, their own candy land of natural splendor. For most of my life, Doug and Nancy had seemed like extremists to me. Their earnestness made me queasy; there was always so much singing and hugging in their house. *How sweet*, I thought, *and awkward*. My parents were hippies, I told myself, but not like Doug and Nancy—neither of my parents wore felt hats or sang about Gaia before dinner.

How could I so powerfully agree with their politics and also feel so uneasy with their form of expression? We were not marching in sync. I felt proud of their activism, but with an acute sense of remove. Was it my dislike of rigidity? Was I part of a generation that did things differently? Was it an issue of style? Did I feel judged and thus defensively want to judge in return?

For years, I couldn't decide if Doug and Nancy were the most idealistic people I knew, always chasing heartfelt dreams, or the most pessimistic, forever lapping at despair. Were they modeling a more humane way to live, one that I could learn from, or were they escaping into a hideaway for the privileged few? What is the line between vision and delusion? I respected the community Doug and Nancy helped build, and yet I questioned its equity, inclusiveness, and future viability. I was both an admirer and a critic.

But if I'd learned anything from all these visits to Port Townsend and the infinite bowls of gruel eaten there, it was that it's impossible to predict the exact results of your efforts. It's easy to fault idealists when their visions fail to live up to their initial grandeur. The myth of continual progress leads us to call these efforts "failures," but they are experiments in the petri dish of the moment, shaped by their contexts and with long afterlives. The impacts of our actions aren't always obvious or linear, and the story isn't over when we think it is.

Doug and Nancy were haunted by nightmares of societal and environmental collapse. So was I, honestly. But instead of accepting dystopia, they experienced their alarm and fear as an urgent clarion call. Even after Nancy's aneurysm, they continued to dream bold dreams. Repeatedly, talking to Doug and Nancy, I noticed their fixation on helping to create a world where children can dream silly dreams. Looking at the little picnic table, I imagined my cousin Amanda's daughters sitting there, lost in their own sweet fantasies. I thought of the brightly painted carousel in Jalapa, of children being children and what that requires of adults. I thought of the adult I'm still becoming.

How did Doug and Nancy metabolize difficult things? I thought I'd gleaned a partial answer. Doug gave Nancy fortitude. He saw possibilities among the ruins, the scraps, the refuse. His self-deprecating humor kept his spirit limber. Nancy's experience with tragedy and sense of horror added gravity and urgency to their life together. There was a powerful chemistry between them, a kind of wild energy. But they weren't alone. They were actively engaged in their Quaker and RoseWind communities, their choir, their bingo-parlor home, the Nootka rose thickets and the creatures within, and their extended family's lives. Fellowship flowed through them and offered places for their energy to travel and spark.

I'm obligated neither to reject nor to replicate experiments of the past. I simply have the option to engage with them, to

possibly build from them, which is a privilege. I see the greatest promise in what writer Kiese Laymon calls "revision."
Exploring both how we write and how we live, he said, "I was
beginning to understand 'revision' as a dynamic practice of
revisitation, premised on ethically reimagining the ingredients,
scope, and primary audience of one's initial vision. . . . If revision was not God, revision was everything every God ever
asked of believers."

Doug and Nancy's slog upriver might not have taken them to
the destination they'd hoped for, but it had shown other people
routes that worked and routes that didn't. It had allowed others
to revise. Across the street, another cohousing community began
to form, founded by two former RoseWind members. They
benefited from the work RoseWind had done with the city. This
new community focused on creating affordable options, including rental duplexes and tiny houses. Doug participated in planning meetings and helped build some of the homes. RoseWind
had become a mother log, nursing new life. Unlike RoseWind,
where the average resident was over sixty, this new community
filled with young families.

One morning, letting myself into their home without knocking, as I usually did, I found Doug and Nancy sitting together
at their computer. They were fretting over language.

"We can invite the Spirit of Life to . . . ," Nancy read aloud,
unsure of their next word choice.

"Strengthen us? Help us to awaken?" Doug mused.

"Fill us?" Nancy added. "Imbue us?"

"Or maybe it should be: 'Stop the insanity! Change course
before it's too fucking late!'" Doug joked, not joking.

"Or just keep it as is, and go right into the song?" Nancy wondered.

They paused when they saw me.

"We've been working on this since two thirty in the morning," Doug told me, clasping his enormous hands together. "We need to finish the invitation today to get it printed in the *Kitsap Sun*."

Over their shoulders, I read:

Join us for a Quaker Vigil on
War and Peace, Patriotism and Profiteers
JUNE 20TH FATHER'S DAY NOON TO 4
at the LL Good Memorial PARK across the road from
THE NAVY WEAPONS TRANSFER DEPOT
(NavMag Indian Island) near Port Townsend

Speak your inner truth! Share silence and deep listening.
Bring food and something to sit on. Acknowledge
the death and destruction Our country is causing.
At the cost of trillions of dollars WAR bankrupts our ability
to provide healthcare for all, create adequate public housing,
repair critical infrastructure, grapple with global warming . . .
Many of our veterans are ill and homeless,
thousands have committed suicide.
American weapons and the bombing of critical
infrastructure have killed Millions in our lifetime . . .
WE CAN Invite the Spirit of Life to
Open my eyes to truth
Open my hands to give freely
Open my lips to good words, to
pure words

Open my heart to love.
Song by Judith Silver
WAR IS NOT THE ANSWER.

A younger me would have felt itchy all over reading those heartfelt, wildly capitalized words, filled with so much candor. *It's true*, I would have thought, *but isn't that a little* much? Too ranty, too preachy, too on the nose. But I didn't feel as judgmental as I used to. I felt something closer to delight.

"I'll bring my parents," I told them.

Amalia's Cantaloupe-Seed Horchata

Recipe by Amalia Sierra

MAKES 4½ CUPS

I've always known Doug to have an appetite for scraps and for what others see as refuse or don't notice at all—a cracked countertop, an ancient anchor, an abandoned bingo parlor. He's more at home in a junkyard than a mall. He practices a gentle delight in small life that extends to the material realm. For Doug, the whole world is alive—he calls earth "our garden planet," always with a twinge of heartbreak—which means even inanimate objects have significance. Nothing leaves the earth, so nothing is truly disposable. He expresses his creativity by reanimating objects with life, sometimes transforming them into something entirely new.

With that spirit in mind, this ingenious recipe salvages cantaloupe seeds, which are always discarded but shouldn't be. I learned it from Amalia Sierra, who runs Tierra del Sol, an exceptional Oaxacan restaurant in Portland. Unlike the horchata most people in the United States are familiar with—sweet and creamy cinnamon-scented rice milk—this Oaxacan version uses melon seeds and almonds in place of rice. Doug always serves me his homemade hemp milk, ground up in his Vitamix, when I visit, so I've taken to bringing him this horchata in exchange.

During the summer, whenever I open a cantaloupe, I scoop out the insides, rinse the orange flesh, put the clean seeds in a container, and stash it in the freezer. Then, whenever the craving hits, I have cantaloupe seeds on hand to make perfect horchata.

¾ cup sugar

1 cinnamon stick

⅓ cup almonds

Seeds of 2 cantaloupes

Zest and juice of 1 lime

Put 4 cups of water, sugar, and a cinnamon stick in a pot. Bring to a boil; then reduce heat to medium and simmer for about 5 minutes. Let cool completely. Discard the cinnamon stick.

Boil 1 cup water and pour over almonds. Let sit for 10 minutes; then peel off the skins. (This is easier than it sounds.) Discard water and set almonds aside.

Place melon seeds in a colander under the faucet in your kitchen sink. The orange flesh around the seeds can be challenging to remove, but running them under steady water can make it easier. Discard the orange membranes and reserve the seeds.

Combine melon seeds, skinless almonds, and 1 cup of water in a blender. Blend very well until it becomes pulp. Strain through a cheesecloth. Once you've squeezed as much liquid from the seeds and nuts as you can, discard the pulp that remains in the cheese-cloth. Combine the almond-cantaloupe seed milk with half of the cinnamon syrup. Add lime zest and juice. Taste and add more syrup until it reaches your desired sweetness. Chill in your refrigerator and serve over ice. I usually drink half a cup right away so I can fit the rest in a quart jar. The drink will separate as it sits, so shake it before serving.

KANOM KO RONA

The second weekend in March 2020 was supposed to be a big one for Zak. For almost a year, my brother had worked around the clock on an animation with his longtime boss and collaborator, Rose Bond. Their assignment had been to create a piece that visualized Luciano Berio's 1968 composition, *Sinfonia*, to be projected on the auditorium walls while the Oregon Symphony and the experimental vocal group Roomful of Teeth performed the piece live. The symphony had rented and installed the projection equipment, at a cost of tens of thousands of dollars; flown Roomful of Teeth to Portland, where they were doing final rehearsals; and were almost ready to welcome audiences. Zak told me, as everything came together, how incredible it all looked and sounded.

Opening night was March 14. On March 12, a declaration of emergency shut it down.

The coronavirus arrived with force, and all our plans ground to a halt. Zak seemed to take it in stride, knowing he wasn't alone in losing something he'd put a lot of love and work into. He acted like his loss wasn't worth acknowledging given the rising death toll. But I felt bereft.

Berio's *Sinfonia* is a very challenging and enigmatic piece with bizarre, alluring vocals, often delivered in whispers, sometimes in layered ravings. The composer was influenced by the events of the late sixties, dedicating one movement to Martin Luther King Jr.'s assassination and nodding to protest movements worldwide. It can be a disorienting listening experience, but Rose and Zak had created a visual compass for navigating the music. He showed me a mock-up on his computer, and even without the full spectacle, the work affected me deeply. The animation mined the past and the present to portend the future. There were scenes of activists in the streets of Hong Kong from the previous year, of protesters and police facing off like opposing gangs. In a few months, these images would come back to haunt me.

When the stay-at-home order came down, our household was a group of seven. In addition to Zak, Chris, Corey, and me, we had three new residents: Chris's partner, Erin, who wanted to be closer to Chris as the aperture of our world shrunk; our friend Tony, who'd come up from Los Angeles in February for a work contract; and Tony's partner, Stef, who'd followed to see Zak's show. Tony and Stef decided to stay past their planned return date and live in our basement.

I'd first met Tony and Stef more than a decade before, when they befriended Chris and Cynthia through the stop-motion world. Chris would invite them over for dinner, and we'd sit side by side at the kitchen island, eating noodles. At first, I didn't like them at all. I didn't trust their overwhelming friendliness—*No one is that bubbly, that gushy*, I thought. But I can remember the first night I saw Stef in a new light. We were eating bowls of *khao soi* together, and she started talking about her love of Mike Leigh, the British director of numerous excruciating comedies, whom I also love.

"His characters are going through such desperate, sloppy pain," she said between bites. "You can feel their layers of shame. I just fall head over heels in love with them."

A pool behind her eyes rippled. For the first time, I sensed that her sweetness was expansive rather than superficial, that it gave her room to love some of the abrasive and uncompromising art that I also loved, which could be so hard to share. I choked on a noodle.

Stef works as a character designer. While she lived with us, she based a character update from the *Rugrats* cartoon reboot, Grandpa Pickles, on my dad. Many nights, we'd sit on the couch and watch movies—her favorites were about old people in love. We'd fold our laundry together and marvel that we both seemed to wear only clothes intended for giants and clothes intended for children—what wild variations!

Tony is also an extraordinary artist; his specialty is fabrication and sculpture. He recognized his calling at a young age and went straight from high school into the film industry, fabricating life-size rabbit puppets for David Lynch's *Inland Empire* as one of his first gigs. Tony is always well put together, his pants neatly cuffed and wrinkle-free, his black hair combed and glossy.

Living with Stef and Tony calmed me. They're effusive, making the rest of our household seem like a bunch of curmudgeons by comparison. "Dreamboat!" Stef would call out whenever someone or something delighted her. Every few days, Stef and I would jog through the neighborhood. She'd always wear an enormous red bubble coat over the tiniest crop top and skintight black stretch pants. We'd run and walk in equal measure, talking through our feelings and watching the spring announce itself with the first ballooning crocuses.

On Fridays, Tony would make pizza dough and Stef would prep toppings. We'd have a "pizza party," which would have felt like a regular dinner in our house at any other time, but during the early days of the coronavirus it became an occasion.

I n those first months, we were trying to acclimate to the daily changes in our routines and to the incomprehensible news. My friend Lauren works as a doctor in midtown Manhattan, and the descriptions she shared froze my blood—of sick patients isolated in sealed rooms with the deafening whir of makeshift negative-pressure fans and flowing oxygen, breathless and filled with fear, and doctors enclosed in whatever protective gear they could find, also overcome with fear. She didn't want to show her patients her terror, but they could feel it through all the plastic. She watched patients and nurses die.

The Holman House felt as emotionally distant from that war-like scene as it was physically. Corey had started working with Chris as a puppet painter at a new stop-motion studio, applying details so small and precise that he sometimes had to use a jeweler's lens. Tony had been hired to work on the same film, making molds and casting puppets. The studio switched to a work-from-home arrangement, and all three set up little stations around the house—in the dining room, on the side porch, in the upstairs hallway. I was glad I left for work.

Umi Organic was continuing to sell products at farmers markets, which remained open because they were outdoors, and to grocery stores. Home-delivery business boomed. I spent many of my days alone in the office or kitchen. This created a small well of longing for company that I could satisfy each night. The time to myself also kept me sane.

Tony started working his way through the films of surrealist director Luis Buñuel, and we all joined. In 1962's *The Exterminating Angel*, a group of around twenty people, fresh from the opera and wearing their finest garb, arrive at a gated villa for a late-night dinner party. For reasons that are never explained, the servants begin to leave but the guests stay. They are unable to exit the room they're in. Across a long night and subsequent day and night, their overt pleasure-seeking transforms into disgust. Relationships of years unravel in a matter of hours. Companions they'd found pleasant turn suffocating and hostile. They point fingers at one another, hungry for someone to blame for their entrapment. They begin pooping in a closet for want of access to a toilet. One of the guests dies and is secretly deposited in another closet. The tension in the air amasses with each breath they take, as though the oxygen might run out.

We laughed at these upper-class socialites caught in the hell of their own company, but the parallel to our small, cloistered world wasn't lost on us. This movie provided a funhouse mirror to our present circumstances. We were also trapped. Would we lose our pleasure in each other's company? Would one of us die of the coronavirus? None of us asked that second question outright, but the thought was hard to escape. Death was omnipresent, but we were joking all the same, trying to find humor and ease alongside unremitting panic.

n March, most of our evenings followed a similar pattern. I'd
bike home to the Holman House from the Umi office. As I
reached the back door, I'd smell dinner cooking and feel the tin-
gle of chilis in my nose. The pink-orange walls of the kitchen
would faintly glow in the evening light. If Chris was making *larb*,
he'd be standing at the island, meticulously picking *rau ram*
leaves from their stems, which he'd deposit in our plastic compost bucket. Since my childhood, our compost had sported a
wooden lid my mom salvaged from her first job at a natural foods
co-op. (It lasted for five decades!) Over time, however, the edges
had frayed, and faint stains darkened the bottom. Erin had made
us a replacement, and its clean wood shone on the counter like a
new toy.

I'd sit down at the island, thumb through a few magazines,
and ask Chris about his day. He'd whine without bitterness about
being given an impossible job fixing a puppet that should never
have been designed the way it was. I'd eat one of the flaky, rolled
Thai coconut cookies he always kept stocked, which crackled
pleasantly between my teeth. Slowly, the household would
gather. Corey would put on a record. Zak would go downstairs to
grab an IPA from the extra fridge in the basement and return to
help Chris prep. I'd start unloading the dishwasher. Stef would
appear first with her hair set in large curlers, which looked goofy
and old-fashioned, and then reappear without them, her hair in
broad, clean, lovely swoops. "Dreamboat!" she'd call out when
Chris announced what he was making. Tony would join, too, and
sit on a stool at the island. The aroma in the room would grow
even more delicious as Chris added a spice mix his mom had

sent from Los Angeles and began chopping fresh cilantro and green onions.

My dad, who lived alone, was the last member of our pod. He'd appear as though in a rush, plopping his dirty red backpack on a stool and passing me a few books. He'd be wearing sandals with socks and cargo shorts, no matter the weather, his white beard covering his chest like a bib. Erin would come downstairs, his skin glistening as usual. He'd set the table, I'd grab each of our favorite utensils, Corey would light candles, we'd each serve ourselves from the rice cooker, and we'd sit down to eat together.

Dinner became the metronome of my life, something even and regular to assure me that time was passing. I looked forward to coming home to a full house where I felt safe and cared for. In many ways, bizarrely, these were sweet days for us. We went overboard trying to make delicious meals for one another and lingered extra long at the table after dinner, making each other laugh.

Yet even with a partner and roommates by my side, I found myself longing for distant friends and family. I wanted to excessively touch their faces, hold them, tell them I loved them without using an app. It was psychologically exhausting to feel that much uncertainty, fear, anger, worry, and disappointment. I was grateful to be going through it with others, and for the additional security that came from sharing the rent among more roommates. We were both more at risk and more resilient for our numbers.

One Saturday morning, Erin texted me at five thirty, as I was packing for the farmers market at our warehouse: "Do you have your mask?"

"Of course," I texted back, annoyed. Why was he awake so early?

It was easy for me to forget Chris's vulnerability, given his seeming good health and imperturbable affect—he tended to wave off concerns about his compromised immune system—but he was the most obviously affected by what was happening around us. He never, ever left the house. His demeanor was constricted, his laughter muted and hard to elicit. I knew he and Erin would talk late into the night, and I imagined they were discussing how best to keep him safe. Erin had become a cyclone of worry and fear.

As a group of eight, counting my dad, we were only as safe as our most exposed housemate—and I was that housemate. Because the coronavirus lurked in seemingly healthy people, no amount of physical distance, hand washing, mask wearing, face avoidance, or general hygiene could ensure that I wasn't carrying the virus into our home. In leaving for work, I was endangering everyone, including Chris.

That day, when I returned from the market, I learned that Chris and Erin had fled the house, taking only a few of Chris's things with them. They'd decided to isolate at Erin's place. It felt abrupt—they told Zak and Stef and were gone within an hour. There was no conversation whatsoever. This tested my ideas about our social fabric: maybe we weren't as good as I'd thought at communication, group decision-making, or compromise.

At first, it'd seemed like all our years of group living primed us for just this moment—for the pandemic—but now I saw that wasn't true. My health made me unable to see that I was deciding for the group. I'd wanted Chris at home, and I'd wanted my life as close to normal as possible. Someone had to sacrifice. And

Chris was in no position to ask me, the daughter of the landlord, to move out, a power dynamic we'd never truly tested before. He had Erin's place as an option, and he took it.

My first and abiding feeling was fury. Not generic rage at the world for putting us in this impossible situation, or disappointed rage at Chris for leaving, or at myself for not seeing the situation from a larger frame, but specific, hot rage at Erin for taking Chris away. Chris was so easygoing and appeasing—he'd never just vanish without a conversation. He'd been coerced! I'd pace up and down the yard that Chris had put so much love into and picture him in Erin's small apartment, with so few private spaces, listening to Erin talking on the phone, because Erin talked on the phone a lot. I'd imagine this and feel testy and bitter. I also felt rejected.

'd begun feeling smug about our house—*Oh, everyone should do this; it's the greatest*—and the extreme social isolation of the coronavirus had seemed to affirm me. Still, Zak insisted it was purely a fluke that made our household run smoothly. And I could see, to his point, that our lives were only possible because of a particular set of circumstances: the big house our mom owned, with lots of separate rooms; our mutual obsession with cooking; our general inclination to avoid muddy conflict.

But there's a difference between an initial fluke and an ongoing commitment. We all valued the Holman House and the relationships we'd created, so we made offerings to it: beautiful potted plants, nice cookware, a scoured sink, a cleaned fridge, snacks, lovingly made dinners, gross jokes, patience when someone was uncharacteristically unkind, verbal appreciation when they were especially sweet. We weren't a random group, just as couples are rarely random. We'd made an unspoken covenant to one another and to the Holman House, a place that demanded a certain generosity of spirit or chewed you up and spit you out. We were united through the culture of this place, our home, which we made together.

Zak and I disagreed on that fundamental point, but in the wake of Chris's departure, I saw clearly that he was right about one thing: we were more fragile as a group than I'd realized. At this point, the three of us had lived together for thirteen years. Chris's departure removed a primary color from my life. My rage waned and was replaced by a moody sadness.

In Chris's absence, our new rhythm started to grate on me. I hated splitting the grocery bill. Because we only sent one person to shop each week, this happened by necessity. It was the era of toilet paper and flour shortages and lines to limit the number of shoppers inside stores. But something about that receipt tacked on the fridge, with everyone initialing their own items (which suddenly didn't feel as okay to share) and splitting the remainder evenly (also weird, since people ate different amounts and had different incomes), vexed me.

I wasn't paying more than before the pandemic, but meals I'd previously experienced as ineffably invaluable now had a precise dollar amount affixed to them, and my share was due at the end of the week, like rent. I felt more peevish when someone bought something overly expensive or cheap. I didn't feel autonomous. My meals were no longer my gifts. In the past, we'd never talked about our systems, but now that they were changing, I found there was a reason I'd liked them as they were.

Three weeks after Chris and Erin left, when the first lilacs began to flower, I realized it was Thai New Year. Every year Chris makes a simple shrine in the kitchen by stabbing incense into a banana and bathing a statue of the Buddha. He also makes sticky rice filled with the little bananas whose bunches look like fat-fingered hands. We talked on the phone and texted, and he walked Stef and me through every step of making a massaman curry, directing us to make sure red oil seeped out of the curry paste in the right way. But I still hadn't seen him in person.

With time on his hands, Chris decided to try something more ambitious for the New Year—steamed sticky rice with a salty mung bean filling, wrapped in banana leaves. He dropped them at the house while I was at the office. These skinny, long pyramids—squishy in their wrappers, which smelled like wet straw and green tea—were new to me. They walked the line between sweet and savory in a way that at first confused my tongue and then delighted me.

On the phone, he told me they were "*kanom ko rona*." This was new to me as well. I knew the word *kanom* from other steamed desserts he'd made. "But what's *ko rona* mean?" I asked. I heard his joke as soon as the sounds exited my mouth.

Even in isolation, Chris's hunger to cook for other people hadn't diminished. He wasn't at the house to see us react in real time or to let us reciprocate. Stef and I left treats on Erin's porch. It was a way to offer care when all other forms were denied.

D erek Chauvin murdered George Floyd on May 25, 2020. It was a Monday. Late on Tuesday and into Wednesday, I heard about the protests in Minneapolis. On Thursday, the emotional frenzy and exasperation in the air increased. This murder stormed the collective consciousness differently. I spent most of the day roiling in my thoughts, secluded on our front porch, staring at the branches of horse chestnut trees writhing in the wind.

Before George Floyd's murder, I'd been thinking about the oxymoronic way the coronavirus made people feel both more alone and more united in shared experience than at any other time in my life. Now I felt it again—alone inside my heart-break, rage, shame, and confusion but ultimately one of many working through these same emotions. This single death echoed through the canyon of death we'd been traversing. It was a landscape of loss.

Alone, together, I tried to process too quickly the things I did and didn't know about how policing works in America. None of it was new. All of it was new. I'd thought of abolition as the call to end slavery and was only now learning that it had evolved into a demand to end policing and prisons.

For a few hours every day, I'd go to the front porch, watch the sky—spitting rain, spitting sun—and think. The horse chestnuts sprouted thousands of tiered, chandelier-like flowers, their white petals flecked with colorful speckles, which then withered and died. Each night, we talked at the dinner table. I was filled with whirling feelings about racism in America and the unjust systems webbed through it. The online discourses overwhelmed me, but I felt grateful, even in my discomfort, for the way these ideas were stretching my mind and heart.

On the porch, I thought about the people—especially Black, Indigenous, and poor people—the police routinely incarcerate and kill. I thought about prisons and our entrenched cultural ideas about criminality and safety. I loved how complex *and* simple the core question posed by prison abolition was: Does prison serve anyone?

I kept returning to something my mom had told me. Years ago, one of her younger brothers swindled an older brother out of a significant amount of money. Her siblings were angry at the younger brother, but the older one had money to spare and had "loaned" it—something, as I've mentioned, my mom says you should never do. If you have money to give, you should give it. And if someone gives it back to you, that's also a gift. So this swindling situation didn't seem like a big deal to her, but a few of her siblings demanded that they all cut ties with their younger brother. In response, my mom told them: "There are eight of us. One of us was bound to be a scoundrel. Why are we mad that it's him? Why aren't you grateful that it's not you? He needs the money!"

The scale of this story was wrong, but it helped me think through the question of police and prison abolition. I liked seeing a person who did something illicit as one of us, a member of our family, someone who might need more attention, affection, and resources than others. My mom's family felt like a microcosm of the larger society, with ample complexity to reckon with. Would my aunts and uncles acknowledge the abuse their father, my grandpa, had heaped on his kids, and how that might have shaped this brother? What about the abuse that Goyo had experienced as a kid in the Philippines under American occupation and, later, as an immigrant in the United States?

"Where life is precious, life *is* precious," Ruth Wilson Gilmore told Rachel Kushner in a profile I read over and over like a prayer.

This became my rallying cry. Here was a vision I wanted to walk toward: a culture where people's lives are so highly valued and considered that we don't need policing or prisons. In finding language for what I believed, I felt both energized and discouraged for wanting change that gargantuan, change I wasn't certain I'd see in my lifetime. I recognized this combination of hope and hopelessness in people all around me, but especially in my uncle Doug and aunt Nancy.

Corey was the one who encouraged us to march. I was afraid of the coronavirus and large groups. During our first march, on June 2, I felt nervous to stand near anyone. Because of my hearing, I couldn't hear the chants well, except the names: George Floyd. Breonna Taylor. George Floyd. Breonna Taylor. George Floyd. Breonna Taylor. George Floyd. Breonna Taylor. George Floyd. Breonna Taylor. George Floyd. Breonna Taylor. George Floyd. Breonna Taylor. George Floyd. Breonna Taylor. I was crying before we made it one block. It was right to say their names. Every repetition inscribed the heartbreak in us anew, etching it deeper and deeper.

We marched down the center of East Burnside Street and up onto the Burnside Bridge. Organizers instructed us to lie down on the ground in silence for eight minutes and forty-six seconds, the length of time then reported that Derek Chauvin had knelt on George Floyd's neck, asphyxiating him. Thousands of us filled the bridge from end to end. Eight minutes and forty-six seconds felt like eternity. My tears soaked my fabric mask. All around me, people were sobbing. We lay on the Burnside Bridge, finally together, no longer alone—all of us face down, imagining an invisible knee on our necks.

S tef and Tony moved back to Los Angeles in the summer, and Zak, Corey, and I built a new rhythm as a trio. Change had become predictable and so we adapted, but we weren't doing well. I'd stopped blaming Erin, and I missed Chris's and Erin's presence in my life. We never saw our other friends. This wouldn't be the year I'd attend Doug's protest. In fact, I wasn't going to keep any dates or promises, and neither was anyone else.

The Holman House was demanding visitors, but I was too afraid to let anyone in. Corey mysteriously developed extreme dryness on his hands, and they became raw, rough, and pink. Cracks along his fingertips began to split open and bleed. To protect them, he wore white gloves, like Mickey Mouse, and in the bedroom, he'd become dejected, unable to touch my skin without pain. We were removed from each other even in proximity.

The three of us would cook Chris's dishes because we craved them. I loved making *khao tod*, a crispy broken-rice salad. The first time Chris made this salad—was *salad* even the right word?—it'd seemed like a joke. He stood at the kitchen island, his hands meticulously forming perfect rice-and-ground-pork patties. He poured an inch of oil into our black cast-iron skillet and fried the patties until their exteriors were golden and crispy. And then he tore them apart. It was like watching someone build a house and then knock it down, another mandala constructed and then swept away. But after I ate the crispy fried rice, mixed with fresh shallots, toasted peanuts, and herbs, I understood. Frying the patties creates delicious crackly edges, like you find in Persian stuck-pot rice or Korean bibimbap served in a hot stone bowl. By breaking the patties apart and mixing them with fresh ingredients, you create a dish that's both tender and crunchy. It was a textural marvel.

The nature of the protests in Portland was shifting, concentrating on two blocks downtown at the federal courthouse, where police and protestors faced off nightly. When I went, tear gas choked me before we reached the park. Tear gas is a chemical weapon, and local and federal police used it on Portland protesters for more than one hundred days, night after night, during the summer and fall of 2020. The residue lingered in the neighborhood around the courthouse and washed into the river. Later, my friends who protested regularly reported erratic periods and other health concerns. These protestors were treated like enemy combatants, and the police were also exposed in the process.

In mid-July, federal agents entered the scene, grabbing protestors and shoving them into unmarked vehicles. The stakes ramped higher. Strangely, there was a palpable feeling throughout the city that this might be a window of opportunity to set new priorities, centering care instead of punishment. At the same time, the news was reporting that the city was under siege by protesters. I was disturbed by the portrayal of Portland in the national media—that somehow the protestors were more dangerous to our city than the entrenched issues they were trying to fight. People had the proportions all wrong.

In September, a new pestilence befell us: the Santa Ana winds blew in dry and scorching from the east and spread five forest fires in Oregon, each burning across more than one hundred thousand acres. I sat in the yard the first day and watched tree limbs thrash through the air. That night, the wind in the branches outside created thousands of small scratching sounds, and I pictured an army of rodents coming to attack. The sky turned thick and yellow, like it was filled with mustard gas. The old Holman House showed its porousness; I could see the particulate matter blowing about as our ceiling fan spun. Our lungs ached.

The fires grew closer to the city, and we were put on orange alert, to be ready to evacuate when instructed. I didn't leave the house for several days, but when I finally did, I saw people living on the streets with no shelter. Like the coronavirus, this curse would travel along the well-worn paths of poverty and inequity. It was a human and environmental tragedy.

Tomoko, my host sister from Japan, wrote me an email: "Now, I'm worry about fire. World news reported that mountain fire of California is expand to Portland. Are you, your family, garden, and mushrooms all safe? Stay carefully! Love Tomoko."

Are my mushrooms safe? Tomoko cared about the health of the forest and was worried for my life and for my heart. I reread the letter and cried.

Corey suggested we invite someone without housing to stay in the basement apartment. He was feeling the strangeness of there being only three of us at home. I suspected the Holman House had begun talking to him too.

A local organization was facilitating a housing forum for people who were fleeing high-risk fire areas or otherwise lacked a place to stay. Zak was onboard but felt cautious. How long would we invite them to stay? My mom was due to visit in mid-November and would need access to the basement again. What would our boundaries look like? What if the person became violent? What if they carried the coronavirus? We couldn't control their movements—could we expect the same amount of transparency that we demanded of each other? Corey, meanwhile, felt the moral imperative to share what we had. It would cost us next to nothing, and the need was extraordinary. I let them represent my conflicting feelings—thoughtful concern versus indiscriminate generosity—and played mediator. We worked to find a balancing point.

I made a post and soon received a message from someone, sent through an encryption app. We were instructed by the organization to vet one another but were not given advice on how. In our messages back and forth, the stranger seemed even more tentative than I was. They asked a lot of questions about our house and whether I'd share my Twitter handle, as though my feed might prove I wasn't evil. I had to explain that I didn't participate on Twitter but that I was still a sane human being living in the real world.

The day they came—I'll call them Billy—the sky was as thick with yellow smoke as ever. Billy pedaled up on a bicycle with all their belongings strapped to it. They were wearing a rubber gas mask and punk clothing that reminded me of *Tank Girl*, a 1995 sci-fi movie where earth has become a desert and a community of rebels must take back the limited water supply. Billy was in their early twenties, an activist who'd been volunteering with mutual aid groups, sorting donations and feeding people. They were fully employed but undercompensated as a store clerk and lacked a steady place to live. They'd been in and out of motels, on friends' couches, and, when things were rough, at their parents' home, which was not a place they felt safe.

They were so shocked by the size of the basement apartment that they asked if five of their friends could move in, too, sleeping side by side on the floor. Zak quashed that idea instantly. We agreed that we'd let them have the basement to themselves and keep the main part of the house separate but would happily share the food we cooked for dinner.

Billy was tough. They wore bulky military surplus boots and looked like they could beat the shit out of someone. They were also full of questions and kindness. Zak asked Billy about their pronouns, and they answered, "Whatever you want, as long as you're not mean about it."

Billy's presence helped solidify a theory I was just starting to articulate after more than a decade in the house: the best way to ask people for something—to do a chore, for example, and especially to make a behavior change—is to state the request directly and with as little judgment or frustration as possible. And the opposite holds true: if someone asks me to do something that's important to them, I try to do it without getting defensive. We all had different standards. We cleaned as much as suited our own sense of good enough. We were as considerate as we wanted to be treated in return. If we left a mess on the counter, it meant we didn't mind messes on the counter. If these different standards started to become an issue, the person with the issue needed to be very clear, and the person listening had to take their request at face value and do their best.

Chris had taught me how to care for his wok. Zak reminded me to be less aggressive with our nice knives (I had a habit of banging them against pots to get the last of the garlic off). Corey showed me a better method for loading silverware in the dishwasher. We shaped one another in small domestic ways, fluidly trading the roles of parent and child.

Billy approached us with frankness. They'd ask for things they needed, things I could provide: a better kitchen knife, seconds on dinner, clearer explanations of how things should be cleaned and maintained, if and when a guest was welcome, and more. When they spoke, the enormous gas mask often muffled their voice, and I started being more transparent about my hearing loss, which I usually kept secret. They were responsive and compassionate about it.

Billy wanted to have dinner together, so we gathered on our side porch once the smoke lessened. They shared their favorite snack with us, a Ritz-like cracker from England called Mini Chicken Crimpy Shapes. "Flavour you can see," the packaging promised. I was delighted. They wrote urban fantasy, a genre in which creatures like elves and dwarves inhabit cities. They marveled that Corey and Zak were making a living as artists. They loved being where they could dance freely, without their footsteps stomping over someone else's head.

What started as a week became a month. Even after the smoke cleared, Billy stayed. My mom's visit was approaching, and we gave them two months' notice, but as the date grew closer, it became clear that they didn't have anywhere else to go. They showed Corey the bolt cutters they'd bought to break into abandoned houses where they could squat.

One night, Billy and I sat on the side porch. It was late fall and very cold, but we kept up our outdoor dinners. Billy told me they'd never imagined a group of people could treat one another with the kindness we did. I told them they were still very young, which made me feel patronizing.

"It got better for me when I found friends who built me up and I poured my love into them," I told Billy. "For some reason, that got easier as I got older. You can build this kind of community too." And we both sat there, six feet apart, and cried.

When Billy left, they didn't say where they'd go. I invited them over for dinner again, and they came, but after that, they never responded to my messages.

That fall, I had my first vertigo attack. I couldn't tell if it was stress induced or some new development in my inner ears. I was feeling down about my hearing and struggled to isolate that feeling from my general sense of doom. I'd gotten hearing aids when my right ear started to go, but I hated them. They made me sound miked in my own head, which made me feel like a perpetual stand-up comic.

"Hello, hello, so glad to see nobody here with me," I'd joke to myself in the mirror.

My fear of going deaf had changed. I was no longer preoccupied with not being able to locate some song I couldn't remember. I was afraid of losing the sound of other people's voices in their own mouths, of losing the inflections of my loved ones, the cadence of their speech, the way conversations build momentum in real time. For years, my one New Year's resolution had been to become a better listener. It was the work of a lifetime. And now I felt sabotaged.

When I first learned about my otosclerosis, I was told that becoming pregnant would likely exacerbate it. I decided not to let that prevent me from having a child if I wanted one. When I told Corey about my prognosis, and that I might pass this disease on to our child, he assured me that that wasn't a deal-breaker for him. But over time, I felt more and more fearful that having a child would sacrifice my hearing.

I had plenty of other reasons to not want kids—financial strain and ecological collapse among them—but I also had my household for support. I'd talked to Chris and Erin, and we'd daydreamed about raising a kid inside our community. Parenting with more people felt like it might bring some significant ease (as well as some challenges). Yet even with that bolster, I wasn't ready to accelerate my hearing loss because I was already struggling. My deafness caused me personal pain, frustration, and embarrassment, and my future felt full of unknowns.

As sounds disappeared, I decided my resolution to listen wouldn't change. My hearing might diminish, but I'd keep trying to strengthen my attentiveness. I'd ask the people in my life to be present, patient, and curious as I lost sound. We'd find other ways to communicate. I dreamed our household would adapt alongside me.

One night in late December, with the holidays just barely behind us and my spirits low, Corey suggested I take molly, also known as ecstasy or MDMA. People usually use this drug in party settings because it unleashes interpersonal affection, which flows unencumbered all over the place. It also makes music really nice. We were sitting in our bedroom. He offered to join me and took a little bit, but at ten inches taller and many pounds heavier, it didn't do much and he was soon asleep. Meanwhile, I was blazing. Doing molly alone, I discovered, sent the love flowing inward. I put on some of my favorite Ethiopian music and began dancing slowly with myself.

Time on molly is languorous and sensual. I felt inside an endless liquid present. I stroked my face and told myself, *You're doing it, Loo. You're becoming who you're trying to become.* I was too high to be self-critical, my cynicism overridden by love. I forgave myself for not being the person I wished I was, for going deaf so young. I hadn't realized I'd blamed myself for going deaf until I forgave myself. For eight hours, until the morning light streamed into our east-facing windows, I danced and whispered, "You're doing it, Loo. You are becoming."

The next morning, exhausted and sober, I went to bed. When I awoke, the whole memory felt brief, like it'd happened instantaneously, not across an entire night. Drugs can be scary because they alter our minds, but sometimes I need my mind altered. As a kid, I experienced unconditional love from my family. In my twenties, I had to find it again from my friends and partner. Now, in my thirties, I wanted to claim it for myself. Long after the molly wore off, self-love adhered inside me. I'd walked over an invisible line into a new space where I forgave myself for going deaf, even though I didn't need to be forgiven.

As we entered 2021, I wondered whether Chris would ever move back in. I missed him so badly. He was in a committed relationship with Erin; he was financially self-sufficient and in his forties. What could bring him back to our home?

I wanted to believe that we could start a new chapter in our household, one with more honesty, more recognition of power dynamics and precarity, more presence of mind. I also fantasized that the pandemic would generate endless silver linings—that essential workers would become vaunted members of society and that their pay would increase in relation to their undeniable value; that the police would stop murdering Black, brown, and poor people; that everyone would embrace and act on common-sense arguments for universal health care, housing for all, and reparations. I was left with an unfulfilled longing for a future that seemed, for the first time in my life, to be part of the collective imagination yet kept receding farther into the distance.

As our household remained constrained, I started looking for evidence of group living outside the walls of a house. Doug and Nancy remained committed activists, protesting US military involvement around the globe. They were looking at interconnection on a macrocosmic level—at what it means to imagine the world as a home. Meanwhile, my own fascination with mushroom foraging was becoming more central to my life. Hunting mushrooms was something I could do outdoors with others. My forager friends and I were engaging with interconnection on a microcosmic level. How did exploring the same idea at vastly different scales change its shape and meaning?

The Holman House was asking for a party again, rumbling insistently that we have one, but it wasn't the right time. New coronavirus variants were emerging, and people were dying every day. But I dreamed about a party anyway. I'd wander from friend to friend, taking sips of their drinks, snacking out of big bowls of chips and salsa, sharing respiratory particles and maybe even some saliva. I pictured every part of the house as its own club; in my mind's eye, I bounced from living room to kitchen to porch, from one group to another.

I imagined helping Chris make *khao tod*, the crispy broken-rice salad, for the party. We'd fold cooked rice, ground pork, toasted coconut flakes, lime leaves, and red curry paste together and form the mixture into patties. We'd fry the patties perfectly, until their exteriors were golden and crispy. And then we'd tear them apart into a raggedy pile, so we could build something new.

Chris's *Khao Tod* (Crispy Broken-Rice Salad)

Recipe by Christopher Rabilwongse

MAKES 6 TO 8 SERVINGS

Khao tod is a great use of day-old rice but good enough that I'd cook rice just to make this dish, which is so fresh, crunchy, and thrilling. Chris says there are endless variations, but the classic would include the fermented sausages called *nam* his mother was famous for making. When we can find them, we add one, cut into large coins, along with the cilantro and green onion, and omit the ground pork—but they're not necessary. *Khao tod* is always served with a plate of leafy greens, like lettuce and cabbage, and herbs, including mint, basil, and *rau ram*. These leaves become the vessels for your rice. Make this as a gift for your friends and family. Make this for a party!

PATTIES

1 cup shredded unsweetened coconut

6 to 8 *makrut* lime leaves, fresh or frozen

Cooked jasmine rice, made from 3 cups raw rice

1 pound ground pork

1 4-oz can red curry paste (we use Maesri brand)

High-heat oil (like sunflower)

SALAD

½ bunch cilantro, leaves plucked, washed, and coarsely chopped, stems discarded

3 stalks green onion, trimmed and sliced

4-inch knob fresh ginger, peeled and julienned

1 cup sliced raw shallot (from approximately 1 large or 3 small shallots)

1 cup toasted peanuts

SEASONING

3 tablespoons fish sauce, plus more to taste

Juice of 2 to 3 limes

Chili flakes (page xxiii) to taste

SIDE

2 heads butter or Bibb lettuce, washed

1 head cabbage, sliced into eighths and cored

Rau ram, Thai basil, spearmint, or other fresh herbs, washed and plucked

OPTIONAL

Dried whole Thai chilies, fried in oil until brown and crisp

Prepare the Pork-and-Rice Patties

In a flat skillet, toast the coconut flakes in a single layer over medium heat, stirring constantly. They will darken from creamy white to golden brown. Don't settle for a light toasting—take the coconut all the way to deep golden. Be attentive so it doesn't burn. Set aside. If you have fresh lime leaves, very finely julienne them. If you're working with frozen ones, chop them into a coarse powder.

In a massive bowl, add the cooked rice, toasted coconut, lime leaves, ground pork, and red curry paste. Mix well with your hands until thoroughly incorporated. Form the rice mixture into baseball-sized rounds and then flatten into patties the size of large hamburgers, no more than one inch thick, and set on a baking sheet. At this point, you can set the patties, covered, in the fridge for several hours until ready to fry, or even freeze them and defrost when you're ready to continue.

Fry the Patties

In a frying pan, pour oil ½ inch deep and heat over medium until it shimmers. Add rice-pork patties in a single layer, leaving at least a ½ inch between each. You'll have to work in batches. Fry the patties until crispy and golden on the bottom, approximately 3 minutes. Flip. Continue to fry until the second side is crispy and golden and the pork has cooked all the way through, another 3 minutes. Remove patties from the pan and drain on paper towels. Repeat, frying the remaining patties in batches.

Assemble the Salad

Crumble the cooked patties into a large bowl. Add the cilantro, green onion, ginger, shallot, and peanuts. Break up and mix everything together. Season generously with fish sauce, lime juice, and chili flakes. Taste it. Does it need more salt? Add more fish sauce. Do you like more acid? Add more lime juice. More spiciness? Add chili flakes or bring the optional fried whole dried Thai chilies to the table for people to sprinkle over the top if they choose. Serve alongside a platter of lettuce, raw cabbage leaves, and herbs and let people dig in.

NUCLEAR FAMILY

A few days before Father's Day in June 2021, my parents and I drove up to Port Townsend. We'd all gotten our initial coronavirus vaccines and were starting to see friends and family for the first time in a year. My dad stayed at the bingo parlor with Doug and Nancy, and my mom and I shared a futon on my cousin Amanda's floor one block away. I quickly got used to Amanda's daughter Inez, age five, running outside to the garden to pee standing up.

On Father's Day morning, I made *hiyashi chūka*—cold sesame noodles. Amanda was working all day, so she couldn't join our flock of odd birds—her husband and two daughters, my parents and me, some RoseWind members, and a handful of Quakers—who were headed to Naval Magazine Indian Island, across the water from Port Townsend, for Doug's annual holiday protest and celebration. I'd kept my promise to my aunt and uncle.

D oug staged his first Father's Day protest in 2016. He invited
friends to join him in a four-hour vigil at a park that sits across
the street from Naval Magazine Indian Island, a storage facility
and way station for military weapons. NavMag, as it's often
called, is the only deep-water facility of its kind on the West
Coast. Ships pull in directly from the Pacific to load up on
weapons—missiles, land mines, cluster munitions, bombs, phos-
phorous weapons, napalm, and other ordnance—which are stored
in more than one hundred aboveground concrete domes onsite.
Doug emailed me about the protest afterward, in what turned
out to be an invitation to his arraignment.

"For the vigil," he wrote, "I erected two temporary stick and
string sculptures on the park lawn, creating imaginary cylinders
sized to hold the bloodshed in the Middle East."

Doug had read a report from Physicians for Social
Responsibility estimating that 1.3 to 2 million people died in
Afghanistan, Iraq, and Pakistan between 2001 and 2013 due to
US military intervention. (The United States itself never tried to
tally those numbers.)

"Each person has on average 1.35 gallons of blood," Doug
continued. Doing a little math and thinking like a builder, he
determined that a cylinder eight feet tall with a diameter of 193
feet (almost two thirds the length of a football field) would
accommodate the blood of 1.3 million people. The park lawn
wasn't large enough, so Doug did what he could, using poles and
straps to demarcate a circle almost 140 feet across, "enough to
hold the blood of 682,321 people, one half to one third of those
killed."

I was shocked by his gruesome death geometry. I couldn't decide if he'd reduced people's humanity to literally nothing—a gallon of invisible blood—or honored their existence by memorializing them. But who was I to judge? If I was being honest with myself, I hadn't sat with the deaths from the wars in Iraq and Afghanistan, not really. I'd sheltered myself from returning to the anger and pain I'd felt during the war, enabled by knowing few people who'd fought. Doug called avoidance like mine the "obedient psychology of denial." I thought of it as coping.

"Much of the weaponry that caused these deaths was shipped from Naval Magazine Indian Island," Doug wrote. "At 4:00 p.m., I walked across the highway and sat down in front of the entry gate." After more than an hour, three Jefferson County troopers came to the depot. Doug told the officers that he intended to block the entry until he was arrested. He'd brought a sleeping bag. They promptly scooped him up and took him to jail, where he received a disorderly conduct citation and was released.

"[I will] have an opportunity to speak to the judge about why I blocked the entry," he concluded. "Please come to the courthouse."

I attended Doug's arraignment with my dad. It was a disorienting experience. The judge was a middle-aged woman with short-cropped hair who sounded like she'd been nipping Tanqueray all day. She presented the crimes of Jefferson County one defendant at a time: peeping, driving without a license, animal neglect, domestic abuse, violating a restraining order. The defendants rarely spoke. The lawyers stated their pleas, and the judge banged her gavel and moved along. The only emotion she displayed was mild annoyance as she described situations that ballooned in my imagination: A man who kept hanging around the convenience store where his ex worked. A couple who'd run out of money and stopped feeding their horses. A migrant farmworker caught driving to work without a license or legal status.

The defendants sat around me, morose and resigned. The lawyers skittered in and out like busy restaurant servers.

I'd never been to an arraignment and didn't know that it's simply when the judge informs the defendants of the charges filed against them and lists their rights. The defendants can enter a plea. This wasn't the courtroom drama I was familiar with from TV. Instead, it was a heart-wrenching roll call of the kind of mundane tragedies usually hidden from sight.

After three hours, it was Doug's turn. He was the last defendant. The judge finally showed some powerful emotion: fury.

Standing before her, tugging at his bolo tie, Doug announced that he had a statement he wanted to read, but she wouldn't permit that. The prosecuting attorney announced he wouldn't press charges, and she dismissed the citation of disorderly conduct. No one would give him the gift of a day in court where he could wax poetic about his conceptual art installation. Still, somehow, before she could cut him off, Doug managed to voice his belief that our country's militarism was connected to its overall culture of violence and all the small but bleak infractions we'd heard all day. The judge ignored him, banged her gavel, and left the courtroom.

Outside the courthouse, Doug's friends paced around him, jittery with exhaustion. Like me, many hadn't known what an arraignment was and were discombobulated by the last three hours.

Although Doug's citation had been rescinded, I knew his actions weren't a one-time performance. He'd return to Naval Magazine Indian Island. His activism was central to his life—inextricable from what home and group living meant to him.

D oug and his Quaker community have been actively protesting the military sites around them for more than forty years. NavMag isn't the only weapons depot nearby. In 1984, Doug was arrested at the Naval Submarine Base in Bangor, forty miles southeast of Port Townsend (and twenty miles northwest of downtown Seattle). In the *Bulletin of the Atomic Scientists*, Hans Kristensen and Matt Korda estimate that Washington State has the second-largest stockpile of nuclear weapons in the United States, containing roughly one-quarter of the 5,500-plus nuclear warheads in the nation's supply. (Combined with NavMag, this makes the Puget Sound one of the most weaponized places in the world.)

In particular, the base in Bangor is home to eight submarines that are each armed with up to twenty of the ballistic missiles known as Tridents. As Kristensen and Korda write, "The submarines operating from this base carry more deployed nuclear weapons than any other base in the United States." Each Trident typically carries four nuclear warheads; one of these bombs could, theoretically, do the damage of eight "Little Boys," the atomic bomb dropped over Hiroshima. The math is frightening. The destructive power of the Trident submarines at Bangor alone is 8 x 20 x 4 x 8—the equivalent of 5,120 Hiroshimas.

When Doug was arrested in Bangor, he was protesting a train carrying some two hundred nuclear bombs to the base. He'd broken through the line of police and nearly reached the train when an officer tackled him from behind. Both landed on the tracks as the train screeched to a halt inches from their faces.

Doug remains a committed part of the Bangor protest community, but over the years, more of his attention shifted to Indian Island. The first time Doug was arrested at the NavMag gates was in 2006, along with thirty-five others who were protesting the war in Iraq. In the years that followed, he could never shake its specter. One day, he was sitting on the waterfront looking out at Port Townsend Bay and the shore of Indian Island in deep meditation.

"I was in an altered state of mind," he told me, over a glass of cider at his dining room table. "Peace doves floated over my head, and above them, a military aircraft. 'I am being assigned to pay attention to this military base,' I realized. It was one of the most profound experiences of my life."

His Father's Day protest developed partly from his belief that the best way to be a responsible dad is to fight to disarm his community, a very un-American vision for the role of protector. After all, he thought, why wouldn't someone want to target this place? A single effective airstrike, and you could block US access to a significant portion of its weaponry. Or what if something simply went wrong?

"Let's say a ship loaded with explosives accidentally detonates in the bay," he mused to me, "creating a tsunami and an overpressure of atmosphere that can blow out windows?"

One could accuse him of catastrophizing, but the point of these grim fantasies isn't merely to postulate future scenarios; it's also to critique the present. Doug isn't only asking "What if?" but also "Why?" Why is the destructive power of 5,120 Hiroshimas sitting in these eight Trident-armed submarines? Why are a fleet of outdated nuclear-armed submarines a good use of our tax dollars? Why did the US government spend almost three-quarters of a trillion dollars on national defense in 2021? If the guiding principle for nuclear weapons is to never use them, why do we build more? Why aren't we allowed to interrogate this and imagine other possibilities? What are we protecting with all that money? If people in his community realized the killing power of the armament nearby, Doug thinks they'd be disturbed. But how to make people care and feel connected?

One year, eight people joined Doug at the NavMag entry. "As a citizen of the United States and a local resident," Doug announced to the security personnel across from him, "I arrest the legal 'person' known as Naval Magazine Indian Island. Do not leave."

When the sheriff deputies arrived, he informed them he'd made a "citizen's arrest," and he asked the sheriffs to take over and formally arrest the base. They laughed.

This is performance art, without a doubt. It builds from Doug's wild imagination, curiosity about language, and sense of the absurd. *Is this a joke or not?* one might wonder, the classic response to a Doug project.

But Doug's efforts to raise awareness aren't limited to these annual protests. He ran for Congress twice, once as a Democrat and once on the Green Party ticket, to force local politicians to speak about these military sites. He and Nancy aided a lawyer in bringing a Freedom of Information Act case—which they won, in 2011—to the Supreme Court to force the Navy to disclose information about their weaponry. During one of my visits, Doug met with the mayor of Port Townsend and asked her to join Mayors for Peace, an organization based in Hiroshima that advocates for the elimination of nuclear weapons, which she promptly did.

Taken together, these gestures, big and small, are Doug's way of issuing a constant reminder to his community, like a drop of water falling on the same spot, to hollow out a place of care for people affected by this weaponry around the world.

The word *nuclear* is a strange one. *Nuclear*: the very center. *Nuclear*: total annihilation.

As a high schooler, I learned that, in physics, *nuclear* refers to the positively charged core of an atom, where protons and neutrons goof around. This is the origin of the terms *nuclear power* and *nuclear bomb*, both based on the energy generated when atoms split apart through fission. But in biology, *nuclear DNA* describes the part of a cell containing its genetic material.

Bronisław Malinowski, considered a founder of social anthropology, is credited with coining the term *nuclear family* in the 1920s, using the biological sense of *nucleus* for something core and essential. I think it's a strangely poetic and apt term to describe parents and their children, who are united through their DNA, sit at the center of each other's lives, and often contain within this tight circle the potential for collision, excitability, instability, and explosion.

To go nuclear is to lose your fucking shit. When the world went nuclear—when Einstein's theory led physicists to split the atom and the United States dropped two atomic bombs over Japan—it seems to me that it lost its fucking shit. I've wondered if splitting the atom induced a kind of paranoid schizophrenia in nuclear-armed countries, with delusions of grandeur and siege made real.

Doug, Nancy, and my parents were born into a new collective consciousness that arrived when the United States bombed

Hiroshima and Nagasaki. For the first time, with a single command, an entire city could be incinerated—an absolute, godlike power with few precursors outside of the Old Testament. For decades after the Soviet Union developed its first nuclear weapons, many Americans lived in a state of perpetual anxiety that total annihilation might strike at any moment.

The threat hasn't gone away, but public attention largely has, even though climate change threatens to turn nuclear-armed neighbors against one another. My generation has spent much less time contemplating nuclear war than our parents. Until Putin threatened to use nuclear weapons after invading Ukraine, I wondered if people my age thought about nuclear arms at all.

My mom and I arrived at Lloyd L. Good Memorial Park on Indian Island before almost anyone else. The park consists of a gravel parking lot, a bit of shoreline, a boat ramp, a picnic area, and a modest field of grass. From the water, I could see Mount Rainier in sharp detail, like a chiseled ice sculpture.

My dad appeared, looking like a cross between Rajneesh, Santa Claus, and ZZ Top—huge fluffy white beard, frizzled halo of white hair, black baseball cap, black sunglasses. I placed my sesame noodles on one of three picnic tables under a tin-roof shelter. A couple had stopped for lunch at the park; my dad offered them some of my noodle salad, and they accepted.

Before we arrived, Doug and my dad had begun constructing the sculpture. They'd hammered low stakes into the ground at twenty-foot intervals, marking the circumference of a large circle. Around the circle, they'd laid out white straps made of tightly woven plastic, the kind typically used in lumberyards to strap two-by-fours together, which they'd then attached to longer, eight-foot stakes.

I walked over to Doug. He was wearing messy work jeans, suspenders, and a blue T-shirt, the same vivid color as his eyes and the sky. It was very hot for a June day on the Olympic Peninsula—heading toward eighty degrees—and sweat was pouring off his broad brow. I followed his instructions and helped him drill an eight-foot stake into one of the low ones. As we moved to the next post, a white strap rose into the air. Soon they were all aloft, hanging between the tall stakes like string lights.

Doug had tied hundreds of pieces of red construction tape—reading "DANGER PELIGRO DANGER PELIGRO DANGER PELIGRO"—along the length of the straps. Here, decorating the periphery of an imaginary pool of blood, the meaning of the words felt more existential. As we walked in and out of the ring, the wind caught the strands of red tape, and they danced in the air like May Day streamers.

When my cousin Amanda's husband, Gabe, arrived with Inez and her three-year-old sister, Brighten, both girls were wearing bucket hats to shade their faces from the pounding sun. Inez had added black cat ears on top and immediately grabbed a loose length of red tape for a tail. "PELIGRO DANGER," I read as it flapped behind her. The first thing we did was eat noodles.

Other people began to flit in, calling out "Happy Father's Day" as they joined our little group. A woman wearing a hat that read, simply, "QUAKER" sat down across from me. Her name was Caroline Wildflower. Her hair was pulled back in a low ponytail and her face had a determined, no-nonsense cast to it. This woman couldn't be fazed, I thought. Another woman, with a goofy smile, appeared sporting her purse like a necklace and a rolled bandana tied around her wispy hair like a headband. She clearly didn't follow the rules, I determined.

When Nancy arrived, she was wearing her silvery hair down, a periwinkle linen shirt, and checkered baby-blue pants—the picture of tenderness. I wanted to help her sit down, stand up, move across the lawn, but she was fine on her own, maneuvering with a cane that looked like a ski pole.

My cousin Danny arrived with his daughter, Gitte, a few months younger than Brighten. Then my friend Tassie arrived with her husband, her two-year-old daughter, and her plump infant. For two hours, I chased the little girls around. We sprinted between the posts demarcating the imaginary pool of blood. We pretended to be eggs cracking open to birth monsters. We tackled one another and they all tried to ride on my back, which I accepted and refused in equal measure. Aside from the kids, hardly anyone entered the ring Doug built. *Does it feel sacrilegious to bathe in invisible blood?* I wondered.

At some point, I took a break to catch my breath, and Doug approached me, holding a small basin filled with water, a box of food coloring, and a tiny battery-powered fountain. He asked me to go to the center of the circle, set up the fountain, and dye the water the color of blood.

"Use red and a little blue," he instructed.

Brighten and Inez appeared at my side. I gave one the red dye and the other the blue.

"What is it?" they asked me.

"It's a little fountain."

"Do we get to play in it?"

"Um, I guess not. It will dye your clothes." This felt like an unfair answer, given how hot it was.

"Can I have the yellow?" Inez asked, nodding at the box.

"Sorry, no yellow."

"Why?" She cocked her head.

"Because your grandpa wants me to dye this the color of blood."

They both accepted this answer for some reason, helped me dye the water (three drops red, one drop blue, three drops red, one drop blue), and ran off. The water didn't look like blood. It wasn't viscous, for one thing. And the little fountain didn't work well at all. It sucked up water from the bottom of the basin and spewed it in arcs from the top, but the water overshot the rim and landed in the grass, leaving the basin empty and the fountain sucking air.

"It's not gonna work," I told Doug, back at the picnic shelter.

"Oh well," he responded, "we'll figure it out next time," and he returned to his conversation with Caroline Wildflower.

Around two in the afternoon, Doug called us together to sit on the ground in the shade of an old cherry tree. Danny got a camping chair for Nancy, and Gabe took all the kids down to the water.

Doug thanked us for joining him. He told us a bit about the history of the place. That the federal government took the island from Indigenous people in 1939 through eminent domain. The S'Klallam tribes have confirmed there are some fourteen archeological sites and an untold number of burial sites there, but that didn't stop the Navy from opening the ammunition depot in 1941.

Then, he briefly described the sculpture and its invisible contents. "It's so easy to avert our gaze," he told us. "How can we comprehend invisible suffering on unimaginable scales? This sculpture is just an aid to help perceive what it is we're talking about. I wanted to invite their ghosts to be present."

We sat in silence. I decided to take his request seriously and to try to think about the 1.3 to 2 million people who died in Iraq, Afghanistan, and Pakistan. I didn't know how to begin. I thought about the size of Portland, which has some 600,000 residents within city limits but more than 2 million people in the greater metro area. I thought about all those people dying. I pictured their bodies dropping to the ground simultaneously—in the middle of shooting a jump shot, taking a bite of a sandwich, swiping something from their baby's mouth. I began to feel seasick. I looked around at the others. Tassie was nursing her baby. Doug sat as still as a statue. My mom had her eyes closed and her legs out in front of her, her feet rocking back and forth. Behind us, the red ribbons were flying.

The sound of cars in the gravel parking lot carried above the sound of the breeze. A dog nearby whined softly for attention. I tried again to think about the 1.3 to 2 million people who had died. My mind drifted to Father's Day one year earlier. My dad and I had driven from Portland on a meandering route to the coast. We stopped at one of the last remaining passenger ferries over the Columbia River, then at a secret rope swing under an old covered bridge. At Cape Disappointment, facing the ocean, I suddenly wondered for the first time in my life about its name. "Who named it the Pacific?" I asked aloud. My dad told me Ferdinand Magellan had given it that name because he thought it seemed calm. He reminded me that *pacific* means "peace-making" and *to pacify* means "to soothe." "But a pacifier is not real food," he continued. *Pacify* also means "to make submissive, sometimes through violent threat." We both wondered at the contradictions while staring at the turbulent Pacific, which was alternately crashing and lapping at our feet.

Doug broke the silence. How long had it been? I felt disoriented and embarrassed, as if I'd been caught asleep, drooling. Doug invited people to speak if they wanted to, and one by one they did, never hogging the spotlight for too long. They recalled their own fathers, who fought in various wars. They described feeling "called" to the park. Caroline Wildflower said, "We act without being attached to the result. You cannot know what the results of your actions will be." Her words reminded me of a quote Doug often cited, from a prominent Quaker named E. Raymond Wilson: "We ought to be willing to work for causes which will not be won now but cannot be won in the future unless the goals are staked out now and worked for energetically over a period of time."

When it was his turn, Doug read one of his poems about NavMag, gesturing passionately with his enormous hands. Most of the words whizzed past me, but I caught "Atomic bullets fired into the heart of the future" and "Oh, for more indecision! For more backing about!"

I listened. Nothing coalesced that I wanted to share with the group. For a long time, we were all quiet. Then, once again, Doug broke the silence and asked us if we wanted to join him in walking to the entrance of NavMag. He planned to hold silence at the gate. If we were arrested, he explained, it would be considered a trespassing offense on a county road. There would be a citation and a fine, and we'd be called to the courthouse. No one should feel pressured to join him, but all were welcome.

"Those who feel called for transformation, are we ready?" Doug asked us. My mom was the first to walk toward him. I searched my feelings and discovered I was nervous. Since the stakes were low, I felt ashamed, and that shame propelled me toward Doug, my parents, and eight women, all fifty or older, who'd begun walking together up the park driveway.

Doug and my mom took the lead. A busy road separates the park and the NavMag entrance, so Doug walked us along the shoulder to the safest spot to cross. An SUV appeared behind the base's fence and drove our way. A guard inside began speaking into a megaphone.

"Stay on the other side of the blue line," he commanded. "Stay on the other side of the blue line."

I saw it in front of me: a two-foot-wide line painted on the asphalt in a lovely robin's-egg color. I felt its power like a force field, but Doug and my mom breezed right through. My mom looked very beautiful to me. She was wearing a bright-pink linen shirt, a wildly patterned skirt, a baseball cap, a fanny pack, flip-flops, and cheap turquoise sunglasses, like a lady headed for the beach. She walked with buoyancy, her small frame bouncing beside Doug's sturdy, broad one. This was delighting her, I could tell.

When we reached the gate, Doug and Caroline Wildflower stood in the center of the road and the rest of us fanned out behind and to the sides. Assembled together, we looked puny. Four guards approached us, and then a fifth. They'd been waiting for us, I realized. Of course—I suddenly remembered that Doug always invited the NavMag commander to this protest. They knew we were coming.

Doug spoke to the guards: "In the spirit of life, we are offering our hearts." He brought his hands to his heart. "We are not looking for enemies. We are looking for transformational change. We ask you to close down this base, for your kids and my kids."

The guards tightened their lips and remained silent.

A few others piped up. "Please close this base," they requested.

"Happy Father's Day," my dad told the guards, in a change of tack. He shuffled his feet. "Many of our fathers fought in wars. We honor your fathers."

"We appreciate that," the main guard replied stiffly.

"We are going to stand in silence, praying for peace for ten minutes," Doug continued. "Bear with us."

I caught my dad's gaze. He was wearing a black T-shirt that featured a cartoon armadillo sitting in the road and the words "Get Out of the Middle." I assumed it was a critique of political centrism. He chooses his T-shirts carefully, so this was no mistake, but I felt it might have been a miscalculation given where we were all currently standing.

We were silent. I was once again thrown into my thoughts. I watched the guards. There was no fence between us, just ten feet of road leading to the entrance. They looked uncomfortable and hot. Half were wearing black uniforms that said "POLICE," the other half gray security garb, all of it a thick twill. Their guns were tucked into holsters. Their hands were gripping their belts. Four of the guards were white. One was Latino. Besides my half-Filipina mom, all the protestors were white. *How would this scene change if more protestors weren't white?* I wondered. It felt like a very Doug-like response when I then asked myself, *How am I so certain that we're in the right? Are we so different from these guards?* They were also workers, locals—no one there was calling the shots.

I thought about what would happen if Doug succeeded in shutting down the base. A motley crew of white hippies would have removed a military installation from their backyard, but it would undoubtedly reappear elsewhere, where people have less political clout. The military wasn't going to stop transporting weapons. This base might close, but the work would continue.

The military and its weaponry are integral to our economy. But what a horrible bargain that is. Since the late seventies, US companies have moved large sectors of manufacturing offshore, from clothing to cars to computers, while keeping weapons manufacturing onshore. Now, the United States is the top arms exporter in the world—selling weapons to 103 nations and accounting for 40 percent of global sales between 2018 and 2022. For our economy to function fully, we need reasons to make and sell more weapons. Most of us can't comprehend the scale of death US weapons cause, and it's a commitment to unending death in more ways than one. Researchers estimate that the Department of Defense produces more greenhouse gases than entire industrial nations, including Portugal and Denmark.

I could hear the birds chirping and the cars speeding behind us. Time was moving so slowly. How long had it been? Doug had his hands crossed in front of his stomach. A woman with short gray hair was massaging her lower back. My mom had closed her eyes and was holding her hands together as if in prayer.

I turned to watch Danny, with Gitte in his arms, sprinting across the road to join us. I was grateful to have something to look at other than the miserable-looking guards. Gitte was small and muscular. Her long blonde curls were often in tangles. She was usually naked, climbing everything and jumping from any height. She was like a Viking child. This was the first time I'd seen her clothed all day. She wanted to run back to the park, but Danny held her tightly in his arms as he came to my side and nudged me affectionately.

"Will five more minutes do?" Doug asked our group. We nodded. I thought I saw the power of the little girl working on the guards, who seemed even more uneasy. I tugged at Gitte's foot, and she offered me an impatient smile.

It felt transgressive to be in this space, just standing silently where we weren't allowed. It was such a small act. I'd felt our presence as almost buffoonish when we arrived, but I began to wonder: *What is more ridiculous, the scale of our little party or the scale of this base and the quantity of weapons passing through it? Which is out of proportion? Who's making who uncomfortable? Who's afraid of who?* I wished this didn't feel so abnormal, for them or for us. When do we get to mourn and voice our anger? How are we supposed to process tragedies and ask for change?

Caring this much can be paralyzing, I thought. But isn't doing nothing depressing? Had my heart become too hardened? I thought my uncle's protest was futile; so many parts of our lives feel futile. But Doug was asking us to imagine anyway—to imagine that what we do matters, at every scale; to imagine that caring for people we've never met is essential to being fully human. Our country has made a profound financial commitment to violence that reverberates from top to bottom, and we each have a responsibility to envision a different path. Nuclear abolition, demilitarization—these are way-out-there dreams, but if you don't name a destination, how can you walk toward it?

often wonder how we choose our issues, or how they choose us: the ones that lodge in our minds, dog us in our sleep, and follow us through our days. Accrual, exposure, inheritance, inclination, self-preservation, greed, or all of the above? We can't care about everything equally. What makes one person's passions better or worse than another's?

For Doug, one explanation for his devotion to this cause is a lifetime of living near nuclear projects.

As a child, Doug feared hostile bombs from afar, but ironically, the greatest present danger came from the US effort to build nuclear bombs. From 1955 until 1965, two mines near Lakeview, Oregon—the White King and the Lucky Lass—harvested ore containing the minerals uraninite and autunite. This ore was sent to the Lakeview Mining Company, only two miles north of the family's home, and at the plant, the extracted uranium ore was crushed, leached, and concentrated into yellowcake—what sounds like dry store-bought birthday cake but is actually a powder that was shipped offsite to be further refined. These are the first steps in a long process that creates fuel for nuclear reactors. Along the way, the plant was also creating a huge open-air heap of residual radioactive material.

During these years, my uncle Phil, then a toddler, had a series of mysterious, long-lasting nosebleeds that threatened to kill him. (Hemoglobin is highly sensitive to uranium isotopes, and one sign of radiation sickness is excessive bleeding; the very young are especially vulnerable.) At the time, the family had no idea of the source of Phil's ceaselessly bleeding nose, and eventually a doctor cauterized the inside of his nostrils to create a barrier of scar tissue. Years later, both private and governmental agencies would spend millions of dollars trying to clean up the radioactive remains at Lakeview.

In 1961, when my grandparents moved the family to Washington, the yellowcake was also traveling north, to a facility on the Columbia River about an hour and a half from Moses Lake called Hanford. This once completely top-secret complex was the same site where plutonium had been manufactured for Fat Man, the atomic bomb detonated over Nagasaki. Here, the yellowcake was enriched—the usable uranium was concentrated, and the remaining depleted uranium was set aside. (The process of generating nuclear power produces enormous amounts of radioactive and hazardous waste. The Hanford Site contains some fifty-four million gallons of it. No containment system is failsafe—the site has a history of leaking tanks that pollute soil and groundwater.)

"My whole life has been touched by this demon, the nuclear dilemma," Doug once told me. Even Port Townsend, which sits so near Bangor and Indian Island, is part of the supply chain of nuclear weapons heading out to sea.

In one of Doug's wilder poems, he calls our planet "our Rainbow-blessed living Earth, Little Blue Top, spinning in space." He believes the Christian ethos that we're all brothers and sisters, one giant family sharing one giant home. We share air, water, wind, and soil. We also share waste, pollution, deforestation, desertification, toxification, melting ice, and rising oceans.

In Doug's eyes, we're a nuclear family. Our lives are fused. For him, the sheer destructive magnitude of nuclear weapons brings home our mutual responsibility to one another and to the planet. How are we accountable as members of this family? As fathers and mothers and children? How can we show up for one another and intentionally share a world, even when we may never meet or comprehend each other's realities? What does group living mean on a global scale?

Doug's protest stemmed from deep roots and was also deeply Doug, with an idiosyncratic wildness that couldn't easily be commodified. The form of the protest—the bizarre blood sculpture, the poems—was itself a protest against passivity, lack of imagination, and normalcy. I realized the primary audience wasn't the military or the sweating, stressed-out guards. It was us, the people standing around him. We were the ones being transformed. I'd felt uncomfortable, but that was the point: to face my unease, to begin to acclimate to discomfort so I could show up when called. We have enormous power over other people, to sway and be swayed, to love and be loved. This protest wasn't futile, not on a human scale.

I t took ten minutes for the county sheriffs to arrive. There were two cars. The men who exited were both young muscular white men with buzz cuts who moved stiffly.

Doug scanned our group and asked a question with his eyes—*Do we want to stay and get arrested or was this enough for today?* He registered our expressions and nodded.

"We're leaving now," he told the officers.

"Thank you," they replied. They sallied to their cars and drove to block the road in both directions so we could cross safely to the park.

"These men think they work for the US military," my mom said, smirking, as we walked back. "But they work for the people who manufacture weapons."

When we returned to the picnic shelter, the people who'd stayed greeted us warmly. We cleaned up the park, removed all the stakes and straps, and left not a trace, not even a strand of PELIGRO tape. The only remnant of our time was a small patch of discolored grass where I'd tried to set up the blood fountain. I hugged my aunt, uncle, and cousin. Then my parents and I got in my car and drove the four hours back to Portland.

Sakiko's *Hiyashi Chūka* (Cold Sesame Noodles) with Jammy Eggs, Peas, and Pickled Radish

Recipe by Sakiko Setaka-Domreis and Lola Milholland

MAKES 3 SERVINGS

The dish I brought to Doug's protest was a sesame noodle salad based on a recipe my friend Sakiko shared with me when I first started Umi Organic. It was a hit with the protestors, little cousins, and bystanders alike. This is a Japanese summertime classic: chilled ramen noodles tossed in a miso-and-tahini-rich dressing with colorful toppings. I love the way the springy noodles contrast with the crunchy vegetables.

In Japan, the classic toppings are egg omelet cut into "golden threads," julienned cucumber and carrot, tomato wedges, and poached shrimp, ham, or cold shredded chicken. I'm constantly changing up what I include. Below are suggestions for a late-spring version. The jammy eggs and pickled radishes should be made at least an hour and up to a full day before you plan to eat. The dressing can also be made in advance. Feel free to play with other toppings, aiming for several colors and textures.

This one's a crowd-pleaser! When adults and kids are eating the same meal, I like to serve everything separately, including the sauce. Every topping gets its own bowl, all in a line. Then I let people build their own noodle bowls exactly as they like them.

MISO SESAME SAUCE

1½ tablespoons toasted tahini or toasted and ground sesame seeds

2 tablespoons toasted sesame oil

1½ tablespoons miso

1 tablespoon soy sauce or tamari

1 tablespoon rice vinegar

1 tablespoon sugar or honey

1-inch knob fresh ginger, peeled and minced

2 cloves garlic, minced

2 to 3 tablespoons water

NOODLES

12 ounces fresh ramen noodles

½ tablespoon neutral oil (like sunflower)

TOPPINGS

3 jammy eggs (see recipe below) or soft-boiled eggs

Pickled radish* or thinly sliced red radishes

Handful of fresh snap peas, strings removed, sliced

2 stalks green onion, thinly sliced

2 tablespoons toasted sesame seeds or *gomashio*

Chili oil to taste

In a medium bowl, whisk together miso sesame sauce: toasted tahini, toasted sesame oil, miso, soy sauce or tamari, vinegar, sugar, ginger, and garlic. Whisk in water a little at a time until the sauce reaches a smooth, pourable consistency. Set aside. Dressing will keep in the refrigerator for up to one week.

Bring a large pot of water to a rapid boil. Gently pull apart and fluff the noodles. Add noodles to water and boil according to package instructions, stirring often. Drain the noodles, rinse them under cold water until cool, and shake out excess water. In a medium bowl, toss noodles with neutral oil until well coated. Add sauce and toss until well combined. Slice eggs in half. Divide noodles between three bowls and top each with an egg, radish or radish pickles, snap peas, green onions, and toasted sesame seeds or *gomashio*. Offer chili oil on the side.

> *For this dish, I like to follow Junko's recipe on page 40, using one bunch of red radishes sliced into thin coins instead of daikon and carrot matchsticks. The red of the radish skin will turn the entire pickle a gorgeous hot pink if left to sit for a few hours.

Lola's Jammy Eggs

Recipe by Lola Milholland

MAKES 3 EGGS

This is the very simplest version of a soy-marinated egg, with the salt of the soy sauce transforming the yolk into a caramel consistency. For fun, the first time you make these, cut an egg in half each day and watch this alchemy transpire. You can add extra layers of flavor if you simmer the water and soy sauce with aromatics like ginger and green onion or add a little sugar or mirin. Play around, keeping the ratio of water to soy sauce the same. If you do simmer your marinade with aromatics, chill it completely before pouring over the eggs.

3 eggs

¼ cup soy sauce or tamari

1 cup water

Bring a small pot of water to a rapid boil. Using a spoon or ladle, place eggs in the boiling water and set a timer for 7 minutes. Prepare an ice bath. Once the timer sounds, scoop out the eggs and set them in the ice bath, cracking the shells as you go to make peeling easier. Make sure the eggs are submerged, and let them chill for at least 30 minutes.

Combine soy sauce or tamari and water in a pint jar. Peel eggs and rinse them briefly in water to remove any pieces of clinging shell. Set the peeled eggs in the soy-and-water marinade. Cover and put in the refrigerator. Let marinate at least 12 hours and up to 4 days.

TRIPPING

Amy calls it Power Hunting. We're driving toward a lake on the south side of Mount Hood, cruising slowly and peering into the forest, when suddenly she hits the brakes, jumps out of the car, and runs up the hillside. I see her bright-orange T-shirt puffing out from under her coat like a tutu as she takes rapid little steps through the trees. It's a gray, chilly, and damp November day, but no matter how cold, Amy is usually in shorts and cushioned running shoes. I follow her up the hillside, where she calls out, "Not skunked!"—meaning, "I found one!"

"See anything?" she asks as I get closer, her eyes gleaming. It's a test. There is a matsutake in sight. With so many steps taken, can I make the last one?

Power Hunting means hunting by car, going where you know the matsutake are and seeing if they're peeking out. Most of the time, though, Amy and I hunt for mushrooms the normal way, on foot, stalking through the woods with a basket or a bag. Amy Peterson is in her late sixties, around four feet ten inches tall, with transition-lens glasses and an external hearing

implant behind one ear. "One ear has the best hearing the doctor ever tested," she tells me, "and the other is useless." Raised
in Boring, Oregon, the grandchild of Japanese immigrants, Amy
spent many of her childhood weekends on Mount Hood, hunting matsutake and bracken fern. She tells me of years her family would gather rice sacks full of the mushrooms, which they
canned for the winter.

Around twelve years ago, my friend Raf's mom, Valerie—
knowing I'm gaga for mushroom hunting—invited me to join the
annual matsutake hunt that Amy and her cousins lead each year
for *nikkei*, descendants of Japanese immigrants. It felt like being
invited inside the Magic Castle. Our group consisted mostly of
older Japanese Americans, though non-*nikkei* friends and family
were invited to tag along.

Matsutake, or "matsis," as Amy calls them, are prized in
Japan, where they fetch handsome prices, for their complex
aroma. I've heard people describe this scent in many ways: cinnamon, Red Hots, old socks, ripe cheese, earth, and spice. (*Just*
"spice," like in *Dune*.) For me, the experience of smelling a
matsutake is like being attracted to someone else's body aroma,
my adrenal system responding independently of my mind.

In Anna Tsing's book *The Mushroom at the End of the World*, she
describes how the logging of cedar and cypress forests around
Kyoto to build temples left behind denuded, sunny hillsides,
which favor pine trees—and therefore their symbiotic partners,
matsutake (in Japanese, *matsu* is "pine" and *take* is "mushroom").
Their aroma reminded Kyoto citizens of the grander forests that
once stood there, a memory that Tsing argues is collective rather
than personal. For contemporary Japanese, matsutake smell of a
natural world they've largely cemented over. Since they lack an

adequate domestic supply to feed their appetite, they've built informal economic supply chains to bring them matsutake from all over the globe.

For the first Japanese immigrants to Oregon, the matsutake they found in the forests where they worked as loggers smelled of a country and culture they longed for. In 1942, a few months after the bombing of Pearl Harbor, in a moment of irrational paranoia and racism, President Franklin D. Roosevelt hastily signed Executive Order 9066, sending around 112,000 US citizens of Japanese ancestry in the West to concentration camps in remote, often desert locales. The War Relocation Authority assigned around thirty-three thousand of these people to seasonal or annual farm labor.

Many Japanese Americans lost their homes, farms, and businesses. Amy's dad's family went to the farm-labor camps in Nyssa, Oregon, to grow sugar beets, which became critical to the war effort; they were made into alcohol, which was then used to create synthetic rubber and munitions. (In 1943, newspapers reported that "every time a 16-inch gun is fired, a fifth of an acre of sugar goes up in smoke.") Her mom's family went to Tule Lake in Northern California, where her brother-in-law and cousins helped build the barracks that would later house a group known as the No-No Boys—Japanese American men who answered "no" to two questions on a government-loyalty test administered to all detainees in 1943. Her mom, uncles, and grandfather were then moved to Heart Mountain, Wyoming. Amy's parents married after the war, and she was born in 1954.

Living in the aftermath of internment, judged guilty without trial and afterward left with the burden of proving their loyalty to the United States, Japanese Americans have been adept at creating new lives and finding steady, well-paying jobs. But there's a divide between public and private life for many Japanese Americans. In public, especially immediately after the war, their Japaneseness could be a liability, so it was often masked. In private spaces, however, they celebrated their heritage and continued to evolve it. Matsutake culture exists in this sphere—as an intimate activity that brings Japanese Americans together, ignites memories, and reaffirms their relationships with the land.

For Amy, hunting matsutake is less about a connection to Japan, a place she first visited in 2018. Instead, the hunt connects her to Oregon. Every fall she visits what she calls "my mom's tree," an old pine where her mother always found "dinner-plate-sized matsis." She crawls over the craters and underbrush, knowing which trees have been productive in the past. She and her family complete this fall ritual by making matsutake rice and sukiyaki, a delicious and decadent hot pot with thinly sliced marbled beef and loads of matsutake, both perfect ways to capture and convey the mushroom's potent aroma.

I was starting to see group living outside the home enacted within these seasonal rituals, which are connected to place and anchored in the pleasures of community. I'd long been uneasy with the kind of group-making formed around flags and declarative exclusivity. James Baldwin's words from *The Fire Next Time* rang true: "People always seem to band together in accordance to a principle that has nothing to do with love, a principle that releases them from personal responsibility." My Japanese American friends were showing me a different way of building bonds. Admittedly, what brought them together was a shared cultural heritage. At the same time, they were eager to share their love of food and traditions with new people. They renewed their relationships to one another and to their history and the natural world by foraging, clamming, farming, gardening, cooking, and eating together.

Their practices required deep noticing, and because those practices were honed across generations, they were accompanied by all kinds of sweet details. A friend I met on a hunt carried her mother's old mushrooming stick. It had a bit of tinfoil wrapped around the end so that if you set it on the forest floor, the glint would help you find it again. Amy and her friend Connie always shared their matsutake harvests with people too old to join the hunt and relatives who'd moved away. Sharing and remembering were part of the pleasure. When the coronavirus narrowed our social lives, they continued to check in on elders and bring them food, because these acts of care were integral to their routines. These women built a web around the people in their greater community. You didn't have to be Japanese American to enjoy stalking the woods with them. Each fall, these hunts gave me a new feeling of home.

Matsutake still tease me with coy distance and appeal. After years of Amy's mentorship, I'm getting better at finding matsutake, but the hunt can be like the cruelest game of *Where's Waldo?* Often the mushrooms are underground and out of sight. The first clue they offer to hunters is a little bump as they begin to surface. I, however, can't differentiate the tufts of dirt and needles the mushrooms raise from other disturbances in the duff. I find myself poking into empty holes like a daft squirrel who's lost her acorns.

The second clue, for the very adept, is the aroma. I can't smell matsutakes when they're belowground, although I once witnessed a hundred-year-old Japanese American man take a deep sniff, poke a stick into the ground, and emerge with a mushroom almost as long as his forearm. So it can be done. From a distance, I'm sometimes duped by a fatal mushroom charmingly nicknamed the "Angel of Death," which is also a dirty white. Luckily, up close it looks and smells like chalk.

But despite my middling success, I love the hunt, the company, and the familiar cycle, so I eagerly follow Amy into the forest. Starting in midsummer, when experienced hunters begin their pursuit, Amy heads to nearby volcanoes to begin gathering and freezing matsutake for a sukiyaki-dinner fundraiser for the Oregon Buddhist Temple and matsutake rice for New Years' boxes. She also scouts spots for the fall guided trip. I sometimes join her in these early season hunts.

The mushroom world is famous for its reclusive community of survivalists, type A taxonomists, biologists, ecologists, spiritualists, homesick immigrants and their children, hippies and their children, and chefs. Like the scent of matsutake, the musky fragrance emanating from this hodgepodge group attracts me. Finding mushroom people has become its own kind of hunt. Once, looking for matsutake in the woods, I happened upon an old man with a cherubic face, wispy white hair, wire-frame glasses, and smiling eyes gathering white chanterelles and truffles. He introduced himself as Dan Wheeler, president of the Oregon Mycological Society in 1992 and 1993 and longtime president of the Portland chapter of the North American Truffling Society.

I found no matsutake on that hunt, but as he walked me out of the forest to our cars, he told me about his early work to promote and distribute the Oregon white truffle. Wheeler, who had a truffle named for him, *Tuber wheeleri*, claimed to have inoculated the first native truffles in a Douglas fir stand. At that moment, I wondered if I liked finding mushroom people at least as much as mushrooms.

Many devoted mushroom foragers, including commercial pickers, crave invisibility and choose to exist primarily in the alternate reality of the forest. Amy introduced me to Matsiman, who lives off the grid somewhere in southern Oregon and researches the connections between matsutake and precipitation. As a kid, I met Hmong and Lao commercial pickers in central and eastern Oregon forests, whose camps approximate their former lifestyles in Southeast Asia. Some foragers, like Amy and me, only crave regular visits to the forest, which provide an escape from life in the city.

Loving and delighting in these oddballs helps me continually recalibrate my sense of self-worth. Watching Amy hustle up and down hillsides, feeling waves of affection for her, I find a peaceful glee that visits me most often when I'm in the forest. Amy moves with agility and focus, but her manner is giddy and child-like, full of energetic curiosity. She usually puts her long silvery hair up in a loose bun held aloft with a pen, but while she's tracking through the forest, the pen always seems to slip out and the bun slowly unravels without her realizing. When I notice Amy's hair coming undone, she reminds me of myself, even though she's thirty years older, Japanese American, a longtime Girl Scout leader, a Buddhist, a Disney fan, a teetotaler, and a mother of two: nothing like me, really, at all. But she has a sparky horse-power, like a little truck—*vroom, vroom, let's go, let's go*—a goofy carelessness with her appearance, and an eagerness to please and involve other people. I feel completely at ease in her presence, and more at ease with myself.

For years, Amy wore a neon-orange Reese's Peanut Butter Cup T-shirt on every hunt. She got it for free at her security job at Costco and used it like a hunter's vest, to signal her movements among the trees. Lately, in a cheeky turn, she's started wearing a psychedelic tie-dye T-shirt of an orange mushroom radiating green, blue, and purple flames that you'd more likely expect to see on a Phish fan than on a Costco security guard who doesn't drink or do drugs. But its brightness has the same lighthouse effect, and I follow her beam wherever she tracks. Even though we're foraging matsutake, half the hunt is complete for me: I've already found the mushroom person I was looking for.

In my mind, mushrooms occupy the same liminal territory as the narwhal—a realm where fantasy and reality overlap, where the music of childhood keeps playing unexpectedly into adulthood. What we call a mushroom is the fruit of a much larger organism called mycelium, a network of spiderweb-like threads that spread underground. Mycelium is the vegetative portion of the fungus: think of the roots, branches, and leaves of an apple tree. How large are mycelia? Dan Luoma, a professor at Oregon State University, describes walking through the forest as walking on the backs of whales. But it's the mushrooms, which pop up seasonally, that facilitate reproduction, by spreading microscopic single-cell units called *spores*. One mushroom will drop as many as sixteen billion spores during its lifetime, and these spores are easily picked up by the wind.

"Every breath that we take—from first gasp to last breath—we're inhaling fungal spores," Nicholas Money, author of *Mushrooms*, said in a radio interview. "They're always available;

they're always in the air; and they're always trying to exploit the opportunities to grow and reproduce."

The mushrooms I hunt and eat fall into a category called *mycorrhiza*. These mushrooms, including matsutake, chanterelles, morels, and porcinis, exist in symbiotic interdependence with the roots of trees. Mycelium nourishes itself by absorbing nutrients from organic material. It secretes enzymes that break down its food into more easily digestible units (like our saliva does when we chew). By decomposing whatever it feasts on and by increasing the surface area of the roots, mycelium makes it easier for those roots to uptake gas, water, and nutrients like nitrogen and phosphorus. The mycelium acts as an extension of the plant's digestive system. The trees, in turn, give it carbon, obtained through photosynthesis. It's a mutually beneficial relationship. Nutrients can move between plants through fungal networks, and research shows that, along with nutrients, mycelia transmit signals from the largest, oldest "mother trees" to younger ones to maintain the overall health of the stand.

The forest is acting like one large organism, connected through mycelial networks, concerned for its overall health rather than individual survival—a kind of selflessness that doesn't correspond neatly to our understanding of the survival of the fittest. Paul Stamets, a mushroom guru with a cultlike following warranted by his expansive research on mushrooms, including their power to remediate polluted land, calls mycelium "nature's internet." He estimates that 90 percent of plant life depends on mycorrhizae.

Mycorrhizal mushrooms remind me that all life is interdependent. Our borders are porous. What's happening on a small scale with a mushroom (giving and receiving life from trees and other plants) is true of all life on earth. Our health and every (spore-filled) breath we take relies on the actions of plants, animals, and fungi all around us. Mushrooms offer a different vision of survival—not conquering or dominating but collaborating for mutual benefit.

We often use the violent language of human power dynamics as metaphors to talk about plants and animals, and vice versa: parasitic plants and parasitic boyfriends; fungi that colonize and colonizers who rape the land. There are kings of the jungle and financial predators. Even the term *nuclear family* has fallen into this biological blurring for me, thanks to my uncle Doug.

In a gentler turn of that formula, my favorite metaphor for group living, when it works, is a mycorrhizal network. We are all giving and receiving, and through those interactions, we become like one organism. This is true for any group that values its holistic health—the microcosm underground as the macrocosm of our lives.

In my experience, the best way to understand and appreciate the role mushrooms play in the natural world is by ingesting psychoactive mushrooms. They can have a powerful effect on the ego, erasing feelings of isolation and even selfhood. The hard lines between your corporeal body and the universe dissolve. You become open to the magic of nature and your intrinsic place within it. The mushrooms give you a taste of what it's like to be a mushroom—to be in symbiotic interdependence with living things all around you. The experience can also be other things. It's not predictable.

My first experience with psychedelic mushrooms was at age twenty, with my mom at the Oregon Country Fair, hippie mecca. I ate the mushrooms around midnight, and it seemed as though

my mom instantly vanished. Unsure what to do, I walked without purpose through crowds of strangers whose faces I couldn't
make out to the outskirts of the fair, where an old man was playing acoustic blues guitar to a small crowd of stoned, appreciative
young people splayed on blankets. I sat down next to him and
before long found myself singing, or thrumming, bass lines to
accompany his guitar, oblivious to the fact that this wasn't something I'd ever seen anyone else do or had attempted myself.
"Bump, bump, bump, bump, buh-buh-duh-buh-buh-bump,
bump," I sang as loudly as an upright bass would play it. For at
least an hour I kept this up. As the night deepened to two or
three o'clock, the guitarist finally decided to quit. He leaned
toward me and said, in a resonant Sam Elliott voice, "It was nice
playing with you, little lady."

"It was nice playing with you," I answered sincerely.

I walked back to our tent, feeling accomplished, and found
my mom huddled in her sleeping bag, still high and awake. I told
her about my night. I sang her a bass line. After a long pause, she
burst into hysterical laughter. I began laughing, too, unable to
stop until my stomach hurt from being clenched. I couldn't
breathe. We both gasped for air, and then my mom started laughing again, and I followed. We continued like this until suddenly,
unexpectedly, I was asleep. The next day, sober and completely
drained of all my endorphins, I lay on a picnic table, staring up
into the Douglas fir canopy and feeling like human garbage.

I look back on that trip and a few worse ones with amusement,
but they weren't the ideal way to experience mushrooms. This
isn't an invitation to be casual with something that isn't casual.
After my first few trials, it took me many years to try again,

concerned that every trip would lead me back "under the blan-ket," as I call it, from a time when I literally got stuck under a blanket. But that's not what's happened. I've learned to set the stage and make sure that before I start, I feel safe.

A few years ago, Corey and I traveled to the southern Oregon coast, to a state park on the Chetco River among a grove of Oregon myrtlewood trees some two hundred–plus years old. A short hike from the park is the world's northernmost grove of naturally occurring redwoods. We walked through the myrtle-woods to the redwood grove, up and around the towering trees, among native rhododendrons, lady ferns, deer ferns, and huckleberries.

On our walk back to our cabin on the river, I ingested psilo-cybin mushrooms. It was midday. I sat on the pebbly beach, watching the water stream past. I became aware of how loud the river was and lost myself in its roar. I watched sunlight glinting off the ripples like the scales of a fish and felt the sun warming my skin. I watched several cinnabar salamanders pedaling among the rocks. I enjoyed the clean eucalyptus smell of the myrtlewoods.

Tripping on mushrooms, people think thoughts that can sound cliché when they've come down but which are in fact profound—just boringly familiar. The words lose their meaning on the side of a Dr. Bronner's container ("we are all one or none"), on one of my uncle Doug's T-shirts ("love is the answer"), on the bumper sticker of a car ("co-exist"). But when you truly inte-grate those words, it's something else!

Archeologist John M. Allegro wrote a book called *The Sacred Mushroom and the Cross* in which he proposed that the New Testament was written as a way for fertility cults to pass down information about using magic mushrooms to commune with

God. I first found out about it from a video where an interviewer says to Allegro, "I'm puzzled. Are you really seriously suggesting that Jesus Christ was a mushroom?" "Put pretty blankly," Allegro responds, "yes." Allegro, who was famous for his work on the Dead Sea Scrolls, was discredited and humiliated for his blasphemy, but I love its goofiness. I also think it contains a kernel of ecstatic truth, which is that mushrooms help us commune with nature as divine.

On the riverbank in Oregon, I remembered how to sit in awe and why it's important to slow down and observe the natural world. In day-to-day life, most of our senses aren't fully engaged, which protects us from the onslaught of experience; mushrooms swing the doors of perception and empathy wide open. *I'm a swirling bit of matter in an infinite universe*, I thought. *My body and spirit are porous to all living and nonliving things. I'm a process of growth and decay, living and dying every second, a corpse and a newborn, a source of life and a parasite. I am impossibly small, and I am part of everything.* And then I fell asleep.

Earlier that year, on a drive from Boise to Portland, my dad insisted we visit the largest known living organism in the world. In the Malheur National Forest on the eastern edge of Oregon, a network of mycelium stretches underground for 3.4 square miles, an area as big as 1,665 football fields. Somewhere between 2,400 and 8,650 years old, this mycelial behemoth, jokingly called the "humongous fungus," or *Armillaria ostoyae*, is something of a parasitic monster, killing the conifers in its wake. (Not all mushrooms are mycorrhizal.) The mushrooms that sprout by the thousands are known as honey mushrooms because of their sweet flavor. We think of mushrooms as a product of wet forests dripping in moss, but much of the hunting that goes on, especially for commercial matsutake, is in the drier forests of central and eastern Oregon. In terms of mushrooms, the entire state of Oregon is fecund.

There are no road signs or landmarks to point you to the enormous patch of land sitting atop this mycelium, so we drove for miles, to where my dad imagined it might be. We parked, stomped our feet on the ground, walked around a burbling stream to a spring, and then got back in the car and drove to the nearest town, Prairie City, for dinner. That night we camped in the Strawberry Mountain Wilderness. As the sun set, we hiked up to alpine Strawberry Lake in time to see the last rays hitting the namesake strawberry-colored, iron-rich gabbro rocks towering above us. My mom says she fell in love with my dad because he opened the desert to her.

"Your mom and I knew we wanted to have a little girl," he told me, while we looked up at the mountains and shared a beer. "We came out here, took mushrooms, and conceived you."

Amy's Matsutake Rice and *Onigiri* (Rice Balls)

Inspired by Amy Peterson, recipe by Lola Milholland

MAKES 4 SERVINGS, OR 8 TO 10 RICE BALLS

Matsutake are best cooked in ways that amplify and encapsulate their powerful aroma—they're not a mushroom you should ever sauté in oil. Steaming rice with matsutake allows a handful of mushrooms to infuse an entire pot of rice. Amy doesn't make small quantities of matsutake rice—she's always making it to share—so I've shrunk and adapted her recipe. My favorite way to eat matsutake rice is as an *onigiri* with the Korean-style sea-weed called *gim gui*, which is fried in toasted sesame oil. Japanese nori also works great.

Rice balls are a perfect food for taking on a mushroom hunt. If you can't get your hands on matsutake, use a combination of maitake and shiitake. I love matsutake rice with a side of miso soup and something crunchy, like a pickle or a salad. You can make this in a rice cooker or on your stovetop—I've included instructions for both. For the stovetop, be sure to use an enamel or cast-iron pot with a heavy bottom and a tight-fitting lid.

2 cups Japanese short-grain rice

6 ounces matsutake (or substitute a combination of maitake and shiitake)

¼ cup soy sauce or tamari

1 tablespoon mirin

½ teaspoon salt

OPTIONAL

½ pound boneless, skinless chicken thighs, cut into small bite-size pieces

2-by-3-inch piece kombu seaweed

Rinse the rice in several changes of cold water until the water almost runs clear. In the bowl of your rice cooker or pot, add the rice and cover with water by an inch or so. Set aside. After 30 minutes, drain the rice in a strainer and set the strainer aside for 15 to 30 minutes to air-dry. This helps the rice cook perfectly.

Matsutake are often sandy. Clean them using a small brush or by swishing them aggressively in water. Slice the mushrooms thinly.

Combine 2 cups of water with the soy sauce or tamari and mirin. Place the rice, water, soy sauce or tamari, and mirin in the bowl of your rice cooker or pot. Place the mushrooms on top of the rice. Sprinkle the salt over the mushrooms. Add optional chicken, if using, on top of the mushrooms. Set optional kombu on top of the mushrooms or chicken. Do not stir anything into the rice—let everything sit on top.

If using a rice cooker, close the lid and set to cook, following the instructions of your device. For the stovetop, place your pot over high heat and bring the water to a boil. As soon as bubbles are visible, immediately turn the heat to low, cover with a lid, and cook for 25 minutes or until all the water is absorbed. Turn off the heat.

After the rice cooker clicks to "warm" or you turn off the heat, let the rice stand, covered, for 10 to 15 minutes. Discard the kombu. Using a rice paddle or spatula, gently fold the mushrooms and chicken into the rice, bringing the bottom to the top and vice versa. Let stand, covered, for another 5 minutes. You can eat the rice as is or make yourself rice balls following the instructions below.

Onigiri

Once your rice has cooled just enough to handle (it should still be hot), fill a bowl with ice water. Dip your hands in the water and clap once to remove any excess. Grab a handful of rice a little smaller than a baseball. Form a loose ball with the rice, just compact enough to hold its shape. You can stop right here—you have a nice round rice ball! If you want to make a traditional triangular shape, like the roof of a wooden block set, squeeze gently from the bottom with one hand while shaping the top into a roof with the other. Rotate the triangle in your hands three times, squeezing, so every side is uniform.

To make more, dip your hands in the cold water and clap each time before forming a rice ball. Wrap each in plastic wrap or place inside a container with a lid. Rice balls taste best when kept outside of the fridge and eaten within one day, but you can store them in the fridge for up to a week or in the freezer for several months. Just be sure to reheat fully before eating. Only when you're ready to eat, pull out the *gim gui* (Korean-style seaweed). Cut each sheet of seaweed in half and wrap one half around an onigiri. Eat before the seaweed goes limp!

COMPOST

I n May 2022, as Mother's Day approached, I drove to the Jefferson County Fairgrounds, where Doug and Nancy's bingo parlor once stood. I arrived at dusk. The darkness was ushering in cold sea-salt air. There were a couple hundred cars in the parking lot, and nearby I saw a few women around my age sitting on the rear bumper of a Volvo. One was dressed in a chocolate-brown turtleneck and flared orange linen pants. She was passing a joint to a woman wearing patchwork jeans, a corduroy jacket, and a floppy suede hat. Walking toward the entrance, I saw a woman in her fifties sashaying in an urban cowgirl outfit—all black, with tassels. *Port Townsend is lost in another era*, I thought, shaking my head. And then it dawned on me: *This must be a costume party, and I'm the one who's out of place.*

I'd come to the fairgrounds because my cousin Danny was organizing the Port Townsend Food Co-op's fiftieth anniversary, and he'd invited me. The co-op was founded in 1972. Back then, it was a hole-in-the-wall where Nancy bought brown rice, tamari, and kombu. Now, five decades later, her son was requesting permits, setting up tents, hiring food vendors, organizing volunteers, and throwing a big seventies-themed costume party for a thriving grocery store in the twenty-first century.

Inside the fairgrounds, several hundred people were milling around, eating slices of chocolate cake. It didn't take me long to find Gabe, my cousin Amanda's very tall husband, who was dressed in a wildly colorful paisley shirt. Amanda was in her usual outfit of jeans and a fleece, her curly dark hair in a bob and her bright blue eyes full of affection. She hugged me tightly and scratched my head.

Kids were flying around everywhere, like insects in a wildflower meadow. I spotted Inez and Brighten among them. Danny and his crew had set up a play area with Hula-Hoops, bubble wands, and piles of ribbons attached to plastic sticks. The kids were using these props as swords and wands, bashing them into the ground and parading around like triumphant armies. Broken plastic and shredded ribbons littered the wet grass.

I saw Danny zoom by in the natural way of an event organizer, heading toward someone who had a question before zipping elsewhere. As night fell, Amanda and her family headed home.

"Next up: Uncle Funk and the Dope 6," I heard Danny announce from the stage.

Standing alone, I felt the familiar, itchy discomfort that arrives when I come too close to a certain earnest, hippie-inspired scene. I felt out of place, judgmental, and awed. The hippies who moved to Port Townsend fifty and sixty years ago wanted to build an alternate world, and, in some ways, they succeeded. They dreamed they could mount a resistance to ecological collapse and endless war. Instead, they built an enduring social fabric. Hippie culture can seem superficial, only an aesthetic one can dress up in. Consumer culture has so thoroughly commodified its language, style, and philosophies (many of them originally appropriated from other cultures) that they now represent consumer culture itself, as well as its pacifying feel-good vibes. But here, at the beating heart of hippiedom, there's substance and energy—and long-lasting relationships—beneath the costumes.

I walked around the field, now empty of children, and, by the light of my cell phone, picked up the play props turned garbage. Danny was hustling around, folding up tables and carting off equipment with helpers, as the band played on. When I was done cleaning the kids' area, there was still a lot to do, but I was very cold, so I begged off and drove to Amanda's house. There, I climbed onto the futon in Gabe's office and fell instantly asleep.

When I woke up the next morning, I realized that Inez and Brighten had climbed into bed on either side of me. I didn't have my hearing aids in, so I could barely hear their high, muffled voices. I was half-asleep anyway, so we just snuggled for a while. Then I grabbed my hearing aids—which played their funny little jingle into my ears as they turned on—and mumbled that this was like waking up at a sleepover. Brighten, who was four, told me she'd never been to one.

"My friend came over once, but at bedtime she wanted to go home," she explained, glumly.

"I've been to thousands of sleepovers," Inez, two years older, put in. Brighten curled into a tight ball, wounded.

Thousands? I mused. I felt sorry that I'd brought up this touchy subject.

Adjacent to RoseWind, Amanda and Gabe, with help from Doug—as lead contractor—several friends, and his former Blue

Heron colleagues, had built their home from the ground up. They decided not to pay the nominal dues to become RoseWind associate members, which would grant them access to the common house and garden—Amanda liked having some autonomy, she told me—but she loved raising her kids near the community, where she knew everyone. They valued the trails, the green common spaces, the towering flower bushes, and her parents' presence. Doug and Nancy magnetically drew their kids toward home, even if neither chose to join RoseWind.

Staying at Amanda's house is the most aunt-like experience in my life. I become the third adult of the household, offering help so Amanda and Gabe have a little more time and ease. I do the dishes, make snacks, read books, play with the girls in the yard, literally wipe Brighten's ass after she poops—oh, how quickly I forgot that wiping my butt was a difficult thing to learn and requires some acrobatics. In their house, I get to reexperience something I already know, in a new form—that living with someone creates a different kind of intimacy. I'd never know my little cousins as well if I just saw them on holidays, outside their home.

There was a moment a few years before when I still felt undecided about whether to have kids, and I came to stay with Amanda and Gabe specifically to see how I'd respond to spending time with Inez and Brighten. Would my ovaries start throbbing around these cuties? Or would the opposite happen? Would the intensity of this caretaking and its demands on my time and energy repel me? The result was neither. Instead, I discovered that I liked *this*: being an auntie, being helpful to overworked parents, making inside jokes with my little cousins that only we understand. I like that I have energy to bring to our interactions and that I want to play and play.

I don't have anything quite like this in Portland, in part because our culture has largely reserved this role for blood family. I feel uncomfortable inserting myself as aggressively in my friends' kids' lives. My Portland friends with children say, *Oh yes, come by anytime*, but I don't believe them, or I don't quite know how to start. And yet I miss spending time with kids.

When I came downstairs, Amanda was about to leave for work. She manages the Jefferson County Farmers Market and needed to prepare for the upcoming Saturday. A week before, at my request, she'd emailed an introduction to the founders of the cohousing community across the street from RoseWind, and I had plans to visit them in a few hours.

"There's hot cereal if you want some," she said, hugging me, because she's always hugging me.

"I'm heading over to Kees and Helen's in a bit. I'll try to be back before bedtime," I told her.

T he walk from Amanda's to Kees (pronounced *Case*) and Helen's house took me five minutes. I let myself in a gate with a hand-painted sign that read, "CAUTION BEEHIVES NEARBY!" The house was two stories and cedar shingled, with a forest-green metal roof that fell steeply, creating the illusion of an A-frame. When I knocked on the front door, no one answered, but when I turned around, there was Helen biking toward me in full rain gear, a little mirror sticking out from her helmet to help her see traffic. She had white hair in a ponytail, aquamarine eyes, and a reserved but friendly smile.

As she pulled up and dismounted, Kees appeared in big black rubber boots and a thin down coat, carrying a bucket. He was fit and lanky, with short white hair and a lean, lined face.

"Beneficial nematodes," he was telling me the moment I said hello. "They attack 230 different pests. It's natural pest control! They're carnivorous and burrow deep into the soil to eat pests buried within. I was just distributing them under apple trees near Apiary Hill." He motioned to a small mound behind their home, near several squat, flowering fruit trees.

We conferred about our plan: Kees would give me a brief tour, and then I'd sit and talk with Helen.

"I'm going to make myself a piece of toast. Want one?" he asked before we headed off. I got the feeling that his metabolism demanded constant fuel, even at his age.

As we walked to a small pond where mallards were bathing, Kees told me that he'd worked as a pediatrician for about twenty years in Seattle, and that Helen had written curricula for teachers, worked as a Planned Parenthood educator, and volunteered as a dispute mediator. They'd lived on Capitol Hill and raised two kids. But over time, Kees and Helen needed a change.

"I was worried about the environmental impact on my patients," he continued. "I became more concerned about the health of our planet and how the global climate catastrophe is killing us, as well as all other species." He spoke these grim words in a surprisingly relaxed voice. In 1995, Kees retired from his medical practice. For one year, he and Helen moved to the highlands of Peru, where they volunteered for the Mountain Institute, an environmental and community nonprofit, and wrote, photographed, and illustrated, along with indigenous Quechua speakers, a bilingual field guide to the flowers of the Cordillera Blanca, one of the mountain ranges of the Andes. When they returned to Seattle, they didn't want their old life anymore.

In 1996, they visited RoseWind with friends. The setting and concept enamored them. They immediately bought a four-acre property due north of RoseWind, across the street from Doug and Nancy's house, for $360,000. Several years later, they bought an adjoining three and a half acres.

Kees and Helen became full RoseWind members. For the next six years, they participated in community life, "always with the understanding that as soon as we decided, we would step out," Kees emphasized. They dreamed that someday their own land would become the site of an intentional community, but in the meantime, they wanted to learn about cohousing directly. Kees became the chair of the common-house committee and helped shepherd its creation. Helen served on the facilitation committee. On Christmas Day, 2003, at a shared meal in the newly built common house, Kees and Helen announced their decision to separate from RoseWind. They now had the energy and vision to focus on their own land.

RoseWind gave them a model for what they did and didn't want in their new community. They envisioned four significant points of departure: first, they wanted to adopt a more radical legal structure than a homeowners' association; second, they wanted to live in a multigenerational community, with younger families; third, they wanted to create more affordable housing; and fourth, they wanted environmental commitments from members to give the community a lighter footprint.

They decided to call their new community the Port Townsend EcoVillage. I dislike the prefix *eco-*, which seems so meaninglessly do-gooder-y. The name reminded me of Findhorn, where Doug stayed in Scotland, which bills itself an "ecovillage" as a marketing tool to attract "ecotourists." Kees didn't necessarily disagree. He told me the term "ecovillage" doesn't have an agreed-upon definition. "The language of intentional communities is all so mushy," he said. Coming from me, this would be a jaded criticism, but from him, it simply sounded factual.

A dozen people came to their first meeting in 2004. Kees, Helen, and their friend Laurence, all in their fifties, were the oldest ones in the room. For the following six years, the group met every weekend. Throughout that time, the future members of the ecovillage were trying to determine their ideal legal structure. They explored many options but were most excited about limited-equity housing cooperatives.

In New York City, there are over eleven hundred HDFCs (Housing Development Fund Corporation co-ops). In the seventies and eighties, the city acquired residential buildings abandoned by their landlords, rehabilitated them, and gave tenants the opportunity to become shareholders. No matter the size of the apartment, all shares of the building are equal and all shareholders have equal voting rights. These co-ops benefit from reduced real estate taxes in exchange for maintaining affordable membership, which means that if someone wants to sell their apartment, they have to do so at a price that low-income people can afford, and a portion of the profit must be returned to the co-op for upgrades, maintenance, and other collective needs.

Limited-equity co-ops are a powerful tool to provide affordable housing and create broader ownership opportunities, but the ecovillage's timing was off; the Great Recession hit just as they were ready to invite people to buy in. The banks said no. "People needed traditional forms of funding, even though we don't like that idea," Kees told me. "But that's part of reality."

And so they ended up with the same legal structure as RoseWind: a homeowners' association. There were now twelve private lots in the Port Townsend EcoVillage. Each was four thousand square feet. Ownership came with one-twelfth of the common areas. To the first goal, then—a more radical legal structure—they failed.

To the second goal—creating a multigenerational community— they largely succeeded. The youngest member of the community was a month old; five families had kids; three had grandkids who visited frequently. One key was marketing. They went out and solicited families. But the second was turning one large building into two rented duplex apartments. The lower upfront cost of rent made them more accessible. The homeowners' association owned the apartments, and the profits went to cover collective expenses, like insurance and taxes. Eventually, they built a second duplex to encourage more young families to join the community.

We were walking through the center of their community, past houses in the same muted colors I recognized from RoseWind. There were bountiful community gardens in all the open spaces. The ecovillage was one Port Townsend city block wide by about three or four blocks long, with no roads within its bounds—a long rectangle that began under open sky and moved into ever-green forest at its western edge. The houses were much denser than at RoseWind, without the sweeping green spaces.

We passed three tiny houses, a recent addition. Intentional-community-curious people often inquire about the ecovillage, so the residents decided to create a space specifically for tiny homes, where someone could build and own one and join the community at a lower cost. The housing association leased them the land, bridging ownership and rental.

The common house was still being built, and Kees led me into the construction site. The building contained two washers and two dryers. (Neither are allowed in private homes.) The ecovillage also split only two city garbage cans, and Kees and

Helen lent their car to a neighbor who had a young child. The next room we entered was a workshop, filled with a table saw and all kinds of tools. Kees told me that Doug always dreamed RoseWind would include a shop, but the members didn't want to fund it. Seeing this community up close, I wondered how many of Doug's dreams had blossomed in his friend Kees's head.

Kees and I walked back to his home, past Apiary Hill. At their front door, I took off my shoes, and Helen offered me some slippers from an impressive collection. The coronavirus was still a threat, so we put on masks. Kees offered me more toast as he made himself a second piece, slathered in honey, and dipped his mask down to take bites. He told me that Doug had helped them build this home, with foot-thick walls to lessen heating costs. In fact, Doug had helped with a lot of the construction onsite. Kees finished his toast and left, and Helen and I sat down to mugs of tea.

Where Kees was matter-of-fact but gentle, with a hopefulness that sweetened every statement, Helen headed into the hard stuff faster, with less instinct to show the bright side. She seemed more private than Kees, but I found her easier to relate to.

I asked her about the power dynamics in the early years, when they owned all the land but were committed to group decision-making. In meetings, everyone went around and around, trying to come to a consensus about legal structure.

"Did you tire of that?" I asked, and Helen answered "Yes!" before I finished the question.

After all those meetings, Kees and Helen made an executive decision to move forward as a homeowners' association

and asked who'd join them. They'd promised a consensus process and then abandoned it, but this act of hypocrisy broke the
gridlock. Everyone remained, and the power dynamic shifted.

After having sold most of their land to shareholders, Kees and
Helen were no longer in a position of primacy. The ecovillage
returned to a consensus system, but they'd recently switched to
a model called sociocracy, where they organized themselves into
committees, or "circles." Each circle sent two people into a "hub"
for decision-making.

"The idea is that each circle makes decisions for their area.
It's supposed to be more efficient." I could hear a drip of doubt
in Helen's voice, and I asked how it was going. "It doesn't always
work that well, but we're trying. We have a lot of meetings, and
that's the challenge."

This system was intended to distribute power, but when I
asked about her commitments, Helen told me, "I'm part of the
people's circle, conflict group, retreat planners, the hub, and the
board. In sociocracy, you're supposed to limit your roles. But if
you don't have a lot of people who can spend the time, then you
end up with a concentration of power anyway. And yet we're trying to get input from everyone. It's a balancing act."

People who don't have kids or work around the clock have
more time to meet. People who aren't exasperated by endless
meetings have more energy to do it. I suddenly understood that
it's more than just the cost of RoseWind that might be unappealing to younger people: these communities require a lot of time
and patience.

"Conflict is hard," Helen continued. "Sometimes we have
dealt with conflict better than at others. We were trying to have
the renters and owners be on equal footing. But the renters aren't
owners."

At first, the relationship between owners and renters was informal—the idea was "we're all in it, we're all equals," Helen said. But the owners were the landlords, and decision-making became increasingly uncomfortable. "Now there's a rental-management circle, so renters know where to turn" with issues, she continued. This replaced nice feelings with real structure, which acknowledges who holds what powers and who doesn't.

Limited-equity co-ops solve for the uneven power dynamic between owners and renters, but they are rare, due partly to banks' unwillingness to participate. I thought of my own home, where we'd remained in the soft darkness of nice feelings until the coronavirus came to force us into the light, and how, even now, I was uncertain how to navigate our different levels of power.

I asked Helen why she liked living in the ecovillage.

"I enjoy being with people," she replied. "I can always find someone to talk to. Collectively, we take care of each other."

She started telling me about a family that had recently moved in: Ocean, Hillary, and their two kids. "They're just wonderful," she said excitedly. I could feel the energy their presence was giving her, and I suspected it went both ways. Like RoseWind, I realized, this place would provide life for the next generation, a vision to spark revision.

Walking back to Amanda's, I began thinking about my own disinclination toward communal living on this scale. Intentional communities don't inherently create the conditions for what I love about group living—camaraderie, intimacy, synchrony. I'm drawn to something less structured than an intentional community but less atomized than the nuclear family, some squishier in-between place. I'm unwilling to participate in the amount of process these communities demand. In fact, I find it almost comical: Helen was part of *how* many circles that met *how* many times a month? But that level of commitment also moves me.

I thought about the making of decisions outside of autocratic systems. It's not easy. It's lovely that my roommates and I mostly get along, having initially chosen one another for some whiff of compatibility. *How nice*, I thought, *and fleeting, and uncommon.* There are so many challenges we haven't faced, including how to ask someone to leave or how to vet someone new. In numerous ways, as a group, we're still inexperienced.

Whenever I talk about group living, people point to the worst manifestations—and there are plenty—to pan the entire enterprise, but I believe we need something different than the status quo. That these experiments often end up leading back to oppressive forms of social control seems more about the difficulty of humans getting along, overcoming larger cultural forces, and moving in sync than about something inherently broken in the impulse to try.

I thought about Adrian Shirk's book *Heaven Is a Place on Earth*. She asserts that utopian experiments are never all that far from their opposite and that they often become them when power becomes too concentrated. "Ephemerality is a virtue," she writes. Failure and transitoriness should be endemic to the utopian attempt. Despite our cultural ideas about finding the *right*, lasting models, disagreement and transience might be essential components of a healthy community. Says Shirk, "All movements that are truly pure of heart will die quickly and return to the compost heap and show up later in the soil of society in some other form."

The ecovillage is an experiment in how people can live together, and it primes its residents for civic engagement. You'd think that attending all those meetings for all those years wouldn't leave time for anything else, but actually, since retiring and moving to Port Townsend, Kees and Helen have kept busy: Kees has served terms as president of the Jefferson Land Trust, chair of the local Climate Action Committee, on city council, as Port Townsend's mayor, and, currently, as an elected commissioner of the Jefferson County Public Hospital District No. 2, advocating for universal health care. Helen has volunteered with the nonprofit Northwest Earth Institute and the Quimper Unitarian Universalist Fellowship, and she has co-led wilderness retreats.

Making positive strides on all the challenges we face, from climate change to structural racism to labor and environmental exploitation, requires extraordinary levels of cooperation. It's very hard, and the mainstream culture is working against us. We'll always fail on some level, but the effort is never futile. There's no perfect structure. We need a multiplicity of ongoing experiments at every scale and people who are willing to try and fail and try again, to keep looking backward and forward, to never throw anything away and never accept anything as it is, to put in the time. We need junkyard lovers, repairmen, inventors, historians, fantasists.

Kees, Helen, Doug, and Nancy remind me of the power generated from a sense of purpose. These four chose home lives that exceed their borders, where they interrogate their values, hone their diplomatic skills, and build energy to funnel into the greater world. Residents of their communities actively practice communication, sharing, and conflict resolution and explore different models of governance and social structure. In short, they've created the home as training grounds, practicing skills to bring into the world. What kinds of kids come out of these places? I can think of two: Danny and Amanda.

To reach Danny's property, I drove about fifteen minutes out of Port Townsend, turned onto a dirt road, and followed its meandering path past faded Trump signs, tucked-back homes, a junkyard, and the occasional pop of gunfire. The road terminated at Danny and his wife Meredith's ten acres. The driveway bifurcated the land. To the right was a large shed. Beside it, propped up on stilts, was a sailboat in need of repairs and, just beyond that, an Airstream trailer. To the left, sloping downhill, was a pasture where several trailers and a bus sat. Farther along, there was a garden with a chicken coop, an outbuilding that had been turned into a duplex, a kids' play structure, a giant trampoline, and their house.

Meredith, who works as a midwife, wasn't at home. Danny and I sat on their porch in the light rain, Gitte resting just inside and the baby, Keenan, asleep in the stroller beside us. We drank beer and talked under the low, wet sky.

The Danny I grew up with was a mischief maker and tantrum thrower—a big, loud, brassy boy, chubby cheeked and strapping. Now, as a father, he's learned to channel his youthful fire into a kind of hot current he can point with almost-mathematical precision toward his projects. He's strong, like his father, with curly brown hair, a booming voice, and eyes that look feral and electric when he's excited.

Three years ago, Danny and Meredith purchased this land with financing from a friend and from Doug and Nancy. There are seven home units onsite, including the duplex apartment,

Airstream, trailers, and bus. They charge three hundred to eight hundred dollars a month per place, depending on the size. Among the people living there are nine adults and seven kids. They also raise animals for meat: six cows, a flock of sheep and goats, and chickens.

"This is not an intentional community per se," Danny said. Meredith grew up in a community that was even more regimented than RoseWind: "She spent a ton of time doing intimate circle work, listening and speaking from the heart," he told me, not poking fun but just describing it frankly. He and Meredith wanted a property "where we're in charge, and we don't have to run everything by everybody—it's not run by consensus; it's a benevolent dictatorship."

What Danny was solving for far more rapidly than cohousing could was affordability. "If it was up to me, each one of those RoseWind houses would have, like, three families in it. Then there'd be a couple dozen tiny houses for lower-income people. You could have two or three times as many people living there comfortably, and it would be a much more lively, wild, fun place."

Danny's guiding impulse is to make spaces lively, wild, and fun. He makes his living as a civic event planner, organizing everything from the Port Townsend Fourth of July celebration—with its fireworks display, cake picnic, and parades—to the Department of Emergency Management's All County Picnic, which taps into the community of local preppers to help ready other residents for natural disasters. Later in the summer, he was hosting a roundtable with tribal councils from around the Olympic Peninsula.

A mother and two kids, who live in one of the trailers, walked to the play structure and began swinging. Danny waved. The rain remained light, and we went to feed and water the new chicks.

"My own relationships to Jefferson County and Port Townsend are certainly riding on the shoulders of my parents and everything they've built. I inherited a network," Danny reflected. "My calling includes bringing a lot of people together. I can't make it happen alone. As you find your calling, you are hopefully inspiring other people to find their calling."

Danny could wrangle a lot of human energy. He was experienced at navigating disagreement and bringing people together toward a shared goal. His parents' activism, and his mother's aneurysm specifically, pushed him into positivity—extreme, spewing, gleeful, jumpy positivity. He has a rah-rah quality he inherited from his dad, without Doug's inclination to sound the alarm bells. He can talk about grim things but doesn't linger there for long.

I recalled something Doug once told me about his son: "Danny's got a big soul. He told me to be less full of blame and shame. 'How else can we create a civil society?'" Doug paused for a long moment and then flashed me a mischievous look. "I still like blame and shame quite a bit."

We walked from the chicks to the far field to see the new lambs, nuzzling their moms and leaping through the tall grass.

"I tend to invite a lot of people in, which then doesn't always give enough space for depth and intimacy because of bandwidth," Danny continued. "I think Meredith is more like a smaller-circle person, who wants intentional space. And I'm more: 'Everyone's welcome! It can be this great big thing.' It's something we work on. There's no compromise found—you know, move on to the next thing. It's part of our process."

Striking the balance between letting new people in and pulling your existing community close—between inclusiveness and intimacy—is a tension at the heart of most groups, a tension that I see as innate to being a human among other humans.

The route from Danny's back to Amanda's took me past Redmen Cemetery on Discovery Road. The Red Men were members of a fraternal organization established exclusively for white men in the 1830s. It spread across the United States—at its peak, there were half a million members—and Port Townsend had an active chapter. The Red Men pantomimed Indigenous culture, dressing in redface, assuming invented titles, and performing secret rituals.

I was shocked the cemetery retained the name of this racist group, which had fringe membership into the twenty-first century, but there was something clarifying in it too. Seeing the name of the cemetery reminded me that we're still living in a world owned by white Americans. That's literally true—the five largest landowners in the United States are all white and own more rural land than all Black Americans combined. The greatest blight on our society is not names from a racist past but unending injustice.

Discovery Road was another name pointing to white power. Before I left, Danny and I talked about the Doctrine of Discovery. European monarchs invented this framework to claim that any land not inhabited by Christians could still be "discovered," which meant conquered, colonized, and owned. The Doctrine of Discovery was used to justify colonialism and imperialism throughout Asia, Africa, and the Americas and was supplied by Thomas Jefferson as good cause for white settlement of the United States and codified into law by the Supreme Court in 1823.

"I don't own this land. This is native land," Danny said to me as our conversation was ending. I'd just spent several hours asking Danny about the land he owned, but, strangely, this contradiction felt like solid ground. He was expressing the idealism, hope, and hypocrisy of operating within a system as you strive to undermine it—a feeling I knew well.

The next day, I met Amanda for lunch at her office, a tiny house that sits in a yard of tiny houses. Amanda bought me tomato soup and a spinach-and-cheese croissant from a nearby shop, and we sat on the floor and ate. Amanda is the most grounded member of her family. Her energy feels even, determined, and pragmatic. She loves detective novels and board games: challenges with neat and conclusive endings. She's my height but with feet two sizes larger than mine, planted squarely on the ground. She's always been physically affectionate. When I was little, she loved to braid my hair and sleep spooning together in a nightlong hug.

One time, racing to drop me off at the Bainbridge ferry, we talked about her parents' political passions, and she said, "How nice if more people could be this way. And, also, how could you survive if you were?"

Amanda's form of group living is not in her home but in public. Her inheritance is a work ethic oriented toward the commons. She organizes the farmers market with devotion and clarity—a bureaucrat who manages a contentious board and supports farmers who come with their own agendas and passions.

We finished our croissants, licked our fingers, and stuck them to the last flakes of pastry clinging to our plates. Amanda was scheming about a more permanent home for the market so they wouldn't have to set up a stage, tents, and tables every time. Should they continue on where they hosted the market now and only build a covered bandstand, she mused, or should they develop something larger, meeting more of their needs, in a different spot? Who at the city level should she speak to, and what was her next step?

I'd see what she meant on Saturday, Amanda told me. Doug usually helped her set up and take down the market, but both he and Nancy had the coronavirus and were holed up at the bingo parlor. Gabe and I had offered to join in his place. The process, Amanda explained, would take several hours to complete—both before and after the market. Although I was a vendor at other farmers markets, this would be my first time experiencing setup and takedown from the vantage of the market manager.

I changed topics and told Amanda what had been spinning in my mind all morning: that more and more, I find myself questioning the paradigm of private property. It's a tool for hoarding power, used very effectively by white Americans. I'm disturbed by the honest answer to the question of who gets to own land in the United States. Historically, it was white men. Now, increasingly, it's the wealthy, a group that looks fundamentally the same.

In the United States, home ownership is presented as the primary foundation of financial security. This is a natural extension of our country's basic principles. The Founding Fathers rebelled against the European aristocracy by plotting out a nation of landholding "yeoman farmers," aspiring to equality through property ownership. These new citizens, of course, were exclusively white men, and this project required massacring and relocating the Indigenous people who already lived here, as well as dehumanizing and exploiting everyone else. Centuries later, property ownership is still the only dependable way to build personal wealth that you can pass to your kids, and it's still the same contradiction: an exclusionary right that's presented as egalitarian. In some countries, there's much lower property ownership than in the United States but a greater social safety net, which gives people lasting security.

Currently, co-ops—where ownership exists within a collective—are the closest thing to true, long-term equity that I know of. Paired with land trusts, they have the power to create affordable housing into the future. Each person's participation creates security for the whole. They encapsulate the reciprocal spirit of group living on a slightly larger scale. The mainstream narrative tells us a meaningful life is one where we prioritize ourselves and our nuclear family unit, but I sense the exact opposite is true.

My instinct is to fight the paradigm of property ownership—safe, stable housing should be a human right, not a status marker—yet I'm obsessed with the Holman House. I see the contradictions, and so does Amanda. She told me she knows about this kind of closeness with a house. She built her home with her father and husband, and her garden is even more superabundant than mine. Every square inch of ground plumes with irises, kale, bluebells, and poppies. But that's the point. Everyone deserves that opportunity—to see their gardens bloom.

A ll week, Amanda had been nervous about the weather during the farmers market on Saturday. The forecasts promised torrential rain and strong winds. It was Mother's Day weekend, a big one for families, and the market stalls would be filled with strawberries, rhubarb, peas, and flowers. She'd been planning

activities for months and was starting to fear the whole day would
be ruined.

Saturday arrived and the sky was bright and blue, but the
wind was ripping. Gabe took the early morning setup shift, and
while he was gone, Inez showed me her caterpillar terrariums in
yogurt containers and Brighten ate two bowls of oats. When
Gabe returned and it was my time to head to market, I found
Amanda at the information booth. She squeezed me tightly and
introduced me to her volunteers.

The aisles between booths were packed with people, arms
overflowing with flowers—I saw mothers with little babies and
older women with their grown kids, walking hand in hand. One
year before, I'd been with Doug on Father's Day, and here I was
with his daughter on Mother's Day, witnessing a very different
vision of community building. It was lunchtime, and I bought
soup from a surly old woman, the kind I always want to win over,
with weathered hands and squinting, distrustful eyes. The soup
was deliciously weird—stinky broccoli rabe and sorrel with huge
amounts of lemon and herbs. It smelled and tasted like forgotten
pickles.

Taking down the market required a crew of volunteers. The
wind was picking up the tents and flinging them at us, using the
canopies as sails, so four of us each held down a corner as we
planned every step: lowering the legs, closing the canopy. Gabe
returned with Inez and Brighten in Doug's truck, and we loaded
the speakers, picnic tables, benches, and stage floor in pieces
into the truck bed. He drove to the storage sheds a few blocks
away, our team of volunteers met him, and then we all unloaded,
standing in a line like a bucket brigade, passing each piece from
one person to the next. And then we did it again with tents,
weights, large plastic storage bins, and sandwich boards. It was

physically demanding, and I thought of Doug here in my place, week after week, helping his daughter construct and deconstruct this vegetable town.

After the market, Amanda and I met a group of her mother friends to drink and kvetch about children, partners, and over-filled lives. We sat on the deck of a mariner's bar called Sirens and watched the rain clouds arrive over the water in the dimming light of sunset. Our server, an older woman with wrinkles that seemed to recess forever, described a rainbow she'd seen just moments before we arrived. "It had the deepest shade of violet," she said, in total wonder, and I felt as though I'd seen it, too, and felt the power of its fleeting beauty.

I looked out at the dramatic sky and the water of the Strait of Juan de Fuca. Across the way, I saw a massive blue crane that sits on Indian Island, loading ships with weapons, a lasting monument to war.

People take longevity, scale, wealth, and fame as the important measures of success in any undertaking, I thought, but what matters to me is the level of care, imagination, and camaraderie while it lasts, however brief or enduring. These qualities reverberate through the people who participate and create waves of energy that give life to new projects. Giving and receiving care changes us, which in turn changes our culture.

Danny and Amanda were attempting to build on their parents' activism, which they'd witnessed at both high and low moments. But rather than breaking with society or rejecting it, Danny and Amanda were working to build bridges. Their vision of cultural change is more inviting than their parents', more party-like, localized, and achievable. Compared to committing to RoseWind, or spending four decades protesting military sites that don't budge, one can readily shop at the farmers market, giving money to a local farmer, or attend a preppers' picnic, learning survival skills and ways to shelter your neighbors. Maybe Amanda's and Danny's activism would prove more durable, in some ways, because it was less motivated by grief or terror.

Yet I felt like something was lost in this generational shift—the big-picture vision, the incisive critique, the fire. Something was always lost, and gained, in generational shifts. I could hear Amanda's voice in my head, reflecting on her parents' mode of being in the world: *How nice if more people could be this way. And, also, how could you survive if you were?*

On my second margarita, listening to the mothers laugh and conspire, I thought to myself that if group-living experiments, at their best, were compost, then so were each of us. We live, die, and feed back into the soil of the communities we inhabit. In a few generations, we're gone. Aside from the rare genius or celebrity, we're remembered—if we're remembered at all—not as individuals but as parts of generations, movements, and communities. In life, we're individuals. In death, we're collectives.

Later that night, drifting off to sleep, I recollected a family photo that my grandparents had framed at their house in Moses Lake. Amanda, eight years old, had climbed onto Doug's sturdy shoulders, and Danny, five, had mounted onto Amanda's small shoulders, and they stood like a towering, wobbly, three-headed creature. Tiny Nancy grasped Doug's hand and grinned. Behind them stood an old-growth Douglas fir tree, disappearing out of the frame into the sky.

I loved this photo of my aunt, uncle, and cousins. It embodied them to me—strong Doug bringing carnival energy everywhere,

turning everything into a sculpture. Nancy determinedly standing on her own, smiling and mischievous. Amanda and Danny, so
game, so goofy. I'd always read the photo as a joke about how
small humans are, even piled on top of one another, compared to
trees. Now I thought about my cousins standing on the shoulders
of their parents. They'd become parents themselves and were
offering their shoulders for someone else to stand on. This was
not a triumphant march toward a great and absolute solution. It
was a cycle of growth, death, decay, and regrowth. It was repeti-
tive and singular. It was the work for us all, everywhere, at every
scale, forever.

Amanda's Rhubarb-Strawberry Crisp

Recipe by Amanda Milholland

MAKES 8 SERVINGS

Amanda makes my favorite crisp. She's a passionate gardener, and
everything she tends grows overlarge, including rhubarb plants
that resemble prehistoric succulents. The secret to her recipe is
cooking the rhubarb ahead of time so it becomes velvety and
melts into the berries, making every bite sweet and sour.

Rhubarb and strawberries are a perfect match. Strawberries
are often the first berries to arrive in the spring, alongside rhubarb, and their taste captures the seasonal transition from
Mother's Day to the summer solstice. That said, any berry—or
even cherries, nectarines, or other stone fruits—will work in
place of either rhubarb or strawberries, although you should cut
the sugar in half if you omit rhubarb.

FILLING

1½ pounds rhubarb (about 6 loosely packed cups)

2 tablespoons butter

1½ cups sugar

1 lemon, juice and zest

¾ pound strawberries (2 to 3 cups)

2 teaspoons cinnamon

2 tablespoons flour or arrowroot powder

Pinch of salt

TOPPING

1 cup whole-grain or all-purpose flour

¾ cup walnuts

½ cup rolled oats

8 tablespoons (1 stick) butter, room temperature, cut
into pieces

2 tablespoons brown sugar

Pinch of salt

Preheat the oven to 375 degrees.

Rinse dirt or debris off the rhubarb stalks and discard rhubarb leaves if they're attached. Cut the stalks into ½-inch pieces. In a medium-heavy saucepan over low heat, melt 2 tablespoons butter. Add rhubarb and stir. Then add 1 cup sugar (reserve ½ cup for later) and the zest and juice of one lemon (about 2 tablespoons juice). Cook, stirring occasionally, for about 10 to 15 minutes or until rhubarb is tender and falling apart. Remove from heat.

Wash and slice strawberries. Mix berries and cinnamon into the rhubarb compote. Taste for sweetness. If it's too tart for your taste, add another tablespoon of sugar and taste again, repeating until the sweetness level is as you like. (You can do this in advance. Cool the compote to room temperature and store it in the fridge for several days until ready to finish the crisp.) Mix in 2 tablespoons flour or arrowroot powder and a pinch of salt. Pour into an 8-by-8-inch-square or 9-inch-diameter-round casserole or cake dish.

In a separate mixing bowl, add all topping ingredients. (I leave the walnuts whole because I like the crunch.) Pinch the butter with your fingers or a pastry cutter into the dry ingredients until there are no more clumps of butter left. Cover the fruit filling with the topping. Place the pan on a baking sheet so that any juices that boil over won't fall on the floor of your oven.

Bake, uncovered, for 50 minutes to 1 hour, or until the topping is turning golden brown and juice is bubbling up the sides. Cool slightly and serve, still warm, with vanilla ice cream.

ALWAYS COMING HOME

Chris moved back into the Holman House after his first vaccine series in 2021. I would grin from ear to ear as I headed home from work, laughing to myself about nothing in particular. When Chris cooked dinner, I lingered at the kitchen island to admire his elegant handiwork and enjoy the collision of my impatience with his slow precision. I knew none of this was permanent, but I enjoyed it so much that it no longer seemed relevant that it might not last.

More than a year after Chris moved back into the house, in late summer 2022, we threw our first big party. Our friend Jordan was moving to Mexico City—Jordan, whom I'd fallen in love with at Chopsticks III: How Can Be Lounge so many years before—and a few days before he departed, we invited all our friends over to bid him farewell. The day of the party, Jordan came over early to decorate. He brought all the fixings for Sonoran dogs, along with everything that remained in his fridge and liquor cabinet, including—I'm not kidding—eight kinds of mustard.

While Chris made *miang kham*, a Thai appetizer of betel leaves wrapped around peanuts, ginger, shallot, toasted dried shrimp, coconut, and little pieces of lime with the skin on, I made salads, and Jordan showed us the three outfits he'd brought for the night. Then he described an orgy he'd gone to in Colorado in the basement of a cool industrial cement building. The space was full of naked men, and as Jordan wound his way through it, peering into one room after another, the air echoed with wet slapping sounds—*whap whap whap!*

I was giving Jordan bites of broccoli I'd sautéed with garlic and laughing at the image forming in my mind: I'm walking through a colorless underground bunker right out of a Cold War spy movie. Icy water is dripping onto the rusted metal beneath my feet. I look into one of the dim cells, but instead of filthy, bearded prisoners, I see naked men having loud, wet, glorious sex. *Whap whap!* Oh, the pleasures of friendship and of getting to inhabit experiences I've never known!

When people started arriving, I took on the role of grill master and tried barbecuing the bacon-wrapped hot dogs, but they dripped fat onto the coals, and it was gnarly. Luckily, a friend brought down a sheet pan from the kitchen and placed it on the grill as a frying pan, which worked perfectly. Zak walked around taking photos, and Corey started a bonfire in our firepit. I'd made a ridiculous ice cream cake, covered in frozen bananas and dribbled with sweetened condensed milk—its own kind of orgy— but before I served it, Jordan suddenly left. We later learned he'd contracted hand, foot, and mouth disease and had become feverish during the party.

Jordan was gone, but the party continued, which felt strangely apt. I felt sad about his departure, but here we were, still partying, still loving him as vividly as before—not so unlike when Chris and Erin went away. The night was warm, and I was alternating between soda water and mezcal with lime. Friends were arriving and departing in waves. The side doors of our porch were flung all the way open, connecting inside and outside. Corey put a pile of dancehall albums next to the record player in our kitchen. My friends and I pushed the tables aside and danced and danced, our chins nodding to the upbeats, our bodies bouncing in slow sync with the rhythmic bass notes. After two and a half years, the Holman House was finally filled again.

The pandemic put significant strains on Umi Organic, but we weathered them with surprising agility, thanks to the rise in home cooking and grocery delivery. Early in the pandemic, with so many people out of work, Patrick, who ran Umi's farmers market program, encouraged us to move to a sliding-scale model. The farmers market turned out to be a good venue for the experiment because it's an economically diverse crowd. I was shocked at how seamlessly the system worked. People who had less paid less. Some didn't pay at all. Others added a few dollars more and sometimes slipped us an extra twenty. Over and over, we had to explain what sliding scale was, but once our customers grasped the system, they seemed to have a gut sense for what the right level was for them. We pocketed neither more nor less overall, but now a wider range of people was eating our noodles.

I started to think about our whole business as existing within a sliding-scale system. We can't tell grocery stores to offer our products on a sliding-scale basis. (I wish!) We are contractually obligated to sell to all distributors at the same wholesale price, and they decide what price goes to each store they serve. But we can make our products available in other venues, like public schools. We can use parts of our business to subsidize other parts that make less money but are just as important to us. Equity does not mean charging everyone the same price.

I began bringing sliding scale into my personal life. When I order food with a group of friends, I ask them to hit me back based on a sliding scale. When Zak and I rented a gym to play pickup basketball and needed upfront cash, I asked our regulars to contribute on a sliding scale. I was looking for a new system to help me think about my business in a fresh way, and sliding scale loosened the rigid pieces of my mind. As with home, it's so easy to feel like there's only one way to do things, but that's never true.

M y life has returned to its rhythm, for the most part, even as the pandemic continues. Every week or two, I bike to my dad's apartment for breakfast. He makes me something either very wet or very dry. One morning, it'll be eggs covered in melted cheese, cooked with saucy pinto beans, bacon ends, and *longganisa* sausages. The next time, it's a crumbly multigrain muffin studded with odds and ends from his cupboard. He's unwilling to abide by set recipes. "Guess the ingredients," he'll often say, and that's how I know he's included something especially esoteric. "Hmm, I'm not sure, Pops," I'll answer, and he'll reply, "Banana powder, *HA!*" delighted to have stumped me.

My dad is what I call "beverage prepared" because, well, he's always prepared with many beverages. He invariably serves me a smoothie, his latest version of a mocha, and water he's chilled in the fridge—such an abundance of drinks! While we eat, he'll describe the plot of a book he's just read. Recently, it was *Doctor*

Mallory, the first novel written by Alan Hart, a trans doctor who began his practice on the rural Oregon coast in the early 1900s. The novel, a bestseller of its time, is about carving out a medical career in a community whose doctors resist the protagonist's presence.

"He's in a putt-putt boat, crossing the Coos Bay estuary, heading toward a timberman who's lost his arm," my dad begins, as he gleefully waves his signed 1936 first edition in the air. Sometimes I listen attentively and other times, unexpectedly, I zone out and the words transform into a blur of sounds. Out his window, I survey a small community garden filled with hummingbird feeders.

I look around. He moved into this modern, fairly nondescript apartment two years ago. The rooms are cluttered. I want to help him clean, but it's not easy, because everything he owns holds a story about people he's known and cared for. In truth, though, I'm just washed by a gentle wave of relief that he has this place.

"I'm sure you've heard this one before," he segues, as he retrieves a different book, this time a memoir written by his friend Marjorie Sharp about her time living in a cave in Thailand. She was being menaced by a local drug dealer's wife, who suspected adultery, and one day she returned to her cave and found her dog literally crucified to the wall. The story is horrifying, but my dad is letting out his usual shouts and waving his hands around excitedly because life, especially in its wildest moments, never ceases to thrill him.

For several years, I was constantly afraid my dad would get evicted from his previous apartment. He hasn't had a steady paycheck in thirty-odd years and is often penniless. I love him for choosing a creative, community-focused life, but there's little romance in aging in this country as a poor, working artist. He can be secretive and proud, and I feared he wouldn't tell me if he was evicted.

He'd been living in a foul place that he couldn't afford in the Hollywood neighborhood of Portland. It had a leaky ceiling, a broken refrigerator, a clogged sink, and minimal natural light. But it was huge, and he filled every crevice. His apartment was the only residence in a three-story commercial building and had once been the home of a dollar store magnate who'd brought his chintzy business philosophy to designing this place. Many of the walls were thin wood paneling. The ceiling tiles fell down in chunks and crumbled between my fingers like asbestos.

My dad was often late on rent, and I worried that if his landlord evicted him and he *did* tell me, we wouldn't have enough time to figure out what to do with his stuff. I felt guilty that I lived in the Holman House and he didn't. *What a hypocrite I am*, I'd think, *espousing group living and multigenerational households but unwilling to have my own dad move in*. But I knew that if he did, our relationship would suffer. It wasn't off the table, but it was the last resort.

He was reluctant to find a new place, so I undertook the search for an affordable, federally subsidized apartment in a city with far too few options. We made lists of all the buildings he qualified for and visited them surreptitiously, walking around their perimeters and trying to imagine what it would be like to live there. Because of the pandemic, we weren't allowed inside. The building managers I talked to didn't keep waiting lists because half the people on the lists would have moved on by the time an apartment opened. To secure my dad's place, I had to call the building he wanted to move into every week for ten months.

His new apartment was for low-income people who are over the age of sixty-two or are disabled. Everyone in my household helped my dad move. We stashed many of his boxes at the Holman House but also had to get rid of vanloads of things, which was miserable for him and made me feel cruel. Among his life's treasures, he'd also hoarded hundreds of plastic bottle caps, knowing they couldn't be recycled now but believing that someday they would.

"This is potential energy," he told me as I carted bags of colorful plastic to the dump.

My dad's stress about housing insecurity had impacted his mental health. He seemed on edge all the time, less focused, less present. When he finally moved into his new place and I knew he wouldn't be evicted, I felt such intense relief my body felt physically lighter. His personality lightened too. I was reminded that the person living on the street is never that different from my father, or my friends, or me. We can't take care of everyone personally, but we can believe that everyone deserves care and fight for a society that enacts that belief.

For a long time, I'd wanted to see one of the lost documentary films my dad made in the seventies. All I had was a framed poster of one—a beautiful black-and-white illustration of a large family with a big, happy baby in the center. It haunted me that I hadn't seen these movies, which were about multigenerational communal households. My dad learned that one of the movies had survived, the first of the series, called *Living Together*. It was in the archive at Portland State University. I wrote to the

librarian and just one hour later they sent me a link to the film on
YouTube. After all these decades, there it was, immediately, in
my inbox. I stopped what I was doing and watched.

Living Together is a thirty-five-minute documentary made
collaboratively by my dad and six other young filmmakers in
1972 as part of the Center for the Moving Image, then a program at Portland State University. The film was commissioned
to welcome the celebrated anthropologist Margaret Mead, who
was coming to speak in Portland, and it features four profiles of
living experiments wherein loose or organized groups are raising kids communally: a single mother on welfare who cares for
toddlers as part of a co-op; a group of queer women and their
kids who intentionally live without men; three middle-aged
families in a large house; and a collection of young political radicals and anarchists.

The audio consists of interviews played over footage of each
group in their home, doing domestic things like teaching their
kids how to tie their shoes, peeling potatoes, baking a pie, laying
down linoleum flooring, and laughing around a dinner table.
Sometimes the filmmakers follow the people to their day jobs
making sandwiches, welding, and running a women's health
clinic. The film doesn't advocate for any one model; instead, it
shows everyday moments and gives each group the chance to
describe why and how they are experimenting outside the status quo.

I was riveted by every profile in this short film. The people
featured ask the same questions I've been writing about, but
they come to more radical conclusions. The mother who opens
the film says, early on, "People in this neighborhood don't have
anything except each other. . . . If you don't help each other, then
you have nothing." She was teaching her son how to cook, clean,

wash his clothes, and do dishes because she didn't want him to be dependent on a woman. I liked that framing—that men were being denied skills and this was a chance to reclaim them.

The next group continues the same theme but with a decidedly sharper critique. "I think it's more important to talk about why we don't want to live with men. . . . It's not just everything that we get from women but all the negative shit that we don't want to get from living with men," a woman states. "When you live with women you can fight over who gets to wash the kitchen floor, but when you live with a man it's your job."

One of the women living in the queer collective insists, very calmly, that we should do away with the concept of family entirely because it ties people together out of obligation. People lose their capacity to identify for themselves why they show up for one another, what they can offer, and what they need.

The third group of families have only recently moved in together and are filled with excitement. A man with a voice like a radio announcer's articulates with spite, "The pure waste of living in single-family units is so gross." Over footage of a group eating around a dinner table lit up by an *enormous* candelabra, one of the men ponders whether communal living is more significant and necessary for people raising kids and growing old together than it is for young people.

After the portraits, Mead reflects on all she's seen. My dad told me he'd filmed the interview, and I can imagine him behind the camera, overeager, wanting to interrupt to share his own ideas. I see him in the same vivid black and white as the film, his curly dark hair and beard framing his face like a lion's mane and his thick glasses enlarging his excitable light eyes. Mead, with her hair in a bob and dressed in a vest and white blouse, slightly resembles a schoolgirl, but her tone is stately and adult. She looks like she's never shown any strong emotions, only orated presciently, confident that her slow, steady voice will be heard.

"In a country as heterogeneous as the United States, we have a great tendency to impose one style on everyone," she observes, but "we can't insist in this country on a lifestyle that we simply cannot give to the rest of the world."

"As the United States has been the country that developed the overcapitalized individual home, our problem is to develop a new lifestyle. . . . People willing to try extreme experiments as a way of criticizing the narrowness, the fragmentation, the over-emphasis on material things and the social injustices that result . . . are exceedingly valuable."

I loved that term, the "overcapitalized individual home," because it takes the entire world in its purview: *Overcapitalized* because someone else is undercapitalized. *Overcapitalized* because we don't need all the things we have, although capitalism makes owning them the highest proof of our worth. *Individual home* because "home" has been reduced to a place for small family units. *Individual home* because those two words aren't innately connected—there are more expansive ways to imagine home.

When the movie finished, a strange ecstatic mood overtook me. I could imagine watching this movie seeing only that these experiments didn't take, that they didn't become the norm. But instead, what I saw was much more personal: the run-up to my own childhood, my young dad making intimate domestic portraits of people who fascinated him, something I also love to do. Here was the compost that fed the soil of my whole life.

I already knew that I'd inherited unconventional ideas about how to build a home, but I now saw that my dad's documentary impulse is in me too. I want to capture what I appreciate about the people in my life, to refine an eye for specifics, contradictions, and tenderness, and to delight in the things I see. This impulse feels inseparable from my love of group living—both are an extension of my desire for closeness with lots of people and for the way intimacy makes me feel. I crave voyeuristic peeks inside other realities. This is why I read, why I watch movies, why I sit with friends for hours, why I live in a group house. This is one reason why I write.

By and large, my explorations of an unconventional home have been less radical than those of my parents' generation. I can't tell if my experiments contribute to a contemporary cultural movement. To me, they feel both deliberate and inevitable, given the impossible costs of housing. A few of my friends are attempting similar experiments. My friend Sarah lives with her partner, her elementary-aged son, her father, and a rotating cast of roommates. She's looking to take that further on a small piece of land with outbuildings, similar to Danny's compound. My friends Sofie and Andrew moved to a southern suburb of Portland and bought a place that they share with housemates. They hope to live communally into old age and dream that someone with kids will join them. In every case, my friends choose these arrangements in defiance of the attached social stigma.

Some of the ideas that seemed controversial when my parents were young have become unexceptional parts of my life: sharing domestic chores with men; sharing material things like a car, a television, and a washing machine; not getting married; growing into middle age in a house with more than just my romantic partner. I've sublimated things that were hard won but lost the thread on others. The radicalism of the past bled away somewhere, and I once again sense that something has been lost and something found. I find myself longing to be more radical, wishing it would burst into flame inside me—cheering when I see that fire in others but finding that I'm a more staid person. My inheritance is a calm, durable relationship to living communally.

Although our starting places are different, I think the questions underlying my interest in group living are similar to those that inspired my dad, my mom, Doug, Nancy—and Margaret Mead, for that matter. How can we begin to experiment outside the status quo? How can we learn to see companionship itself as both home and wealth? How can we take more of the world into our daily consideration and care for people we may never know? How can we live with joy and humor in the face of crises, without shying away or diminishing others?

What if we get everyone together and get a good feeling between us? How about we work out anything and everything that lies unexpressed? Uh-oh—am I about to write a group-living recipe?!

What is a recipe? It's someone else's record of how to do something, captured at a specific moment in time. It's also cumulative—the product of many people, cultures, places, and histories linked in a chain that brought us to this moment. To see a recipe as definitive is to misunderstand its nature.

For that very reason, perhaps, I also see recipes as contradictions. Writing a recipe is both an act of generosity and an act of dogma. The author grants themselves authority and then gives up control. If, as Lewis Hyde wrote, "the gift must stay in motion," the gift is the recipe, which was passed in some form to the author, transformed in their hands, and then sent back into the world to convey their expertise. The moment it reaches the hands of another cook, it becomes something altogether new. The cook is a different person with their own tastes. The air, the context, the ingredients themselves are different. The goal of following a recipe is rarely to make a perfect replication but to experience pleasure and nourishment. Who, then, is the expert, when nothing is absolute or fixed?

As cooks, our relationship to recipes works best when we feel empowered to break the rules—when we commit to understanding them as they are and then embrace our own preferences. This push and pull—between authority and independence, between collective wisdom and self-knowledge—is how we transform a static recipe into a dynamic part of our life.

How we learn from one another is just as interactive and confounding. There are no definitive recipes, just a lot of material to draw from, yet too often the same tired narratives dominate. The nuclear family is one of them. Any overprescribed form of group living could be another, which is perhaps reason enough not to reduce it to a definitive set of instructions and fall into the same conventional trap that Mead called out: the attempt to impose one style on everyone.

Zak has mostly stopped using his refrain "*That's* group living." But sometimes it still comes, unbidden, to my mind. When it does, I think about compromise: what we sacrifice and what we gain. I also think about paradox. In ecology, *paradox* describes a setting that combines contradictory features: places where the desert meets the rainforest, for example. These places may seem strange or extreme to us, but only because they're unfamiliar. We don't necessarily believe dissimilarities can or should coexist, but that's a limit of imagination rather than a reflection of what's possible.

I don't have a recipe for group living, but I do have guidance. Endurance in group-living settings requires living inside contradictions. But contradictions can be complementary; qualities that seem like opposites may be essential to each other. Heavy dressing needs crispy lettuce. Sweet mochi needs bitter matcha. These interlocking dichotomies are infinite. *Freedom and structure*: Too much freedom is meaningless. Too much structure is stifling. Some structure creates space for free experimentation. *Being together and being alone*: One creates the pleasure of the other. Without one, the other becomes oppressive. *Power and surrender*: Sometimes we need to be unyielding and determined; at other times, we desperately need to learn to let go, which is also a form of power. *Vulnerability and strength*: The intimacy that comes with time and attention allows us to be vulnerable with others. This intimacy, across a group, can become a durable network—like mycelia. We are strongest when we feel safe being soft.

Living inside these paradoxes allows what seems like dogma to soften into stories. It allows recipes to become fairy tales and asks us to learn from them, then tear them apart and build them anew. It gives us the limberness to find our way forward, together.

In the novel *Always Coming Home*, Ursula K. Le Guin writes, "When I take you to the Valley, you'll see the blue hills on the left and the blue hills on the right, the rainbow and the vineyards under the rainbow late in the rainy season, and maybe you'll say, 'There it is, that's it!' But I'll say, 'A little farther.' We'll go on, I hope, and you'll see the roofs of the little towns and the hillsides yellow with wild oats, a buzzard soaring and a woman singing by the shadows of a creek in the dry season, and maybe you'll say, 'Let's stop here, this is it!' But I'll say, 'A little farther yet.'"

Until she died in 2018, Le Guin lived in the northwest hills of Portland, across the Willamette River from me. She seems to me to be describing home not as a fixed destination but as a process. The destination is always a little farther. The journey is never complete. We shape our homes, they shape us, and over time, we belong more and more to one another, and we're never done. We're always coming home.

I have many questions about the future of the Holman House. Should we actively pursue a model of collective ownership? We could! If either or both of my parents need more care, will they move back in? I don't know! Sometimes a vision of our household as deranged elders flashes through my mind, a return to my *Grey Gardens*–induced paranoia. We're wandering the house in ragged bathrobes, spreading cat food on crackers, sorting and resorting the piles of clutter that have come to represent the totality of our lives. I've wrapped a scarf around my head like Little Edie, and I prance erratically through the rooms.

I wonder what old age will look like for us without children. Who will care for whom? When our generation passes, who will inherit the Holman House? I don't know the answers to these questions, and they aren't mine to decide alone. We have time to explore their contours and the expanse of the unknowable future ahead of us. At this writing, the soup isn't done. The Brotherhood Spirit in Flesh Soup will never actually be done, which isn't sad—I didn't want to eat that soup anyway! We still have time to revise the recipe, to laugh at the recipe, to laugh at ourselves. We still have a little further yet to go.

David's Seedy Granola

Inspired by David Milholland, recipe by Lola Milholland

MAKES APPROXIMATELY 8 CUPS

I hesitate to end this book with a granola recipe. Isn't it too on the nose—this quintessential hippie food that's become so casually mainstream? But I love how flexible it is. And this recipe, especially, feels like a fairy tale to me: *Once upon a time, there was a hungry old man who liked things very wet and very dry . . .*

Boy oh boy, does my dad love to make granola. Almost every month, he hands me a new iteration he's made, with a thousand ingredients inside. He's never written down the recipe, so I've taken inspiration from his model and offer you my own loose instructions. This uses five forms of coconut—coconut oil, coconut sugar, coconut-milk powder, shredded coconut, and large coconut flakes—which feels like the most David Milholland thing possible: all coconuts are invited to the party.

I think of this granola as dark-roasted because I bake it to a deep color, which tastes rich and delicious to me. It's important to add the coconut flakes near the end of baking so they don't burn and to only incorporate dried fruit after the granola comes out of the oven so it doesn't harden. This granola bakes into big, crunchy clumps with a beautiful glossy sheen.

You can decide which nuts and seeds to use and in what ratios, but I recommend using as many different kinds as you have on hand. There's something about the abundance and diversity of nuts and seeds that makes this granola especially satisfying. For the seeds, I go heavy on sunflower, pumpkin, and sesame, using about ¼ cup of each, and then add less flax and chia—2 tablespoons or so of each—but you can follow your own whims. Somehow, the coconut is the solid base note, and the high note, the real showstoppers, are all the seeds!

DRY

1½ cups old-fashioned rolled oat, barley, or rye flakes

1 cup seeds (mixture of sesame, sunflower, pumpkin, flax, nigella, and/or chia)

¾ cup whole raw nuts (mixture of almonds, walnuts, pecans, cashews, and/or hazelnuts)

2 tablespoons coconut-milk powder or milk powder

1½ teaspoons cinnamon

WET

¼ cup honey

¼ cup coconut sugar or brown sugar

¼ cup fruit jam (homemade or store-bought)

¼ cup coconut oil

1 tablespoon vanilla

½ teaspoon salt

LATER

1 cup unsweetened shredded and/or flaked coconut

¾ cup dried fruit (raisins, cherries, or chopped apricots)

Preheat the oven to 325 degrees. Lightly coat a large baking sheet with oil (I use olive oil).

Measure all the dry ingredients into a large bowl and toss to combine. Measure all the wet ingredients into a heavy-bottomed saucepan and heat over low, stirring continuously until everything is melted and combined, about 1 minute. Be attentive—don't walk away from the stove. Pour the wet mixture over the dry and stir until everything is incorporated and glossy.

Spread the mixture in a single layer on the baking sheet. Bake for 15 minutes. Remove from the oven and stir the granola, bringing the edges to the center and the center to the edges, so nothing burns. Bake for another 15 minutes. Remove from the oven again and repeat the thorough stirring; then sprinkle the shredded and/or flaked coconut over the top and return to the oven to bake for 10 to 15 more minutes. Check the color after 10 minutes, in case your oven has hot spots. Total baking time is 40 to 45 minutes.

Take the baking sheet out of the oven and sprinkle the dried fruit over the top. Let cool slightly and then stir to combine, scraping the bottom of the sheet pan, which can get sticky, with a metal spatula. Cool granola to room temperature and then transfer to jars and store in a cool, dark place. Will keep for 3 weeks at room temperature or several months in the freezer.

Eat a big bowl, and then package some and share it with your family and friends!

ACKNOWLEDGMENTS

How strange that I wrote most of this book about group living while I was alone—which is to say, not in my home but in quiet, empty places. Writing can feel antisocial and solitary, but I never *felt* alone. This book is the product of a loving community.

First, thank you to my editor, Joey McGarvey, who said no to my outrageous idea for a parody commune cookbook but yes to what also felt unreal: my first book! Her edits transformed the book you're holding in your hands, and I feel so powerfully grateful to her that I'm a little beside myself.

To my loved ones who make the world so fascinating. Thank you for allowing me to tell your stories. To my sun, Theresa Marquez; my moon, David Milholland; my love, Corey Lunn; my rock, Zak Margolis; and my noodle, Christopher Rabilwongse. To my dearests: Erin Long; Cynthia Star; Doug, Nancy, Amanda, Danny, and Meredith Milholland; Gabe Van Lelyveld; the little Impu monsters; and Junko, Tomoko, and Nobuko Yamaguchi. And to those who've passed but remain forever present in my life: Walt Curtis; Rhonda Kennedy; my grandparents; and Wendy the cat, RIP.

To the Holman House, my home, which remains so generous and mysterious.

To my consistent readers who gave me new ways of seeing the work; told me when it was sluggish, aimless, or too yummy; cheered me on; and kept me company when I felt lost: Stef Choi, Sasha Davies, Peter Field, Gabi Lewton-Leopold, maya rose, Margarett Waterbury, and Rachael Guynn Wilson. To my favorite bookmaker, Gary Robbins, whose honest, uncomfortable, and, in the end, deeply loving conversation was the push I needed to pursue a formal publisher. And to Barrett Briske, for attention to detail.

To Julie Grau and Celina Spiegel, for offering a lovingly built home for my book, and to the team at Spiegel & Grau, for being the facilitators of dreams.

To my amazing coworkers and friends who helped me create Umi Organic and keep it afloat as I disappeared for weeks at a time to work on this book: Patrick Barrett, Fannie Chen, Ayla Ercin, Shawn Linehan, Dino Matt, Stephen Pierce, and Amanda Plyley.

To the people and organizations who gave me places to write, money to live on, and votes of confidence: Kerrie Richert, Oatmeal Creek, and the little donkey, emu, and armadillo; PLAYA Summer Lake and its long shadows at dawn; the Rice Place and the shoopies; Hedgebrook and the Cedar Cabin spirits; Nancy and her Elyria Canyon cabin; Peter and the Sou'Wester; Emi and Larry's prefab in Cayucos; the Regional Arts and Culture Council; and, of course, the Kettle Lodge, my home away from home.

To the magazines that provided the original homes for parts of this manuscript, in different forms. Elements of the prologue, "Butter Sculpture," and "Driftless" all appeared in *Oregon*

Humanities, and my first iterations of "Bitter and Sweet" appeared in the *Amherst Circus* and *Gastronomica*.

To Judith Silver and Lucy Horton for permission to quote their work.

To my recipe writers, recipe testers, and the life-changing friends and sources who directly shaped this book: Andrew Barton, Yuri Baxter-Neal, Jordan Behr, Tony Candelaria, Sarah Magrish Cline, Joanna Cowan, Mae Culbertson, Jessie Eller-Isaacs, Laura Ford, Alley Frey, Tracy Gagnon, Lila Jarzombek, Love Jonson, Kees and Helen Kolff, Diane Linn, Connie Masuoka, Jerome McGeorge, Kacy McKinney, Jamie Melton, Ana Mikolavich, Amy Peterson, Althea Grey Potter, Lizi Robbins, Alix Jo Ryan, Sakiko Setaka-Domreis, Patty Seward, Sofie Sherman-Burton, George Siemon, Amalia Sierra, Sam Smith, Claire Stewart, Sean Pierce Sumler, Emi Takahara, Manu Torres, Sage Van Wing, Lauren Wessler, Nancy Wong, and the kittens Weetie and Miles.

To the Big Worms, Friendship Basketball Guild, JMPers, the Amherst Prince fan club, Ecotrusters, Little Nuts Big Nuts, Free Spirits, Hollywood and King Farmers Markets, and all the other collectives webbed through my life.

To the many unnamed friends, family, and teachers—too many to thank—I love you! Your name belongs here:

_____

_____

_____.

And to Valerie Otani, who drew me maps.

NOTES

xviii **I wanted to make a commune cookbook** For more information on commune cookbooks, see Stephanie Hartman, "The Political Palate: Reading Commune Cookbooks," *Gastronomica* 3, no. 2 (May 2003): 29–40, https://doi.org/10.1525/gfc.2003.3.2.29.

xviii **"Get everyone together"** Lucy Horton, *Country Commune Cooking* (New York: Coward, McCann & Geoghegan, 1972), 33.

xxi **Zak's Chili Oil with Fermented Black Beans** Recipe adapted from Barbara Tropp, "China Moon Hot Chili Oil," *The China Moon Cookbook* (New York: Workman Publishing Company, Inc., 1992), 10–11.

59 **"The gift must stay in motion"** Lewis Hyde, *The Gift: Imagination and the Erotic Life of Property* (New York: Vintage Books, 1979), 146.

60 **"gift exchange is more likely"** Hyde, 18.

63 **"One man's gift"** Hyde, 4.

63 **"property is plagued by entropy"** Hyde, 23.

73 **Land trusts have an extensive history** For more information on land trusts, see John E. Davis, ed., *The Community Land Trust Reader* (Cambridge, MA: Lincoln Institute of Land Policy, 2010).

76 **The co-op formed in response** CROPP Cooperative, *CROPP Cooperative ROOTS: The First 25 Years* (La Farge, WI: CROPP Cooperative, 2013), 5.

76 **"the most severe financial stress"** Jerome M. Stam et al., "Farm Financial Stress, Farm Exits, and Public Sector Assistance to the Farm Sector in the 1980's" (United States Department of Agriculture, Economic Research Service, Agricultural Economic Report Number 645), 4, doi.org/10.22004/ag.econ.308151.

78 **more than eighteen hundred farmer members** CROPP Cooperative, *CROPP Cooperative ROOTS*, 175.

81 **US propaganda that described Filipinos** Sean McEnroe, "Painting the Philippines with an American Brush: Visions of Race and National Mission among the Oregon Volunteers in the Philippine Wars of 1898 and 1899," *Oregon Historical Quarterly* 104, no. 1 (Spring 2003): 30, http://doi.org/10.1353/ohq.2003.0089.

109 **"Each subject lives"** Roland Barthes, *How to Live Together: Novelistic Simulations of Some Everyday Spaces*, trans. Kate Briggs (New York: Columbia University Press, 2013), 6, https://cup.columbia.edu/book/how-to-live-together/9780231136167.

109 **"something like solitude"** Barthes, 6.

110 **"because their structure"** Barthes, 8.

110 **"a zone that falls"** Barthes, 9.

111 **Racist housing policy had laid the tracks** This letter to the first known Black resident of Oregon, which traverses Black history in the state since, should be required reading for everyone in Oregon: Mitchell S. Jackson, "Prologue: Dear Markus," in *Survival Math: Notes on an All-American Family* (New York: Scribner, 2019), 1–12.

121 **one-third of US adults live with an adult roommate** Richard Fry, "More Adults Now Share Their Living Space, Driven in Part by Parents Living with Their Adult Children," Pew Research Center, January 31, 2018, https://www.pewresearch.org/fact-tank/2018/01/31/more-adults-now-share-their-living-space-driven-in-part-by-parents-living-with-their-adult-children/.

121 **The nuclear family is a surprisingly recent formula** David Brooks, "The Nuclear Family Was a Mistake," *The Atlantic*, March 2020, https://www.theatlantic.com/magazine/archive/2020/03/the-nuclear-family-was-a-mistake/605536/.

122 **Racist housing policy during this same period** For more information on the history of racial segregation in cities, see Richard Rothstein, *The Color of Law: A Forgotten History of How Our Government Segregated America* (New York: Liveright, 2017).

128 **Today, Findhorn is famous as an "ecovillage"** Find a personal account of the founding of Findhorn in Dorothy Maclean's *Memoirs of an Ordinary Mystic* (Everett, WA: Lorian Press, 2010).

140 **the United States had been funding and providing military support** For another description of the Quaker-led Witness for Peace trips to Nicaragua,

see Joyce Hollyday, "The Long Road to Jalapa," *Sojourners* 13, no. 2 (February 1984), https://sojo.net/magazine/february-1984.

143 **"It's something about that intermediary"** Fred Moten, quoted in David S. Wallace, "Fred Moten's Radical Critique of the Present," *New Yorker*, April 30, 2018, https://www.newyorker.com/culture/persons-of-interest /fred-motens-radical-critique-of-the-present.

147 **Two centuries ago, Port Townsend** The general context about Port Townsend's history is drawn from Jefferson County Historical Society, *Port Townsend* (Charleston, SC: Arcadia Publishing, 2008), 7.

148 **Fourier designed the structure** Charles Gide, introduction to *Design for Utopia: Selected Writings of Charles Fourier*, by Charles Fourier, trans. Julia Franklin (New York: Schocken Books, 1988), 11–45.

149 **In 1964, a Danish architect** Kathryn McCamant and Charles Durrett, *Cohousing: A Contemporary Approach to Housing Ourselves* (Berkeley, CA: Ten Speed Press, 1994), 12.

161 **"I was beginning to understand"** Kiese Laymon, "What We Owe and Are Owed," *The Highlight*, Vox, May 17, 2021, https://www.vox.com/the-highlight /22419450/kiese-laymon-justice-fairness-black-america.

162 **"Open my eyes to truth"** Judith Silver, "Open," YouTube video, 1:47, song, posted by Judith Silver, June 3, 2015, https://www.youtube.com /watch?v=BX7BcPjkq8U. Hear more of Silver's music at www.judithsilver .com.

178 **"Where life is precious, life *is* precious"** Ruth Wilson Gilmore, quoted in Rachel Kushner, "Is Prison Necessary? Ruth Wilson Gilmore Might Change Your Mind," *New York Times Magazine*, April 17, 2019, https://www .nytimes.com/2019/04/17/magazine/prison-abolition-ruth-wilson-gilmore .html.

194 **more than one hundred aboveground concrete domes** Julianne Stanford, "Little-Known Island the 'Logistics Backbone' of Pacific Northwest Navy Fleet," *Kitsap Sun*, November 26, 2017, https://www.kitsapsun.com/story /news/2017/11/26/little-known-island-logistics-backbone-pacific-north west-navy-fleet/886272001/.

194 **1.3 to 2 million people died** Physicians for Social Responsibility, *Body Count: Casualty Figures after 10 Years of the 'War on Terror,' Iraq Afghanistan Pakistan* (Washington, DC: Physicians for Social Responsibility, March 2015), 15, https://psr.org/wp-content/uploads/2018/05/body-count.pdf.

197 **second-largest stockpile of nuclear weapons** Hans M. Kristensen and Matt Korda, "Nuclear Notebook: United States Nuclear Weapons, 2023,"

Bulletin of the Atomic Scientists 79, no. 1 (2023): 30, https://doi.org/10.1080 /00963402.2022.2156686.

197 **up to twenty of the ballistic missiles** "Trident II (D5) Missile," America's Navy, September 22, 2021, https://www.navy.mil/Resources/Fact-Files /Display-FactFiles/Article/2169285/trident-ii-d5-missile/.

197 **do the damage of eight "Little Boys"** "Trident Missile Factfile," BBC News, September 23, 2009, http://news.bbc.co.uk/2/hi/uk/4438392.stm.

197 **some two hundred nuclear bombs** Don Mosley, "This Train Is Bound For . . .?" *Sojourners* 13, no. 2 (February 1984), https://sojo.net/magazine /february-1984/train-bound.

199 **three-quarters of a trillion dollars** "Discretionary Spending in Fiscal Year 2021: An Infographic," Congressional Budget Office, September 20, 2022, https://www.cbo.gov/publication/58269.

204 **the federal government took the island** Julianne Stanford, "Metal Nets and Homesteaders All Part of Indian Island's History," *Kitsap Sun*, April 9, 2018, https://www.kitsapsun.com/story/news/local/2018/04/09/metal-nets -and-homesteaders-all-part-indian-islands-history/489832002/.

206 **"We ought to be willing"** E. Raymond Wilson, quoted in Alicia McBride, "Systems, Relationships, and History: Advocating for Peace Today," Friends Committee on National Legislation, September 17, 2020, https://www.fcnl .org/updates/2020-09/systems-relationships-and-history-advocating-peace -today.

209 **United States is the top arms exporter in the world** Pieter D. Wezeman, Justine Gadon, and Siemon T. Wezeman, "SIPRI Fact Sheet: Trends in International Arms Transfers, 2022," Stockholm International Peace Research Institute (SIPRI), March 2023, https://doi.org/10.55163/CPNS8443.

209 **the Department of Defense produces more greenhouse gases** Neta C. Crawford, "Pentagon Fuel Use, Climate Change, and the Costs of War," Watson Institute for International and Public Affairs, Brown University, November 13, 2019, https://watson.brown.edu/costsofwar/papers/Climate ChangeandCostofWar.

211 **the White King and the Lucky Lass** The general context for the two Lakeview mines is drawn from different pages here: "Mining Records— Lake County," Oregon Department of Geology and Mineral Industries, accessed May 16, 2023, https://www.oregongeology.org/milo/ohmi-lake.htm.

212 **The Hanford Site contains** US Government Accountability Office, "Hanford Cleanup: Alternative Approaches Could Save Tens of Billions of Dollars," GAO, September 27, 2023, https://www.gao.gov/products/gao-23 -106880.

219 **the logging of cedar and cypress forests** Anna Lowenhaupt Tsing, *The Mushroom at the End of the World: On the Possibility of Life in Capitalist Ruins* (Princeton, NJ: Princeton University Press, 2015), 49.

220 **they were made into alcohol** "The History of Japanese American Farm Labor Camps," *Uprooted: Japanese American Farm Labor Camps during World War II*, Oregon Cultural Heritage Commission, http://www.uprooted exhibit.com/farm-labor-camps/.

220 **"every time a 16-inch gun"** W. P. Cooney, quoted in "Value of Sugar in War Told," *Butte Daily Post*, November 19, 1942.

221 **"People always seem to band together"** James Baldwin, *The Fire Next Time* (New York: Vintage, 1993), 81.

223 *Tuber wheeleri* I was saddened to learn of Dan Wheeler's passing in 2020, but this obituary offers a lovely testament to him and to his love of mushrooms and truffles: "Daniel Bland Wheeler," *Oregonian*, June 15, 2020, https://obits.oregonlive.com/us/obituaries/oregon/name/daniel-wheeler -obituary?id=10774959.

225 **"Every breath that we take"** Nicholas Money, quoted in "The Man Who Studies the Fungus Among Us," *Fresh Air*, National Public Radio, January 18, 2012, https://www.npr.org/2012/01/18/145339196/the-man-who-studies -the-fungus-among-us.

226 **"nature's internet"** Paul Stamets, *Mycelium Running: How Mushrooms Can Help Save the World* (Berkeley, CA: Ten Speed Press, 2005), 2.

226 **90 percent of plant life** "Paul Stamets on Mycelium (Part 2)," YouTube video, 0:21, posted by Host Defense Mushrooms, accessed July 10, 2023, https://www.youtube.com/watch?v=WRQGr8GGVbU.

230 **"I'm puzzled"** "John Allegro—Jesus Was a Mushroom," YouTube video, 0:41, from an interview with John Allegro, posted by Hagbard Celine, May 24, 2014, https://www.youtube.com/watch?v=T71gSMOySZ0.

241 **Port Townsend EcoVillage** Kees and Helen recommend this thorough how-to on founding and running an intentional community: Diana Leafe Christian, *Creating a Life Together: Practical Tools to Grow Ecovillages and Intentional Communities* (Gabriola Island, Canada: New Society Publishers, 2003). To learn more about the Port Townsend EcoVillage, visit http:// www.ptecovillage.org.

242 **over eleven hundred HDFCs** "HDFC Cooperatives," New York City Department of Housing Preservation and Development, accessed June 21, 2023, https://www.nyc.gov/site/hpd/services-and-information/hdfc.page. For more information on HDFCs, see Greg Olear, "A Look at HDFCs: Understanding Housing Development Fund Corporation Co-ops,"

CooperatorNews New York, September 2017, https://cooperatornews.com
/article/a-look-at-hdfcs.

247 **"Ephemerality is a virtue"** Adrian Shirk, *Heaven Is a Place on Earth: Searching
for an American Utopia* (Berkeley, CA: Counterpoint Press, 2022), 47.

252 **the five largest landowners** Jess Gilbert, Spencer D. Wood, and Gwen
Sharp, "Who Owns the Land?: Agricultural Land Ownership by Race/
Ethnicity," *Rural America* 17, no. 4 (Winter 2022): 56, https://doi.org
/10.22004/ag.econ.289693.

252 **Doctrine of Discovery** For an Indigenous perspective on the history and
impact of the Doctrine of Discovery, see Sal Sahme, "Lies of Discovery,"
Oregon Humanities, April 27, 2021, https://oregonhumanities.org/rll/magazine
/possession-spring-2021/lies-of-discovery/.

269 *Living Together* **is a thirty-five-minute documentary** David Milholland et al.,
Living Together, YouTube video, 43:12, documentary film from 1972, posted
by Portland State University, December 12, 2013, https://www.youtube
.com/watch?v=7Km78QYPpL4.

269 **"People in this neighborhood"** Interview with mother, in Milholland et al.,
Living Together, 7:18.

270 **"I think it's more important"** Interview with second mother, in Milholland
et al., *Living Together*, 7:47.

270 **"The pure waste"** Interview with father, in Milholland et al., *Living
Together*, 14:35.

271 **"In a country"** Interview with Margaret Mead, in Milholland et al., *Living
Together*, 31:00.

271 **"As the United States"** Interview with Margaret Mead, in Milholland et al.,
Living Together, 34:08.

275 **"When I take you to the Valley"** Ursula K. Le Guin, *Always Coming Home:
Author's Expanded Edition* (New York: Library of America, 2019), 398.

ABOUT THE AUTHOR

Lola Milholland is a food-business owner and writer. A former editor for *Edible Portland* magazine, she currently lives in Portland, Oregon, and runs Umi Organic, a noodle company with a commitment to providing nutritious public school lunch.